FUNDRAISING FOR *The Rest of Us*

HOW TO BUILD YOUR PITCH, NAVIGATE BIAS, AND RAISE CAPITAL ON YOUR TERMS

ALLISON BYERS

Published by Damn Gravity Media LLC, Chicago
www.damngravity.com

Cover and interior design by Bookery

ISBNs
Hardcover: 978-1-962339-25-4
Paperback: 978-1-962339-24-7
Ebook: 978-1-962339-26-1
Audiobook: 978-1-962339-27-8

Printed in The United States of America

TO STEVE AND ZACH AND HANNAH AND PHIL AND MICKEE
AND TONI AND CYNTHIA AND KELLY AND MY FOUNDER
COMMUNITY AND YOU.

YES, ALL THOSE PEOPLE. READ THE
SAPPY STUFF IN THE ACKNOWLEDGMENTS.

WANT TO GO DEEPER?

Readers can access a private resource library at

ALLISONBYERS.COM/RESOURCES

including stories and materials referenced in this book,
downloadable templates, and additional video content.
Use the password *FFRU* to unlock everything!

TABLE OF CONTENTS

THE REST OF US
A Manifesto

We are *The Rest of Us*.
The underestimated. The overlooked.
The ones the system wasn't built for.

We are not broken.
The system is.

We take pain and turn it into progress.
We see injustice and build solutions.
We are the redemptive arc of entrepreneurship.

We don't exist to please gatekeepers.
We don't shrink to fit outdated molds.
We don't wait for permission.

We build.
We lead.
We raise.

We know that checks follow relationships.
That failure teaches as much as success.
That community makes us stronger.

We care less about convincing everyone.
We care more about building what matters.

Nobody is coming to save us.
And we don't need saving.
We are reshaping entrepreneurship.
Rewriting the rules.
Redistributing power.

We are creating companies, communities,
and futures that reflect who we are.

Go raise. Go build. Go take up space.
We need you here.

INTRODUCTION

HI, FRIEND. WHAT BRINGS YOU HERE?

Most books start with the author telling you why they wrote it. I'll get to that, but first, I want to know about you. Who are you, and what brought you here?

allisonbyers.com/ ffrusurvey

By reading this book, you've already taken your first step in joining a community of founders, funders, and changemakers who are rewriting the rules of fundraising together.

If you're willing, please take a moment to go to the link or scan the QR code and answer a few quick questions. You don't have to, but your insights would mean a lot to me, and they'll help shape future editions, resources, and the ongoing conversation this book is starting.

WHO THIS BOOK IS FOR

This book is for founders, all founders, but especially for those who have felt shut out of the traditional fundraising story.

Have you walked into an investor meeting and felt the air shift? Have you looked around and thought, *People like me don't usually get funded.* Have you questioned your own abilities because others made you feel like you didn't belong, or that you didn't know enough to stand a chance? Have you entered a crowded room at an event, realized no one looked like you, and had to fight the urge to turn around and walk out?

If these questions sparked memories or imagery, you're not imagining it, and you are the person I wrote this book for.

People love to compare building a company to a hero's journey. You set out as the protagonist to right a wrong or better the world, and along the way you face seemingly insurmountable odds, gather allies, battle resistance, and confront test after test that challenges your will and stamina before you even get a shot at realizing your vision. After twenty-plus years in Startupland, I can tell you that metaphor is accurate, but it shouldn't have to be.

I've wandered that labyrinth and been blindsided because I didn't realize there were secret doors to networks, knowledge, and capital. Enough with the opaque. Transparency is how we exit the protagonist's individualistic mindset and create a new land where we can all succeed and even have fun together along the way. I'll walk you through the real fundraising process, define industry terms without jargon, and break down concepts in plain language, all while calling attention to what this means if you identify as underrepresented and sharing strategies to employ.

You should never feel like you're not smart enough or hold your tongue because you're worried about asking a "silly" question. If you're new to something, especially something as inaccessible and mystified as fundraising, why would you expect to already know everything? If you were in an emergency and needed to perform CPR without training, would you feel silly asking a medical professional to walk you through it? Of course not! There's power in asking until you understand. That's what gives you confidence and agency. It's what makes action possible.

Oh hey there, investor, I see you taking a peek! Please, keep reading. You'll gain a better understanding of the unique challenges founders encounter, identify unconscious bias, and be part of creating change. Once you understand the barriers you can help dismantle them, and when you do, EVERYONE wins, and EVERYONE gets money in their pocket.

If you've ever thought, *I'm not sure if I belong here,* or *This wasn't made for someone like me,* I wrote this for you. You do belong. You don't need to change who you are. You can learn how the system works and use that knowledge to your advantage. This book will help you do exactly that. You have power here, more than you realize. Let's unlock it.

THE REST OF US

The startup world calls us "underrepresented." Statistically, we are indeed that in terms of the percent of capital we receive relative to our share of the population. Let's not define ourselves by our representation in the venture capital space. *The Rest of Us* represent the majority of the market. *The Rest of Us* are most of the world. *The Rest of Us* are powerful. Throughout this book, that's how I'm going to refer to everyone building businesses and driving our economy who hasn't been funded according to our economic value because of systemic bias—we are *The Rest of Us.*

The heart of this book is about connection. Finding the people who instinctively "get" you and what you're building. Your story, background, and mission ring familiar to them. When people recognize a thread of themselves or someone they care about in your work, the perceived risk of your opportunity drops and the relationship accelerates. You don't need universal approval. You just need the people who resonate with your vision, feel aligned with your energy, and say yes because partnering with you feels natural. Those are your people. They are who you need to find and build with.

NICE TO MEET YOU! I'M ALLISON.

Before we dive into the ins and outs of fundraising, let me start by sharing a bit about who I am, what led me to write this book, and what you can expect to gain from reading it. It's always important to learn about the person you're taking advice from so you can consider it in the right light.

Since we don't know each other yet, here's the lowdown on my style:

+ **Empathetic and experienced:** I've been through the highs and lows of startup life. I've faced bias in fundraising firsthand. I deeply understand the entrepreneurial journey and the structural barriers within the capital landscape.

+ **Supportive and encouraging:** I'm not here to talk down to you or give you the same tired advice from people who've never operated in a system that marginalizes them. This book acknowledges real barriers without discouraging you. It's here to help you feel seen and empower you with actionable steps and realistic expectations.

+ **Action-oriented and pragmatic:** This isn't a book of abstract ideas. We'll break down complex topics into clear guidance that's both practical and understandable.

+ **Transparent and data-driven:** I come with receipts. You'll find data-based statements, cited sources, and stories from entrepreneurs and investors who bring the numbers to life.

+ **Purpose-driven with an advocacy lens:** My voice is mission-driven, and I walk the talk. Changing the funding environment isn't about just posting on social media—it's about creating lasting change. My company and policy work in multiple states are proof of my commitment to this mission.

+ **Humor:** As my 97-year-old grandma says, "If you can't laugh, what's the point?"

If you want to get to know me even better,

watch or listen to some interviews at

WWW.ALLISONBYERS.COM

1

IT'S NOT YOU. IT'S THE SYSTEM.

MY ORIGIN STORY

We raised $9.6 million. Our medical device was registered with the Food and Drug Administration (FDA). We had paying pharmaceutical and clinician customers, and we had published evidence of validity and efficacy in prominent medical journals. Yet, I still couldn't raise our Series B[1] round of funding.

Our Board of Directors and majority shareholders authorized an asset sale. The acquiring company purchased our technology, intellectual property (IP), and customer relationships, and the rest of the company was dissolved. After the sale, the acquiring company, led by an all-male management team, went on to raise $55 million.

---

[1] Fundraising rounds are labeled based on the stage of the company and the type of capital being raised. Most startups begin with a pre-seed or seed round used to build a prototype, validate an idea, or make initial hires. If things go well, a Series A round follows, often led by institutional investors to scale operations. A Series B typically comes next, supporting further growth, expansion, or commercialization. It continues alphabetically from there (Series C, D, etc.). We will cover this in depth, and how there are other ways to think about fundraising for sustainability.

This was a traumatic experience for me, but it was also the start of my redemptive arc. It took me years to understand that it wasn't my failure; it was the system working exactly as designed. A system that excludes millions of people.

I just gave you the TL;DR[2] version of why I do what I do. I'm not here to "fix" people or venture capital. I'm here to build a capital access system designed to serve *The Rest of Us*. Don't worry, we'll get into the full story soon, but to really understand my why and how it impacts *you*, we need to rewind to a moment I never saw coming.

NONLINEAR CAREERS—THEY'RE ALL THE RAGE

My career has been anything but linear, and I wouldn't have grown into the person I am today without such a wide range of experiences.

Over the last 20 years, I've worn many hats: consultant, student, tech operator, chief home officer, entrepreneur, angel investor, advocate for equitable access to capital, and now, author. Each role brought unique challenges and opportunities, shaping the perspective and mission behind this book.

Today, I'm proud to be driving change in the world of equitable capital distribution. I'm the founder of Scroobious, a capital access platform that makes fundraising more human by helping founders and investors build real relationships to activate $1.2 trillion in private wealth to fund innovation. I co-authored California Senate Bill 54, which was signed into law in October 2023 and is now known as California's Fair Investment Practices by Venture Capital Companies Act (FIPVCC). This groundbreaking legislation addresses

---

2   *TL;DR* stands for "Too Long; Didn't Read." Internet shorthand used to summarize a long block of text in one or two quick sentences. Someone once asked me if it meant "Talk Later; Don't Respond," which, honestly, also works depending on the context. I'm using it to give you quick takeaways you can skim and still walk away with the core point. You're busy. I get it.

inequities in venture capital by requiring firms to publicly report diversity metrics on their prior years' investments. You can check out my testimony to the California Judiciary Committee on my website: ALLISONBYERS.COM. I'm working on similar initiatives in other states and welcome conversations with anyone interested in championing these efforts.

Beyond my entrepreneurial work, I was Boston co-chair of the national nonprofit All Raise, contributed as an Executive in Residence at Merck Digital Sciences Studio, served on the Angel Capital Association's DEI Task Force, and sit on the boards of the nonprofits The GK Fund and Project Kesher. I'm also an active angel investor, with 14 investments at the time of writing, and a frequent speaker on navigating the opaque world of fundraising, not just for founders, but for funders ready to activate their capital.

FROM SETBACK TO STARTUP

Entrepreneurship wasn't something I planned. It was something I was pushed into, and in hindsight, I'm so glad I was.

After earning my BA summa cum laude with honors, completing my MBA, and establishing myself as a leader at a venture-backed tech startup, I came back from maternity leave in 2010 and found myself unexpectedly forced out of a job I loved. This came after months of trying to make it work in, you guessed it, a system that wasn't designed for someone like me: a new mother who was ambitious and eager to contribute on her own terms.

I was told to pump breastmilk in the bathroom. I refused. The one conference room with a lock became my twice-a-day battleground. Colleagues complained they couldn't use it. They stared when I walked out with my little cooler bag of milk for my newborn in daycare, which cost nearly as much as my salary. They could hear the pump through the door.

It's an experience that, sadly, is all too common for women. In my case, the "forcing out" came in the form of a reassignment. My role managing our largest client, which was based in New York, was shifted, and I was presented with the "opportunity" to open a new practice area in Los Angeles. We lived in Boston, and we weren't moving. That left me with a choice: nurse my infant or keep my job.

After 11 years of building my career, I suddenly found myself at home with a baby and a self-identity crisis. What followed were four years of unpaid labor. Work that's essential to our economy and society, yet it is rarely recognized. It was also when I strengthened the skills that make me a better entrepreneur today: prioritizing under pressure, strategic communication, empathetic leadership, and relentless self-directed learning.

For any parent who has experienced something similar, please feel free to borrow language I use on my résumé (shown in figure 1.1) to describe this period of growth and contribution.

Chief Operating Officer, Family Division
The Byers Household · Full-time
Apr 2011 - Apr 2015 · 4 yrs 1 mo
Greater Boston

I stepped away from paid work during this period to raise my young children after being forced out of my previous role upon returning from maternity leave, an experience that reshaped my views on equity, power, and leadership.

This was a period of unpaid labor, work that is essential to our economy and society, yet often goes unrecognized. All forms of labor should be valued, and this role strengthened my entrepreneurial skills including:

■ Multitasking and prioritization: making constant decisions by balancing immediate needs with long-term outcomes, often under pressure and with incomplete information.
■ Strategic communication: learning how to understand others' points of view and convey ideas in ways that are received, understood, and acted upon.
■ Empathetic leadership: supporting growth and development while navigating conflict, emotion, and shifting dynamics.
■ Self-directed learning: using this time to explore early-stage venture dynamics, product-market fit, and fundraising models that helped guide my entry to entrepreneurship.

Figure 1.1: Entrepreneurship is how I rebuilt my career.

BUILDING A STARTUP FROM THE GROUND UP

My first venture was joining a team of scientific co-founders in 2014 to launch Digital Cognition Technologies, Inc., a medical device company we spun out of the Massachusetts Institute of Technology and the Lahey Hospital and Medical Center. As the "business one" on the team, I did everything from incorporation, licensing negotiations, and clinical operations to customer success and fundraising. Over five years, we raised nearly $10 million and eventually exited[3] through an acquisition in 2020.

You might be thinking, *Wow, what a success story!* The truth is more complicated. Acquisitions don't always result in financial returns for founders or investors. I'm incredibly proud of what we accomplished, including developing a commercially viable, revenue-generating, class II (exempt) device registered with the FDA with published evidence of its ability to assess cognitive function,[4] but revisiting that period of my life is still bittersweet.

During our final years, we were trying to raise our next round of capital or find a buyer. I regularly flew across the country while raising two young children. The stress was so intense that I experienced true burnout. Not metaphorical burnout. Actual, body-shutting-down, stress-induced illness. I developed shingles in my 30s, on my face no less, which was a first for my doctor.

I did what many founders believe they're supposed to do and tied my identity to the business. Every win felt like a personal triumph and every

---

3   In this context, *exited* means the company was acquired by another business. "Exit" is a common term in startups that refers to a change in ownership, typically through an acquisition or public offering, not necessarily a personal departure or a guaranteed financial gain for everyone involved.

4   Dorene M. Rentz et al., "Association of Digital Clock Drawing with PET Amyloid and Tau Pathology in Normal Older Adults," *Neurology* 96, no. 14 (2021): e1844-e1854, https://pmc. ncbi.nlm.nih.gov/articles/PMC8105970/.

setback felt like a character flaw. I pushed through everything and made it look like strength. Our traction and metrics supported the fundraising strategy, and our pitch was excellent, but it just wasn't working. We'll unpack why as we move through the book.

Ultimately, our board and majority shareholders authorized an asset sale, ensuring the survival of the innovation, but not the company itself. After the acquisition, I learned that the acquiring company, led by an all-male management team, went on to raise $55 million.[5] That was a gut punch, but it also sent me down the path of seeking research and data that clarified what had really happened, and why.

TURNING FRUSTRATION INTO ACTION

When we sold the company, I couldn't help but feel like I had failed. I had poured everything into building something meaningful and innovative, yet I couldn't escape the thought that I had fallen short, especially after learning that the acquiring company went on to raise what I had been striving for. I started researching the world of fundraising and venture capital, desperate to understand what I had done wrong.

The more I dug into the data, the more it became clear: I hadn't failed. I had been operating in a system that wasn't designed to support founders like me.

The numbers were, and are, staggering.

In the United States, $339 billion was invested in startups through venture capital (VC) deals in 2025.[6] Women and entrepreneurs of color, especially

---

5   Andrea Park, "Linus Health Rakes in $55M for Early Alzheimer's Screening, Monitoring Platform," *Fierce Biotech*, July 6, 2021, https://www.fiercebiotech.com/medtech/linus-health-rakes-55m-for-early-alzheimer-s-screening-monitoring-platform.

6   National Venture Capital Association, PitchBook-nvca Venture Monitor Q4 2025, https://nvca.org/wp-content/uploads/2026/01/q4-2025-pitchbook-nvca-venture-monitor.pdf.

Black, Hispanic, and Asian founders, are driving the growth of business ownership, yet continue to face huge funding gaps. Between 2017 and 2022, the number of Black-owned employer businesses grew by 57%, with the number of Black women founders growing by an incredible 72%.[7] Hispanic entrepreneurs launched businesses at a record pace during the same period, but collectively received just 1.5% of US venture funding in 2022.[8]

Despite this growth, capital allocation remains extremely unequal. Women-founded companies secure only 1.2% of all VC funding;[9] Black founders get 0.48%;[10] Latina founders, less than 1.5%;[11] and Black women founders, just 0.34%.[12] In my home state of Massachusetts, women-led businesses receive only 0.5% of venture capital dollars.[13] These statistics make one thing clear: some of the fastest-growing, most dynamic sectors of entrepreneurship

---

7   Andre M. Perry et al., "Driving Prosperity: How Black-owned Businesses Fueled Recent Economic Growth," Brookings, February 19, 2025, https://www.brookings.edu/articles/driving-prosperity-how-black-owned-businesses-fueled-recent-economic-growth/. See also: Governing, "The Number of Black-Owned Businesses Increased by More Than 50 Percent," February 27, 2025, https://www.governing.com/policy/the-number-of-black-owned-businesses-increased-by-more-than-50.

8   Gené Teare, "Funding to Latine-Founded US Companies Falls Sharply in 2022," Crunchbase News, October 26, 2022, https://news.crunchbase.com/diversity/us-based-latine-founded-companies-funding-falls/.

9   Female Founders Dashboard, PitchBook-nvca Venture Monitor Q4 2025, https://nvca.org/wp-content/uploads/2026/01/q4-2025-pitchbook-nvca-venture-monitor.pdf.

10   Chris Metinko and Gené Teare, "Drop in Venture Funding to Black-Founded Startups Greatly Outpaces Market Decline," Crunchbase News, February 27, 2024, https://news.crunchbase.com/diversity/venture-funding-black-founded-startups-2023-data/#:~:text=Last%20year's%20number%20represents%20an,saw%20a%20more%20pronounced%20drop.

11   Alejandra Rojas, "Investors Are Betting Big on Latina Founders," *Forbes*, October 15, 2025, https://www.forbes.com/sites/alejandrarojas/2025/10/15/investors-are-betting-big-on-latina-founders-what-are-they-looking-for/.

12   Sophia Kunthara, "Black Women Still Receive Just a Tiny Fraction of VC Funding Despite 5-Year High," Crunchbase News, July 16, 2021, https://news.crunchbase.com/diversity/something-ventured-black-women-founders/.

13   Female Founders Dashboard, PitchBook-nvca Venture Monitor Q4 2025, https://nvca.org/wp-content/uploads/2026/01/q4-2025-pitchbook-nvca-venture-monitor.pdf.

remain almost entirely excluded from the capital that drives innovation, even as they increasingly shape our economic future.

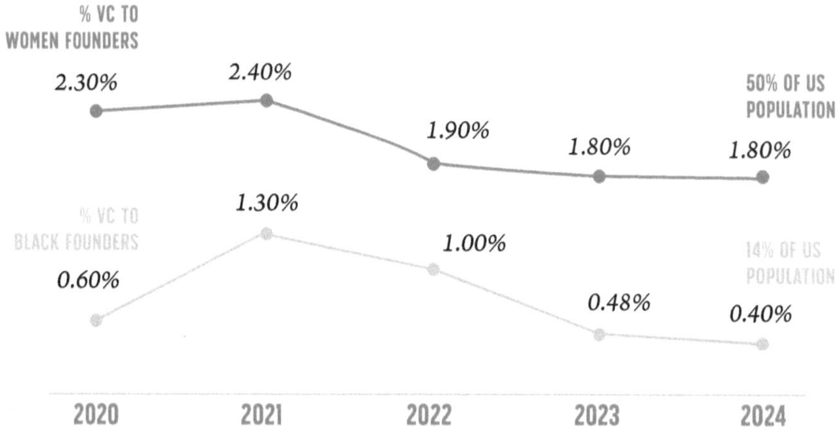

Sources: POCIT, Forbes, TechCrunch, Pitchbook, Morgan Stanley

Figure 1.2

It's not just the US.

While the US leads global VC funding, similar patterns show up around the world. In most developed markets, women and founders of color receive

less than 3% of total VC investment. China and the UK typically round out the top three economies in VC activity, and in India, where startup growth has exploded in recent years, women founders received just 1.5% of VC funding in 2024.[14]

These statistics are disheartening, yes, but they are also liberating. They helped me realize that what I had experienced wasn't a personal failure, it was a systemic one. I could have had the best pitch in the world, and it still might not have mattered. When 98%

---

14   Dealroom.co, "The State of Global VC," 2025, https://dealroom.co/guides/global.

of venture dollars go to men, it's not just about how you pitch. I didn't yet understand that investor pushback and rejection didn't necessarily mean I wasn't telling a compelling story. It often meant I wasn't talking to the right people.

Too often, founders internalize rejection as a reflection of their own inadequacy. We think, *If I were better, smarter, more polished, maybe I could have succeeded.* But the truth is, the system of capital allocation has evolved such that it is designed to marginalize us, to keep us from accessing the capital and resources we need to grow and compete. This realization lit a fire in me. I couldn't unsee what I had learned, and I knew I couldn't let others feel like I had: isolated, defeated, and questioning their worth. That's when I decided to turn my frustration into action and dedicate myself to creating a system that works for all founders, not just the privileged few.

FUNDRAISING—IT HITS DIFFERENT

I encountered systemic bias during fundraising that I hadn't fully understood before. Even after more than 15 years as a woman in tech, being the only woman in the room more times than I can count, this was different. Negotiating with institutions and pitching investors exposed barriers that were less obvious until I was standing right in front of them.

We'll get into the nitty-gritty of bias, how to identify it in the moment, and practical advice on how to handle it, but there is a critical element at play that isn't immediately obvious.

The primary reason for bias in venture capital funding, beyond blatant sexism and racism, is the systemic reliance on pattern matching and signal processing to reduce perceived risk in investments. Investors look for familiar patterns with founders, industries, or business models that align with their past successes. But the dataset for these "successful" patterns is overwhelmingly homogeneous, shaped by decades of predominantly white male decision-makers funding other white men. If you don't come from this demographic, you're automatically less likely to "match the signal," regardless of the strength or risk profile of your business.

The problem isn't just individual bias, it's systemic. The very frameworks investors use to evaluate startups are rooted in exclusion. Criteria like "founder-market fit," "pattern recognition," "warm intros," and "social proof" are all forms of signal processing designed to assess risk, but in practice, they often work against *The Rest of Us* because we don't fit the historical mold of what success has looked like in venture capital. This is why, despite being lower risk or just as qualified, founders from marginalized communities struggle to access funding.

This is also why venture capital as an industry is unsustainable without correcting its trajectory. Businesses founded by women deliver more than twice the revenue per dollar invested than those founded by men.[15] Multiple VC funds have returned better-than-average results with portfolios dispro-portionately featuring women- and minority-owned businesses, including Kapor Capital, Ulu, and Starlight Ventures.[16] To put the opportunity into perspective, if the revenue of women- and minority-owned businesses were proportional to their percentage in the labor force (56%), the US economy would potentially grow by $4.4 trillion.[17]

For an industry defined by the ability to identify undervalued assets and invest in outliers for outsized returns (alpha[18]), it's completely missing the mark. It fails to recognize opportunity where it's statistically abundant.

---

15   Boston Consulting Group, "Why Women-Owned Startups Are a Better Bet," 2018, https://www.bcg.com/publications/2018/why-women-owned-startups-are-better-bet.

16   Morgan Stanley, "Investing in Diverse Startups: A Reassessment," December 27, 2022, https://www.morganstanley.com/ideas/vc-funding-diverse-startups-2022-survey.

17   Morgan Stanley, "The Growing Market Investors Are Missing," 2018, https://www.morganstanley.com/content/dam/msdotcom/mcil/growing-market-investors-are-missing.pdf.

18   *Alpha* refers to the measure of excess return or value creation that an investment generates beyond a benchmark or baseline expectation.

The good news, my friends, is the capital allocation landscape is evolving and diversifying. This book explains alternate sources of capital, their motivations, and how to access them. You'll learn how to pitch the right person, at the right time, with the right message.

FOUNDING SCROOBIOUS

I became determined to help other founders not only avoid the obstacles I'd faced, but also access a new system that values the opportunity their identities present rather than penalizing them for it. As I looked at the capital landscape, I asked a simple question: *If venture capital isn't funding most of us, what's the next-largest pool of money?* The answer was clear—private wealth. According to Bank of America research, if private capital were a country, it would have the second-largest economy in the world.[19]

Most of that wealth sits dormant, however, when it comes to early-stage investing. The system is too opaque, too insider-driven, and too biased, not just for founders, but for potential investors, too. The very people who could be investing in innovative, underrepresented founders don't know how, don't feel invited, or assume they're not qualified to participate.

I founded Scroobious in 2020 to reshape innovation capital access by making innovators and funders more informed, more inclusive, and more connected. Our platform helps founders learn how to navigate the fundraising process, craft compelling pitches, and connect with aligned investors who see the potential for both impact and return. But Scroobious is about more than just tools or training, it's about belonging in an ecosystem that has long told many of us we don't.

---

19   Israel, Haim, Felix Tran, Savita Subramanian, Martyn Briggs, *Unicorns, Decorns and Hectocorns: the Private Companies Primer,* (B of A Global Research, October 21, 2025), chrome-extension://efaidnbmnnnibpcajpcglclefindmkaj/https://business.bofa.com/content/dam/flagship/global-research/private-company-market-research.pdf.

People often ask me what the name Scroobious means, and I love telling the story because it's both meaningful and memorable. It comes from a poem by Edward Lear, in which a group of animals tries to classify a strange new creature, the Scroobious Pip, into one of their known categories. They question if it's a mammal, bird, fish, or insect, but it doesn't fit neatly anywhere. Eventually, they stop trying to label it and instead celebrate it for being unique.

That's exactly how many of us feel in the fundraising world. Misunderstood. Misclassified. Left out. At Scroobious, we help founders and investors embrace what makes them different, craft narratives that reflect their true value, and connect with others who can see their upside because of their uniqueness, not in spite of it.

Since launching, over 1,000 entrepreneurs, investors, and mentors have joined our platform through word of mouth and our intentional partnerships. Through tailored pitch feedback, community-driven learning, and strategic connections, we've helped founders raise millions in funding while staying true to their vision. One of the aspects I'm most proud of is the platform's emphasis on demystifying investor thinking. By teaching founders how investors evaluate opportunities, we're not just improving outcomes; we're building confidence and agency. By exposing investors to founders building in areas of expertise or passion whom they wouldn't have otherwise met, we're debunking the myth that there's a pipeline problem. The pipeline is and always has been there. We've been experiencing a funding problem, and we're taking it into our own hands to fix it.

Our work is rooted in the belief that everyone deserves the opportunity to innovate and create, regardless of their background, from all sides of the table. From day one, we've been about more than just helping individual founders succeed; we've been about changing the system. This means advocating for policy changes, fostering transparency, and challenging outdated norms that perpetuate inequity.

WHY THIS BOOK EXISTS

I've faced barriers firsthand. I've run into walls I didn't even know were there until I hit them. And I've watched incredible founders give up, not because their ideas weren't strong, but because the system wasn't designed to let them through. This book makes the fundraising process clearer, fairer, and a lot less intimidating for founders like you.

This isn't yet another framework from a white male perspective where someone who doesn't share your lived experience talks at you without regard for the inequities and bias you face. I bring my own lived experience as a Jewish woman founder who has navigated systemic bias, but I don't pretend to speak for every identity. That's why I've included the voices and stories of a vibrant, diverse group of founders and investors whose perspectives expand and enrich the lessons in these pages. This book discusses realistic sources of capital and methods for effectively communicating your opportunity to people who are more likely to write you a check based on real-world data.

My goal is to make the fundraising process more accessible, less mysterious, and maybe even a little fun.

This book is part manual, part empowerment tool, and part insider playbook. You'll learn how to:

+ Think like an investor so you can craft narratives that resonate.
+ Identify the right types of capital for your business beyond just venture capital.
+ Build connections and confidence in spaces that often feel unwelcoming.

We'll break down myths, share stories, and provide practical, actionable strategies that you can use immediately. I'll share my experiences, and we'll hear from others who've been in the trenches of fundraising and come out the other side.

THE FOUNDERS AND INVESTORS YOU'LL HEAR FROM

Throughout this book, you'll hear from founders who have lived the realities of raising capital from positions outside the traditional power networks. Their stories are the heart of this work, with each one reflecting a different path, geography, and motivation for building.

Ali Garba, Milwaukee, WI. Ali is an angel investor and venture capitalist with deep expertise across development, investment, and commercial banking. A former first vice president and portfolio management director at Morgan Stanley, Ali has spent decades guiding strategic portfolios while teaching finance and economics as an adjunct professor at the University of Wisconsin–Milwaukee. With a doctorate in business and a lifelong commitment to learning, leadership, and impact, he now focuses on empowering entrepreneurs and expanding access to capital for the next generation of innovators. LINKEDIN.COM/IN/DRAGARBA/.

Amanda Drobnis, Norwood, MA. Amanda is the co-founder and CEO of Hilltop Bio, a biotech startup developing innovative veterinary regenerative products designed to support animals' natural healing processes. A lifelong equestrian with a background in animal science, Amanda discovered the power of regenerative approaches firsthand after a serious hip injury sidelined her at age 29. Her recovery sparked a mission to help bring similar innovations to veterinary medicine. Today, Hilltop Bio offers a growing portfolio of easy-to-use, room-temperature products used by equine and companion-animal practices nationwide. Amanda's work shows how personal experience, scientific curiosity, and practical design can shape the future of animal care from the inside out. LINKEDIN.COM/IN/ AMANDA-DROBNIS/.

Catherine Gray, Los Angeles, CA. An investor, filmmaker, and founder of She Angel Investors, Catherine has dedicated her career to closing the funding gap for women entrepreneurs. She's the executive producer of the award-winning documentary, *Show Her The Money* and host of the long-running *Invest in Her* podcast, spotlighting founders and funders working toward equity. Through her films, fund, and foundation, Catherine is building a movement to ensure women aren't just part of the conversation; they're leading it. LINKEDIN.COM/IN/CATHERINELGRAY/.

Deanna Meador, Nashville, TN. A serial entrepreneur and inventor, Deanna leads Couture Technologies, an AI-powered platform helping fashion brands increase sales and reduce returns with virtual try-on, size recommendations, and AI-powered outfit-building tools. She's launched solutions spanning edtech and fashiontech, translating technical ambition into practical product impact. Over the last two decades, she has supported over

1,000 other entrepreneurial teams as they worked to bring new ideas into the market. Deanna's work reminds us that building with domain expertise and empathy can shift entire industries from the inside. LINKEDIN.COM/IN/DEANNA-MEADOR-99BB5640/.

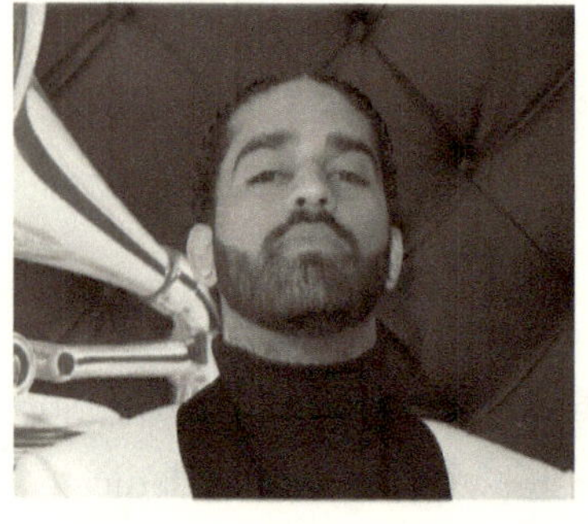

Derek Ali, Los Angeles, CA. A multi-Grammy Award-winning mix engineer (widely known as "MixedByAli") turned startup founder, Derek is building EngineEars, a SaaS platform that provides tools and resources to streamline music collaboration, creator payments, business workflows, and global distribution for music creators. He's worked with artists like Kendrick Lamar and Donald Glover, and he developed EngineEars after realizing through his own experiences that creatives were stuck juggling piecemeal tools for contracts, file sharing, distribution, and billing. Derek's journey demonstrates what happens when a creator becomes an entrepreneur, using intimate domain knowledge to build infrastructure for the next wave of talent. LINKEDIN.COM/IN/DEREK-ALI-964667165/.

Elijah Davis, Dallas, TX. Elijah is the co-founder and CEO of Platinum915, a wellness and life sciences brand offering plant-based products for sober-conscious adults 21+ desiring healthier, functional alternatives to alcohol, opioids, and synthetic stimulants. After sustaining a debilitating spinal injury while serving in the US Army, Elijah turned to plant medicine for healing, an experience that inspired him to build products like CannaShots and Rasta Rocks to promote conscious living and balance.

A ForbesBLK member and Scroobious Innovation Council advisor, Elijah leads with empathy, creativity, and conviction that wellness can be both functional and joyful. LINKEDIN.COM/IN/PEAKPLATINUM915/.

James Valencia, Nashville, TN. James is the founder and CEO of Radical Shoots, an urban microgreens company that grew from a 100-square-foot space into a multisite operation supplying restaurants, markets, and communities across Nashville. A Vanderbilt alum with roots in sustainability and tech, James built his business by marrying design thinking with agtech systems, eventually acquiring CC Gardens to scale further. His story shows how curiosity, persistence, and domain humility can turn a side experiment into a movement toward healthier, local food systems. LINKEDIN.COM/IN/JAMES-MARTIN-VALENCIA/.

Jennifer Kushell, Marina del Rey, CA. Jennifer is the founder and CEO of Exploring Your Potential (EYP), an edtech company transforming how students navigate their lives and careers. A *New York Times* bestselling author and global advocate for youth empowerment, Jennifer has spent over 25 years working at the intersection of education, employment, and entrepreneurship-advising initiatives with the US State Department, the United Nations, and institutions in more than 60 countries. Through EYP, she's helping the next generation gain the clarity, confidence, and strategy to build meaningful futures in an ever-changing world. LINKEDIN.COM/IN/JENNIFERKUSHELL/.

Jennifer Saxton, Los Angeles, CA. Jen is the founder and CEO of Tot Squad, an award-winning marketplace connecting new parents with trusted experts for registry planning, feeding, sleep, car seat safety, and more. With Tot Squad's MotherFund feature, families can add flexible service credits to their baby registry. A serial entrepreneur who sold her first company in 2020, she has raised over $4 million and launched the Baby Concierge program in Target stores in 2025. Jen earned her BS in mathematics from Duke and her MBA from Northwestern Kellogg, and is the mom of two young girls. LINKEDIN.COM/IN/JENBSAXTON/.

Jenny Rudd, Sydney, Australia. Jenny is the founder of Dispute Buddy, a platform that helps people easily collect and export digital evidence for legal disputes. A serial entrepreneur and passionate advocate for equality, Jenny previously bought and sold a regional lifestyle magazine, co-founded The Gender Investment Gap NZ with Dame Theresa Gattung, and became the first New Zealand woman tech founder accepted into Techstars Sydney. Named a finalist in the NZ Hi-Tech Awards "Inspiring Individual" category and ranked among the top 1% of Techstars mentors worldwide, she's on a mission to close the gender gap in entrepreneurship and investment, one woman-shaped puzzle piece at a time. LINKEDIN.COM/IN/JENNYJANERUDD/.

Joel Mutua, New York, NY. A serial entrepreneur and technology innovator, Joel founded TEMBA (formerly Quick Cart Africa) to bank Africa's 53 million unbanked small businesses, enterprises that drive over half of the continent's GDP. He's now building Nurture Connect, an AI-first healthcare platform expanding access to patient-centered care. Joel's journey reveals what it means to pitch across continents and lead with conviction through both success and loss. LINKEDIN.COM/IN/JOEL-MUTUA-409AB1177/.

Julie Moir Messervy, Brattleboro, VT. Julie is a renowned landscape designer, author, and entrepreneur with a mission to democratize sustainable outdoor design. A pioneer in her field, she founded Home Outside, which launched the first online landscape design service and the world's first AI-powered landscape and garden designer. Julie is the author of eight books, including *Home Outside* and *The Inward Garden*, and her design portfolio includes public parks and private gardens across North America, most notably the Toronto Music Garden created with cellist Yo-Yo Ma. A lifelong advocate for access and innovation, Julie's work blends artistry, technology, and climate resilience to bring beautiful, meaningful outdoor spaces to everyone. LINKEDIN.COM/IN/JULIEMOIRMESSERVY/.

Karen Robinson Cope, Atlanta, GA. Karen is a serial entrepreneur and accomplished CEO with a track record of building and scaling high-growth technology and media companies. Throughout her career, she has secured over $100 million in angel, venture, and private equity funding; led multiple successful exits; and served on the boards of public, private, and nonprofit organizations. Karen is also a sought-after keynote speaker on entrepreneurship and women's leadership. She is a recipient of numerous national awards, including Woman of the Year, Investor of the Year, and Entrepreneur of the Year. She has also served as a five-time judge for the EY Entrepreneur of the Year Awards and is an active mentor to women and founders. Karen is currently an investor in more than a dozen companies that range from sports tech and pickleball to e-commerce, healthcare, and women's fertility. Karen continues to champion diverse leadership and inclusive innovation across industries. LINKEDIN.COM/IN/KARENROBINSONCOPE/.

Kelly Kimball, Los Angeles, CA. Kelly is a serial disruptor and co-founder and chairman of Vitu, where he reimagines how businesses and governments interact. He is also co-founder and chairman of F5 Collective, which creates generational change for women through economic empowerment, capital, and policy advocacy. He mentors startups to challenge dominant players, invests in diverse founders, and lectures on strategic disruption. Kelly and his wife Carla are also dedicated advocates for women's leadership through their philanthropy and political activism. LINKEDIN.COM/IN/KELLYKIMBALL/.

Lindsay Kuhn, Providence, RI. Lindsay is the founder and CEO of Wingspans, a platform using authentic storytelling to guide the next generation toward fulfilling careers. With degrees in English and engineering, and a PhD from Brown, Lindsay merges technical expertise with a deep commitment to equity. As a woman in STEM, she believes career exploration is a social justice issue. Wingspans helps students see what's possible and gives employers access to a nontraditional pipeline. If you can see it, you can be it. LINKEDIN.COM/IN/LINDSAY-KUHN-PH-D-7578B8/.

Melissa Wood, Austin, TX. Melissa is an award-winning creative leader with over 20 years of experience helping founders and executives shape brands, products, and cultures that tell powerful stories. Her work spans global companies and startups acquired by Apple and Google, and her passion for storytelling runs through her art, humanitarian work in Ethiopia, and career in design and tech. As founder of Formus, she's reimagining how people experience and design spaces by creating environments that evolve alongside the stories they hold. LINKEDIN.COM/IN/MELISSAWOOD/.

Modjossorica (Rica) Elysée, Boston, MA. A serial entrepreneur and technologist, Rica is the founder and CEO of BeautyLynk, an on-demand beauty service connecting clients and stylists via a few clicks, and co-founder of a stealth retail technology startup. Her experience scaling tech-driven platforms reflects both resilience and reinvention. Rica's story is a master class in confidence, boundaries, and building businesses that reflect who you are, not who you're told to be. LINKEDIN.COM/IN/MELYSEE/.

Rajia Abdelaziz, Boston, MA. A serial tech entrepreneur and the founder and CEO of invisaWear, Rajia built one of the leading brands in personal safety technology, raising millions in funding and scaling to over $20 million in sales. She forged major partnerships with ADT and TELUS, transforming a personal mission into a global movement for safety and empowerment. Rajia's story embodies what it means to lead with both innovation and purpose, and to thrive in an industry that still underestimates women and people of color. LINKEDIN.COM/IN/RAJIAABDELAZIZ/.

Richard Millunchick, Bloomington, IN. Richard is an accomplished professional with more than 30 years of experience in sales and operations management. Employers, clients, and colleagues know him as a goal-oriented individual who is dedicated to corporate expansion and improving the bottom line. He works with early-stage and growing companies that are paving new paths in their industries. LINKEDIN.COM/IN/RMILLUNCHICK/.

Ricquelle Jeffrey, Boston, MA & London, UK. Born in Trinidad and Tobago, Ricquelle leads with a global lens. She brings 15+ years of leadership across finance, healthcare, fashion, compliance, and technology. She has delivered global multimillion-dollar initiatives, led growth strategy securing critical capital and partnerships, and earned one startup recognition in *Forbes France*. Now founder of Cherisse Consulting Group and co-founder of Bloomsuite, she is redefining how the wellness economy scales in a new era, proving that AI's greatest value lies in strengthening meaningful human connection. LINKEDIN.COM/IN/RICQUELLEJEFFREY/.

Stéphanie Joseph, Boston, MA. Stéphanie brings 10+ years of global fintech experience. She co-founded Kura at Harvard Business School and led it from idea to launch—building the compliance, product, and go-to-market foundations for instant, stablecoin-powered cross-border payments serving merchants across Central America and the Caribbean. Under her leadership, Kura integrated with Circle for USDC, built on the Stellar network, and partnered with MoneyGram for global cash-out infrastructure. With prior roles in major tech and financial institutions, she focuses on creating modern financial rails for historically underserved markets. LINKEDIN.COM/IN/STEPHANIEGJOSEPH/.

Suelin Chen, Cambridge, MA. A healthcare executive and MIT PhD engineer/scientist, Suelin founded Cake, the largest end-of-life planning platform, which has served over 100 million users and was acquired by a major funeral services provider. With more than two decades at the intersection of healthtech, entrepreneurship, and strategy, she's helped shape how people plan for care and make their wishes known. A *Fortune* "40 Under 40" honoree and Care100 leader, Suelin's work reminds us that innovation can meet mortality, and that systems change begins where people live and die. LINKEDIN.COM/IN/SUELINCHEN/.

Sydney Robinson, London, Ontario, Canada Metropolitan Area. Sydney is the co-founder and CEO of Vessl Prosthetics, a company transforming prosthetic comfort and performance through innovative socket design. With a background in mechanical and biomedical engineering and training from the Medical Innovation Fellowship, she brings deep technical expertise paired with a genuine talent for connecting with people. Sydney discovered the long-standing problem of poor socket fit while working closely with clinicians and amputees, and built Vessl around a simple belief: solutions should be designed with and alongside the people who rely on them. LINKEDIN. COM/IN/SYDNEYMROBINSON/.

Yousof Naderi, Boston, MA. Yousof, the CEO and co-founder of DeepCharge, brings over 15 years of experience building intelligent, real-world systems where AI, hardware, and software intersect. At DeepCharge, he led the company from deep-tech IP to enterprise platforms that improve device uptime for Fortune 500 customers, architecting full-stack solutions and guiding engineering, manufacturing, and customer pilots. Previously, he oversaw major National Science Foundation-, Department of Defense-, and Office of Naval Research-funded R&D programs at Northeastern University, specializing in wireless systems and applied AI. He excels at translating complex technical challenges into scalable products. LINKEDIN. COM/IN/YOUSOFNADERI/.

Yulkendy Valdez, New York, NY. A founder turned ecosystem builder, Yulkendy's work centers on creating access for diverse entrepreneurs and emerging talent. She co-founded Forefront, a corporate training company that partnered with organizations such as SAP to advance inclusive recruitment and retention. Now shaping early-stage ecosystems through supporting leading accelerators, incubators, and fellowships, she's proof that changing who gets funded starts with changing who gets seen. LINKEDIN.COM/IN/YULKENDYVALDEZ/.

HOW THIS BOOK IS STRUCTURED

The book is divided into two parts to guide you from understanding how fundraising really works to nailing your pitch and securing money.

PART I: WHAT FUNDRAISING ACTUALLY LOOKS LIKE

In the first half, we take a step back and look at the fundraising world from the inside. You'll learn how capital flows, why so much of it stays in the hands of the same types of founders, and what's changing, especially for *The Rest of Us*. We'll demystify terms, expose biases, and explore newer sources of funding that may be more accessible, and quite frankly, a better fit. This section is about clarity, confidence, and seeing the system for what it is so you can move forward with intention.

PART II: BUILDING A PITCH THAT WORKS

The second half gets hands-on. I'll walk you through what makes a pitch resonate, how to structure your deck, and how to talk about yourself and your company in a way that lands. You'll learn how investors evaluate opportunities, how to shift your mindset, and how to tell your story in a way that connects, especially when you've been underestimated or overlooked. This isn't about making yourself fit into someone else's mold. It's about communicating your value clearly, powerfully, and on your terms.

Each part is packed with step-by-step guidance, real-life examples, and advice you can use right now. No gatekeeping. No guesswork. Just the tools and mindset shifts that make fundraising clearer, fairer, and a little less lonely.

PART I

What Fundraising Actually Looks Like

UNDERSTANDING CAPITAL PROVIDER TYPES

No matter the source of the money, it always comes down to a human being making a decision. Whether you're going after venture capital, a small business loan, an angel investor, a grant, or crowdfunding, behind every check is a person (or group of people) with their own motivations, preferences, biases, and goals.

Fundraising is both about pitching the story of your opportunity *and* finding the people who are most likely to say yes to *you*, specifically. Founders can waste a whole lot of time and emotional energy pitching to the wrong people. The goal of this part of the book is to save you from that, so you spend less time chasing validation and more time finding alignment.

We'll start by helping you define your ideal investor profile, which is applicable to any source of capital you're seeking. The clearer you are about *who* you're pitching to, the easier it is to tailor your message, build relationships, and gain traction.

INVESTOR PERSONAS

Just like you would build an Ideal Customer Profile (ICP), you need to build your Ideal Investor Profile (IIP). If you're not familiar with the term, an ICP is a clear picture of the type of customer who is most likely to buy from you—the ones who feel the problem you solve most acutely and are ready for your solution. You figure out what they care about, what motivates them, and how they make decisions.

The same approach works for fundraising. Your IIP is the type of investor who is most likely to "get it" instinctively without a long explanation or deck walk-through. The people who lean in when you talk about your problem space and value your lived experience. Building this profile lets you focus your time, energy, and outreach on people who are more likely to say yes.

I talk to so many founders who try to pitch to *anyone* with money, but fundraising, like sales, is not a game of mass cold outreach (despite what the VC bros tell you). It's about resonance, which starts with finding your people.

Rajia Abdelaziz's company, invisaWear, makes personal safety devices that look like trendy jewelry. Rajia explains how she thinks about her IIP:

> How can you relate to the right person? Everyone has different passions. I could pitch to the most successful person in the world, but if they've never worried about their safety or a loved one's safety, they're not going to understand or think it's a good investment idea. That doesn't mean that it's not a good investment idea, just because that person doesn't see it. Everyone brings their own experiences, and that shapes how they think about opportunity.

Save your breath and energy from trying to convince someone who doesn't connect. You're looking for the person whose eyes light up when they hear what you're building. The one who says, *Oh my goodness, this has to be a thing.* That's your IIP.

WHAT TO INCLUDE IN YOUR IIP

Think of this like persona-building, but for investors. Use these questions to build a detailed profile of the person you're trying to reach:

+ What's their professional background or industry experience?
+ Do they have firsthand or secondhand experience with the problem you're solving?
+ Where do they live, work, or spend time?
+ What do they value among financial return, social impact, innovation, status, legacy, etc.?
+ Have they invested in similar companies before?
+ What networks or ecosystems are they part of?

Go beyond demographics. Think about how they behave:

+ Do they prefer email, calls, face-to-face?
+ Do they move quickly or need time?
+ Are they public about their investing, or more private?
+ Are they online or offline?
+ Do they like big conferences or small meetups?

Don't limit yourself to people who call themselves investors. Many early backers don't even identify that way. At my last company, our early investors were mainly doctors and clinicians who deeply understood the problem and had the means to support a solution.

Think about executives in your industry, exited founders, doctors, lawyers, engineers, and business owners—people with capital *and* a personal connection to your space. When you get this right, it changes the way you fundraise. You're finding people who see the world like you do and want to be part of the solution you're building. The clearer your IIP, the more targeted your outreach and storytelling can be.

QUALITIES THAT RESONATE

Another tip I give in workshops is to think about the kinds of people you enjoy being around. I personally love making people smile and laugh. If someone gets intimidated by or disengages because of that, they're not my person. So, I notice:

+ Do they smile when I talk?
+ Do they respond to the things I say?
+ Can I make them laugh in the first 10 minutes?

If I can't, I know they're not my investor, and that's okay. The same is true for you. Think about:

+ What energy you bring into a room.
+ Who appreciates and connects with that.
+ Who you want to spend time working with.

COMPLETE THE IIP WORKSHEET

Take what you've just read and put it into action. The next page includes a guided worksheet to help you build your IIP and start identifying where to find your people.

IDEAL INVESTOR PROFILE (IIP)

Founders often start raising money within their own network. While a good first step, this approach is limiting. An Ideal Investor Profile (IIP) helps you picture the investor who will naturally connect with your business. Someone who understands the problem, believes in the solution, and sees the opportunity. Use the five sections below to gain clarity. Once defined, you will be able to recognize these investors in industries, communities, online, and unexpected places.

1 — WHO THEY ARE

EXPERIENCE: Do they have firsthand experience with the problem?

BACKGROUND: What industries/roles define their history?

LOCATION: Where do they live, work, or focus (geo/ecosystem)?

LIFE STAGE: What stage of life are they currently in?

YOUR NOTES

2 — WHAT THEY VALUE

INNOVATION: What excites them about change?

PRIORITIES: Do they care more about financial returns, impact, or both?

FOUNDER FIT: What qualities resonate (resilience, lived experience, technical expertise)?

YOUR NOTES

3 — HOW THEY ENGAGE

STYLE: Do they prefer 1:1 interactions or groups?

SPEED: Are they fast decision-makers or slow evaluators?

COMMS: Email, calls, text, DMs, or face-to-face?

ONLINE: Do they post/comment or just observe?

YOUR NOTES

4 — WHERE TO FIND THEM

MEMBERSHIPS: What networks or communities are they in?

EVENTS: What conferences or meetups do they attend?

DIGITAL: What groups, forums, or newsletters do they follow?

GEOGRAPHY: Are they tied to a specific location?

YOUR NOTES

5 — HOW TO CONNECT

INITIATION: What is the most natural way to start a relationship?

THE PITCH: How can you show your vision so it clicks instantly?

THE "AHA": What would make them say "I get it"?

FOCUS: Where will you spend energy finding them?

YOUR NOTES

Figure 2.1

Catherine Gray, founder of She Angel Investors and executive producer of the award-winning documentary, *Show Her The Money*, identified her IIP during a panel where they were both speaking:

> I just really liked her. I loved what she had to say, and we were very much aligned, so we started chatting. Originally it wasn't about the film, we just wanted to connect. After some time I thought, hmm, I'm going to ask her if she would like to invest in this, and she did! I didn't know most of the investors in the film before, but we were kindred spirits from the get-go.

EQUITY VS. NON-DILUTIVE

There are two main types of funding you can raise from outside sources: **equity-based** and **non-dilutive**.

While we often hear about venture capital and equity investments in the news and popular culture, there are many sources of funding. Each funding source has different needs and motivations, and you can mix and match them to build a strong, sustainable funding plan for your business. You might hear this referred to as your "capitalization strategy," which is basically the road map for how you'll fund your business over time.

Remember: The goal is to build a successful business. Any money you bring into the company is to help you build a successful business. Raising money is not the end goal. It is a means to an end, the end being a successful business. Did the main point of this paragraph come through? I can say it again. Raising money *does not equal* a successful business.

Equity-based funding means giving someone ownership in your company, usually in the form of shares, in exchange for money. Think of it like the public stock market: There's a price per share of a public company, and when you buy a share, you now own a piece of that company. As a shareholder, you get to participate in certain votes about how the company is run, and if the stock price goes up, you can sell your shares for a profit.

When you raise venture capital or take on angel investment, it works the same way, except your company isn't on the public stock exchange (yet). That only happens if you go through an IPO, or *initial public offering,* which involves alllllll kinds of legal and regulatory hoops so you can offer your shares to the general public instead of just private investors.

The person or entity giving you the money becomes a part-owner of your business. Their goal is for your company to grow significantly so that their shares increase in value over time. Eventually, they hope to sell those shares for more than they paid, either to a company that acquires you or to the public market, and make a profit.

Non-dilutive funding is different because you don't give up any ownership of your company. That's what *"non-dilutive"* means—it doesn't dilute your share of the company. This type of funding can come in a few forms:

+ Grants or prize money, where you don't have to pay anything back.
+ Loans or debt, where you agree to pay back the money, usually with interest.

In this case, the person or organization giving you the money isn't looking for ownership of your company. They just want to be repaid, ideally after you've used the money to grow your business. They don't care how valuable your shares become because they don't own any.

EQUITY-BASED FINANCING	NON-DILUTIVE SOURCES
✦ Venture Capital Firms	✦ Grants
✦ Angel Investors	✦ Pitch Competitions
✦ Angel Groups	✦ Revenue-Based Financing
✦ Family Offices	✦ Venture Debt
✦ Crowdfunding	✦ Bank Loans

Table 2.1

Who you pitch is just as important as what you pitch. By understanding the different types of capital providers available, you can figure out which kind, or combination, is the best fit for your goals and business model. Once you've settled on the type(s) of capital sources you want to pursue, you can use your IIP to find the human decision-makers who will understand what you're building and relate to you as a person.

These investor personas don't just differ in style and priorities; they also move at different speeds after you pitch them. For example, angel investors can decide quickly, angel groups and corporate venture capital can take months, and debt lenders can have lengthy regulated processes. We come back to this in Chapter 28 when we talk about what happens after the pitch and how to manage investor timelines without losing momentum.

Whether you're raising institutional funding, seeking non-dilutive capital, asking your aunt for $10K, funding your business with customer revenue, or doing all of the above, the throughline is that you are using money as a tool to build your business. There is no one right way to do it; there is only the right way for *you*.

ACCREDITED INVESTORS AND REGULATIONS

Once you decide to raise equity funding in the US, you enter Securities and Exchange Commission (SEC) territory, which means following specific regulations that govern how startups can raise money and who can invest. These regulations were originally designed to protect investors, but they also reinforce systemic barriers that limit access to capital for many founders and potential investors.

UNDERSTANDING ACCREDITED INVESTORS AND THE BIAS IN EXISTING DEFINITIONS

One of the most important regulations to understand is who qualifies as an **accredited investor**. At the time of writing, the SEC defines an *accredited investor* as:

+ Someone with a net worth over $1 million (not counting their primary residence), or an income over $200,000 for the past two years ($300,000 if combined with that of a spouse).
+ Certain types of entities, like venture funds, banks, or trusts, that meet certain financial criteria.
+ Financial professionals with certain securities licenses and knowledgeable employees of private funds may also qualify.

This definition excludes most Americans from investing in private companies. While the original intent was to protect people from taking on too much financial risk, it ends up tying investment readiness to personal wealth and gatekeeping access to private markets. You can spend money on speculative public stock trades, gamble online, or drop all your cash on luxury items without restriction, but you can't invest in a startup unless you meet an arbitrary income or asset threshold.

That's a big problem because these rules favor people with generational wealth. Many individuals qualify as accredited investors because they inherited money or had early access to capital, but they aren't knowledgeable about finance or investment risk. Meanwhile, people with real financial knowledge or market understanding, including many women, people of color, and those outside of major tech hubs, are locked out. The result is fewer diverse investors and fewer funding sources for the very communities we need more representation from.

I have been advocating to modernize the accredited investor definition.[20] Proposed changes include:

- Recognizing financial literacy and experience as qualifiers, not just wealth.
- Lowering income and net worth thresholds to be more inclusive.
- Allowing all individuals to invest up to 10% of their net worth in startups.

Expanding who qualifies as an accredited investor would open up startup investing to a much wider and more diverse group of people. That means more innovation, more opportunity, and more everyday folks having a real shot at building wealth. If we want an economy that's truly driven by innovation, we need policies that reflect how people actually live and work today, and that means removing outdated barriers that keep capital stuck in the same narrow circles. Think about how many teachers, small business owners, or experienced operators you know who could be amazing investors if they were simply allowed to participate.

---

20   You can read the statement for the record I submitted in February 2025 to the Capital Markets Subcommittee in support of modernizing the definition of an *accredited investor* here: http://www.allisonbyers.com/resources.

HOW YOU CAN MARKET YOUR INVESTMENT OPPORTUNITY

When you're raising equity funding, you can't just shout it from the rooftops, at least, not legally, unless you meet certain SEC rules under something called Regulation D (or Reg D for short). These rules are meant to keep things in check and prevent fraud in private investing, but they also make it harder for early-stage founders to get the word out and attract investors.

Let's break down the most common ways founders can legally raise money under Reg D. Basically, these rules tell you who you can talk to about your raise and how.

+ **Rule 506(b): Private raise with limited non-accredited investors**

  - You *can't* advertise your raise publicly. So no posting it on LinkedIn or talking about it on a podcast.
  - You *can* take money from up to 35 non-accredited investors, but everyone else must be accredited.
  - Anyone investing must have a *pre-existing relationship* with you before you talk to them about investing. In practice, this means your relationship should involve some level of substantial interaction before you invite them to invest, not just a LinkedIn connection or someone who liked your Reddit post. A good rule of thumb is, if the SEC asked you to prove this person wasn't a stranger, could you?
  - This is the most common path for startup founders because it gives a little flexibility and doesn't require you to verify investor status up front.

+ **Rule 506(c): Public raise with accredited investors only**

  - You *can* talk about your raise publicly. Go for it on social media, in interviews, at events, wherever.
  - But only accredited investors are allowed to invest.
  - You have to verify that they're accredited, either by reviewing their financial documents or using a third-party verification service.
  - This is more commonly used by new fund managers than by individual startups.
  - If you go this route, you need to file with the SEC before you start marketing your raise.

+ **Reg CF: Equity crowdfunding**

  - You raise money through an online crowdfunding platform (think Wefunder, StartEngine, etc.).
  - All your raise information like terms, documents, and details must live on that platform. You cannot share investment information on your own website, social media, or emails. Instead, send everyone to your official crowdfunding campaign page.
  - You can raise up to $5 million per year through this method.
  - These platforms are tightly regulated, so expect a lot of disclosures and legal paperwork (more on this later).

In the chapters that follow, we'll break down each type of capital, starting with venture capital. You'll learn how they work, who they're best for, and how to approach them with intention. Knowing your options is powerful, and understanding how to use them is even more critical.

Fundraising is about alignment, not approval.
Every dollar comes from a human being with specific motivations, preferences, and biases. Focus your energy on finding people who are predisposed to say yes to you.

Build your Ideal Investor Profile (IIP).
Just like you define your ideal customer, you can define your ideal investor. Your IIP helps you identify the people most likely to understand your business, connect with your mission, and want to support your vision.

Investor fit is personal, not just professional.
It's not just about stage, sector, or check size. Think about how you like to communicate, the energy you bring, and who responds to it. The right investor will get you, not just your deck.

Equity and non-dilutive capital serve different roles.
Equity funding means giving up ownership in exchange for capital. Non-dilutive sources like grants and loans don't affect your ownership stake. Each has trade-offs and there's no single right answer.

Regulations shape how you can raise.

Different SEC rules (like Reg D 506(b) and 506(c), and Reg CF)
govern what you can say publicly, who can invest, and what paperwork
you need. Understanding the rules protects you and expands your
options.

Your capital strategy should reflect your business and values.

There is no one-size-fits-all approach to raising money. The best path
is the one that aligns with your goals, your customers, and the kind
of company you want to build.

INSIDE THE WORLD OF VENTURE CAPITAL

HOW BIAS SHOWS UP IN FUNDRAISING

Systemic bias in venture capital isn't always overt, but it shows up everywhere. It shapes who gets meetings, who gets funded, and who feels like they belong in the room. It also affects investors themselves, not just founders. To navigate this landscape, it's helpful to understand how these biases show up in practice.

Let's break down a few key data points:

- 96% of VC deals come directly from a fund's network.[21] Of those, 89% require a warm introduction or referrals. So, when people say, "You need a warm intro to get into VC," they're stating a hard truth about how access works.

---

21   Morgan Stanley, "Beyond the VC Funding Gap," 2019, https://www.morganstanley.com/content/dam/msdotcom/mcil/Morgan_Stanley_Beyond_the_VC_Funding_Gap_2019_Report.pdf.

+ 90% of check-writing decision-makers at US venture funds are male.[22] And 65% of VC firms have no female partners at all.[23]
+ White men make up 30% of the US population but control 93% of VC dollars.[24] Since people's networks tend to mirror their own identities, guess where most of those warm introductions go?

The bias doesn't stop with founders. Underrepresented fund managers are also building firms, backing visionary entrepreneurs, and challenging the status quo despite facing steep structural barriers. The system limits both who can receive capital and who gets to allocate it. This is about more than just fairness; it's about lost economic opportunity. Studies show that venture firms with at least one female partner generate 10% more profitable exits.[25] Women offer real economic upside and fuel for global innovation.

This is why I want you to think critically about your fundraising strategy. Raising VC isn't impossible, and if it aligns with your goals and business model, go for it. But you need to go into it clear-eyed about the structural challenges at play so you can craft a smart, intentional approach.

22　Dan Primack, "Venture Capital Is Still Very Much a Boys' Club," Axios, February 14, 2019, https://www.axios.com/2019/02/14/venture-capital-women-tech-diversity.

23　PitchBook, "The Majority of VC Firms Still Have No Female Investors," February 11, 2020, https://pitchbook.com/newsletter/the-majority-of-vc-firms-still-have-no-female-investors.

24　Suraj Gupta, "Diversity: The Holy Grail of Venture Capital," *Forbes*, May 26, 2022, https://www.forbes.com/councils/forbesbusinesscouncil/2022/05/26/diversity-the-holy-grail-of-venture-capital/#:~:text=White%20men%20represent%2030%25%20of,staggering%2093%25%20of%20VC%20dollars.

25　Lisa Stone, "WRG's Diversity Paper Featured in *Forbes* Magazine Column," West River Group, September 22, 2020, https://www.wrg.vc/news/wrgs-diversity-paper-featured-in-forbes-magazine-column-by-lisa-stone.

A US-DOMINANT MARKET

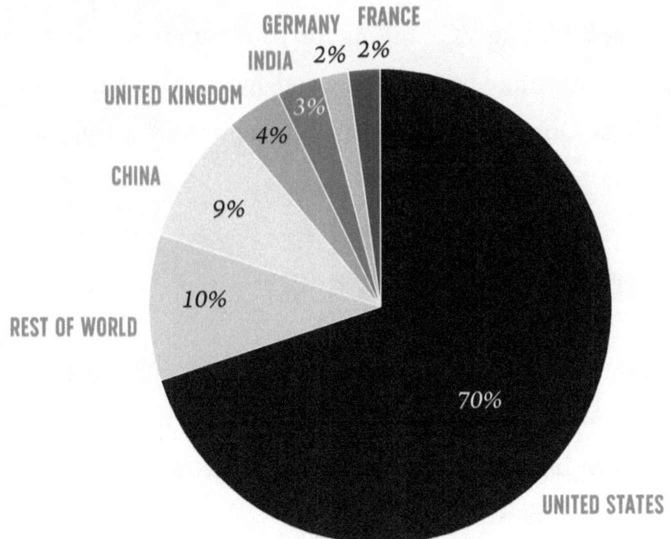

Sources: Approximate distribution of global venture capital investment by country, 2025. Percentages are rounded estimates based on multiple industry data sources (including CB Insights, PitchBook, and other 2025 venture funding reports).

Figure 3.1

Admittedly, much of this book focuses on the US venture capital system, and that's intentional. Estimates of 2025 global venture investment range from about $470 billion[26] to just over $510 billion,[27] depending on how "venture capital" and *late-stage private rounds* are defined. The US alone attracted roughly 70% of that capital—more than every other country combined (see figure 3.1).[28] No other single country comes close to that volume or

---

26   CB Insights, State of Venture 2025 (New York: CB Insights, January 2026).

27   PitchBook, Q4 2025 Global VC First Look and PitchBook–NVCA Venture Monitor (Seattle: PitchBook Data, January 2026).

28   Approximate distribution of global venture capital investment by country, 2025. Percentages are rounded estimates based on multiple industry data sources (including CB Insights, PitchBook, and other 2025 venture funding reports).

dominance in VC, which is why so many international founders aim to raise from American investors even if they're building companies elsewhere.

If you're considering VC funding for your company, it's important to understand how venture firms operate and, more importantly, what drives their decisions. Once you know what they're optimizing for, you can start to see your startup through their eyes.

LIMITED PARTNERS CONTROL THE MONEY

Venture capital firms don't invest their own money, at least not most of it. Instead, they raise money from what are called limited partners (LPs). These are usually big institutions like pension funds, university endowments, corporations, or ultra-wealthy individuals.

The people running the VC firm, the ones making the investment decisions, are called general partners (GPs). They manage the fund, choose which startups to invest in, and work closely with portfolio companies after investing. While GPs may invest some of their own money into the fund, the vast majority comes from LPs. That's an important distinction from individual investors like angels, who are usually investing their own cash and can act more independently.

Because GPs are managing other people's money, they have what's called a **fiduciary duty** to those LPs. That means they're legally and ethically required to prioritize the financial interests of their LPs. Not yours, not the startup ecosystem's, and definitely not innovation for innovation's sake. Every decision they make must be justifiable based on risk, return, and overall portfolio strategy.

THE PORTFOLIO STRATEGY

VC firms don't place all their chips on one startup. They use what's called a **portfolio strategy**, meaning they spread their investments across a bunch of companies to increase their odds of a big win. They fully expect most of those bets not to pan out.

Here's how it typically works:

+ A single VC fund invests in 20–30 startups over the life of the fund, which usually lasts about 10 years.
+ They assume most will fail, a few might break even, and, hopefully, one or two will hit it big and deliver enormous returns that make up for all the losses.
+ To make the math work, they often look for startups with the potential to return 10x their original investment.

This is key to understand because it means a VC might pass on your company even if it's solid and profitable if it doesn't have the kind of massive, high-growth potential they need to balance the rest of their portfolio.

WHY YOUR YES MIGHT ACTUALLY BE A NO

VCs see *a lot* of pitches—we're talking thousands each year. A typical firm might review over 5,000 startups and invest in only 10–20. That's less than a 1% investment rate.[29]

So, if a VC shows interest, it's exciting, but it's not a guarantee of a check. In fact, many founders confuse early enthusiasm with intent to invest, only

---

29 This data comes from multiple independent reports and anecdotal evidence from major investors.

to be ghosted or politely declined later. Here are some common reasons why a "this is interesting" might still end in a no:

- **Portfolio conflict:** They like what you're building, but already invested in a company that's too similar, which would create a conflict of interest.
- **Business stage mismatch:** You're too early (or too late) for where their fund typically invests.
- **Check size misalignment:** Their minimum check size is $5 million, and you're only raising $750K.
- **Sector focus:** Their current thesis is all about AI and fintech, but your startup is in climate tech or consumer goods.
- **LP mandates:** Even if they personally love your company, their investors (LPs) expect them to fund specific categories, like deep tech or enterprise SaaS.

This is why researching VCs before pitching is critical. Don't just go by what's on their website. Look at their actual portfolio, listen to podcast interviews, and read their recent blog posts or deal announcements. What a firm *says* and what it *does* aren't always the same. You should understand not just what they say they invest in, but what they actually invest in. Behavior always speaks louder than words.

That's one of the reasons I co-authored the California Fair Investment Practices by Venture Capital Companies Act (FIPVCC), a first-of-its-kind piece of legislation signed into law in October 2023. It requires venture capital firms with a California nexus to collect and annually report anonymized, aggregated demographic data on the founding teams of the companies they invest in to the California Department of Financial Protection and Innovation (DFPI). The first reports, covering investments made in 2025, are due April 1,

2026. For the first time, there will be real data showing the demographic patterns of who is actually getting funded.

Now, instead of guessing whether a fund truly supports *The Rest of Us*, or just says they do, founders will be able to see the receipts. This shifts power to the innovators. It helps you make data-informed decisions about who to approach, and who's unlikely to say yes, no matter how good your story is. It also provides the data policymakers need to ideate and advocate for programs that encourage a more robust innovation economy.

THE INVESTMENT PROCESS

It's easy to think that if you nail your pitch in a VC meeting, you're all set. But getting a yes from one person is the starting line, not the finish line. Most investment decisions at venture firms go through multiple rounds of evaluation and involve several different people.

Here's how it typically works:

The California State Senate recognized the SB54 bill team members on our advocacy for diversity and inclusion in the venture capital space during their floor session on Thursday June 6th, 2024. Senator Toni Atkins and Senator Nancy Skinner presented each of us with a Resolution commending our work.

Finally, some real transparency with California SB54. It's not always easy to find clear, honest information about where a fund invests. That's a big problem when you're a founder trying to figure out who's worth pitching and where your time and energy will be best spent.

1. **Initial Meeting:** You'll usually start by pitching to a junior investor, like an analyst, associate, or sometimes a partner. If they're excited, they'll do more research (called light **diligence**) and may introduce you to others at the firm.

2. **Internal Discussions:** The person you met with becomes your internal champion. That means they have to sell your deal to their team. They'll frame it in terms of how your startup fits into the firm's strategy, risk profile, and goals.

3. **Investment Committee Review:** If things are still progressing, your company will be formally presented to the fund's **investment committee**, which is a group of senior partners and sometimes LP representatives. These are the people who vote on whether the firm should invest.

4. **Due Diligence:** If the committee is interested, they'll dig deeper. This part is called **due diligence,** and it includes a thorough analysis of your financials, market, team, competition, legal structure, and anything else that could affect the investment. The team will write a **deal memo**, which is an internal document that outlines the opportunity and risk, and makes the case for investing (or not).

5. **Term Sheet:** If they're ready to move forward, you'll get a **term sheet.** This is a nonbinding document that spells out the proposed terms of the investment including how much they'll invest, what percentage of ownership they'll receive, board seats, and other important legal terms.

Each of these steps is a gate, and any one of them can be where a deal falls apart. That's why *no* often takes longer than *yes* and why fundraising can feel like an emotional roller coaster. Even if someone is really excited after your first meeting, they might not have the power to make the final decision, or the rest of the team might not agree.

I'll never forget one of my first meetings with a venture fund while raising our Series A at my last company. It was with a junior partner at a big-name firm, and we met at a cramped little coffee shop, squeezing our drinks and my printed pitch deck onto a table barely big enough for one. He was a practicing clinician recruited for his domain expertise, exactly the kind of person who understood our device.

The meeting was electric. He was engaged, curious, asking sharp questions. When he asked about our fundraising history, I handed him a prepared chart I had made in anticipation. He looked at it and said, "I've never had someone hand me exactly the chart I wanted like that." I walked out floating. This guy got it. I was sure I'd found our lead investor!

I followed up right away. Then again. And again. For over a month, I sent updates and polite nudges. Nothing. Radio silence.

At the time, I didn't get it, but now I do. He was excited as a clinician, not as an investor, and the rest of the partnership likely didn't see what he did. He moved on. And yes, we paid for his coffee.

CHOOSING VC: KNOWING THE RISKS

By now, you've seen that venture capital is high risk, high reward, and often high stakes. You've also read how bias, power dynamics, and opaque decision-making can create frustrating, or even harmful, experiences for founders.

So, why would anyone still pursue it?

For some founders, VC is still the best, or only, path to bringing a bold, world-changing idea to life. Venture capital offers something many other funding sources can't: the ability to scale fast, raise more money over time, and gain credibility by being backed by well-known firms. That stamp of approval can open doors with customers, partners, talent, and media. Jennifer Kushell explained her reasoning like this:

> We've raised $680,000 and generated $2.4 million in revenue. We've trained 50,000 kids. I'm doing exactly what industry says we need in schools, and I have the data to prove it. Yet I still have to hire men

just to build our modeling so investors will take us seriously. It baffles me how hard this is.

I want venture because I want to build something big. I want to set a new global standard for how we prepare young people for the workforce. That's been my mission. The reason I want top VC firms is because they bring credibility. When we say, 'This is the gold standard,' I want institutions to believe it.

I could probably raise from other sources, which maybe I should, but I've been here before in a place where I create more demand than I can serve, like when my *New York Times* bestseller sold out four times before its release. Right now, I have a weighted pipeline between $6 and $54 million. I can't meet that demand without capital. I don't want to keep scraping by convincing people round after round. If I'm with a top VC and we show traction, they can keep funding us and we can all profit in a huge way.

Ricquelle Jeffrey is also going into fundraising with open eyes:

I'm working 100% on my startup and 20% on my consulting firm to pay the bills (yes, 120%). We're fully fundraising our pre-seed right now. We're two women of color. My co-founder is from Pakistan, and I'm originally from Trinidad and Tobago. It's been a very difficult process, and we're seasoned founders with very thick skin. Even for us, we have to remind ourselves of the marathon we're running.

We know the process and how hard it is to raise money, so we've overprepared. We're always questioning: Have we thought about this? Have we thought about that?

Even when I'm contacting someone I know, I constantly have to highlight our team because it's like people forget we have experience.

> Our CTO is one of the original engineers who worked on Apple Siri. My co-founder and I have over 35 years in tech combined. We keep reiterating that again and again. Then I open LinkedIn and see a TechCrunch article about a 19-year-old getting $23 million. They don't have our experience but that is when reality hits you—the funding gap women and people of color experience daily.
>
> We know the rejections are not a personal attack on us, but still, it's painful. So, we stay grounded in our narrative, take it day by day, and focus on finding the people who we know will want to hear about what we're building.

Despite the challenges, founders like Jennifer and Ricquelle pursue VC with clear intent. They're not chasing validation; they're seeking the capital and partners needed to meet the scale of their vision. Choosing VC doesn't mean ignoring the risks, but instead acknowledging them, preparing for them, and making a deliberate bet that this path, with all its complexity, can be the right one. For some, the right kind of VC comes not from traditional firms, but from corporations aligned with their market and mission.

CORPORATE VENTURE CAPITAL: THE SLOWER, STRATEGIC SIBLING

Corporate venture capital funds (CVCs) are the investment arms of large companies. Think tech giants, healthcare systems, retailers, banks, etc. They invest in startups that align with their big-picture goals. That might mean innovation they want to keep tabs on, technology they might want to acquire someday, or future partners who can help them move faster.

That said, a company doesn't need a formal CVC arm to invest strategically. Midsize companies or newer players in the startup world often invest directly off their balance sheet. These one-off or opportunistic investments are sometimes led by a business unit champion who sees clear alignment. In that sense, these informal strategic investors can act a lot like angel investors with bigger budgets.

CVCs have been around for decades, but their presence is growing. In recent years, corporate-backed deals have accounted for roughly a third of all venture capital deal value. Globally, CVC activity has made up 21% of total VC deals over the past decade.[30] Whether it's a structured investment team or a motivated head of innovation with a checkbook, they're investing because your company connects to their strategy.

WHAT THEY'RE LOOKING FOR

Unlike traditional VCs who live and breathe the 10x exit, CVCs care more about how your startup might help their parent company thrive.

They might invest in you because:

+ You're solving a real problem they face internally.
+ You're a potential acquisition target down the road.
+ They want a front-row seat to innovation in your space.

Even if your business is growing fast, they'll likely pass if your product doesn't map to their internal goals. Strategic fit is the whole point.

---

30   Bain & Company, "Global Venture Capital Outlook: Latest Trends Snap Chart," February 2024, https://www.bain.com/insights/global-venture-capital-outlook-latest-trends-snap-chart (reporting that corporate-backed venture activity accounted for roughly 36% of total global VC deal value). See also, Foley & Lardner LLP, "Corporate Venture Capital 2025: More M&A, AI, and Strategic Focus," February 2025, https://www.foley.com/insights/publications/2025/02/corporate-venture-capital-2025-more-m-a (includes finding that from 2014–2024, corporate venture capital represented 21% of global deal count and 46% of total deal value).

IT'S A SLOW RIDE

Even if a CVC is excited about your company, don't expect them to move quickly. Their decision-making process can feel like pitching to a committee that then needs to get approval from another committee.

You might encounter:

+ A business unit sponsor who has to champion you internally.
+ Legal teams combing through how your product fits into their road map.
+ Senior leadership assessing whether your business aligns with their five-year plan.

If you're raising on a tight timeline, this can cause real delays. CVCs are best approached early, in parallel with faster-moving investors like angels or seed-stage VCs. You don't want your whole round hinging on a corporate partner who's still "thinking it over."

READ THE FINE PRINT

The power dynamics here can be tricky, especially if your investor could also be a customer or competitor. That can get complicated.

A few things to keep in mind:

+ Protect your IP. Don't overshare in diligence without a nondisclosure agreement in place.
+ Watch out for exclusivity, right of first refusal, or anything that limits future deals.

+ Ask who makes the decisions. Some CVCs operate like independent firms. Others need board-level approval. Know which one you're dealing with.

If you're not sure, ask other founders who have worked with them. The best way to know how a CVC (or anyone, for that matter) acts in real life is to talk to someone with experience.

THE STRATEGIC TRIPLE THREAT: CUSTOMER, INVESTOR, OR ACQUIRER?

When the alignment is real, corporate venture can be a powerful lever. A strategic investor might open doors you didn't even know existed, like distribution channels, credibility, technical know-how, or insight into industry shifts. But don't go into it expecting a fairy tale.

Many founders dream of landing a strategic investor who will sprinkle magic dust and make everything easier. In reality, the help tends to be targeted and practical with an intro here, a pilot there. They aren't hands-on co-builders but can be strong allies.

Suelin Chen gives us a peek behind the scenes:

> We had a strategic who was looking at acquiring us, but they invested instead. I think this is a source of capital that a lot of founders don't always explore. We considered strategic investment multiple times, and it was through me connecting directly with C-suite counterparts or a dedicated investment arm.
>
> When it didn't work out with a strategic, it was usually for reasons that were harder to read than when fundraising from VCs or angels. There are a lot of shifting priorities all the time in these big companies. What's hot one minute is not the priority the next, so timing is super key.

It's interesting because often when you talk to a company, they could be a customer, an acquirer, an investor, or all three. There are all these potential ways you can partner with a company, and those functions are often owned by different people. So, you have to suss out what's the best way to work with them, and in what order. Sometimes they'll tell you, but it's better for the company to direct this as it is often complicated and leaders in these companies 1) don't always have the full picture, and 2) can be replaced, and then you'll have to build the relationship from scratch.

DECIPHERING VC REJECTION

Venture capital is just one kind of funding, and it's often not the best fit, especially if you're not building a business that's chasing massive scale or a fast exit. Fundraising is all about alignment. If you're raising from venture, you shouldn't focus on convincing someone to invest, but rather finding the right partner. Someone whose fund structure, investment thesis, and goals match what you're building.

I used to take every VC rejection personally. I thought each no was a failure on my part. Once I started digging into how venture works, I realized rejection often has little to do with you. Sometimes it's systemic bias. Other times, it's about timing, fund constraints, or internal dynamics you'll never see. Knowing this can help you stop spinning your wheels so you can focus your energy on what will move your business forward.

Here's a quick guide to decoding what investors say, and what they usually mean:

+ **Investor says:** "We think you're great, but you're too early."
  What it actually means: "We're not convinced, and we don't want to take the risk to find out."

- **Investor says:** "Circle back when you're further along."
  What it actually means: "I'm not excited enough to follow your progress."
- **Investor says:** "We're not sure this is a fit for our thesis."
  What it actually means: "We didn't feel a strong enough connection to the opportunity or to you."
- **Investor says:** "This space feels crowded."
  What it actually means: "We already picked our winner in this category."
- **Investor says:** "Let us know when you find a lead for the round."
  What it actually means: "We're not going to take the lead risk; we're waiting for social proof."
- **Investor says:** "Keep us updated."
  What it actually means: "We're saying no for now, but want to hedge our bets in case you break out."

Understanding these coded responses can save you time and emotional energy. It lets you move on faster and focus on building real traction with people who get what you're doing. Develop your own filters, ask clarifying questions, and surround yourself with trusted advisors and peers who can help translate investor speak into honest, actionable insights.

Suelin puts it well:

Most companies probably shouldn't raise traditional venture. Once you raise venture, you're committing to a particular path, and that path is not always what's best for the business. You're committing to a high-risk, high-reward model, and even if your business could be huge, you're giving up certain other paths. You also now have a fiduciary responsibility.

You can read about how this works and intellectually understand it, but it's so different once you've lived through it. When you're making day-to-day business decisions and trade-offs, you sometimes have to go a particular way because of the type of capital you chose and the kind of business you plan to be. As soon as you take capital, depending on the type, it can restrict how and when you can exit.

The narrative of startup press indoctrinates us into a certain way of thinking that doesn't reflect reality. I meet so many people who want to raise this perfect round because that's what they've read about in startup media. For most people, especially those who are underrepresented, that's just not how it works. It's almost always much messier. It's also not a goal in and of itself—it's just the beginning of a journey. In general, it's usually best to fund company operations with revenue.

STACK THE ODDS IN YOUR FAVOR

If venture capital is part of your strategy, or even a maybe for the future, these four steps will help set you up for success. They'll serve you well no matter what kind of capital you pursue.

1. **Leverage portfolio founders for warm intros.**
   Start by finding founders who have raised from the funds you're targeting. Most VC websites list their portfolio companies. Reach out to those founders and ask about their experience:
   - What was their fundraising journey like?
   - How do they feel about the investors on their cap table (short for capitalization table, which tracks everyone who owns a piece of the company, how much they own, and when they invested)?
   - Would they be open to making an introduction?

This is one of the most effective ways to get in front of the right people.

2. **Research individual partners, not just funds.**

   VC is a relationship business. Funds don't write checks, individual people do. When you're researching firms, dig into the specific partner who would be most likely to lead your deal. Check out their background, interests, and past investments. Also look at the broader team because if your partner leaves the firm, someone else will inherit your deal. Make sure there are others you'd want to work with.

3. **Treat every meeting as relationship-building.**

   Your goal in a meeting isn't to walk out with a check, it's to earn more time. If you show up with "close the deal" energy, you risk skipping over the part where trust is built. Focus on learning, connecting, and showing how you think. Many successful fundraises come from relationships that have been nurtured over years. Investors need to see that you're trustworthy, capable, and consistent.

4. **Build a visible presence online.**

   Be active where investors hang out, especially on LinkedIn and Bluesky. Investors *will* Google or ChatGPT you. At the early stage, *you* are the company, and your online presence reflects your leadership, credibility, and expertise. Share your perspective, your work, and your vision. If investors already know who you are before they see your pitch, you're well ahead of the game.

VC FOR *THE REST OF US*

If you identify as underrepresented, you aren't just raising capital, you're navigating a system that wasn't designed with you in mind. That doesn't mean you don't belong in it. Quite the opposite. The data consistently shows that when diverse founders are given access to capital and resources, they outperform. Your job is to be strategic, intentional, and resilient in how you engage with that system, and to find the right partners within it.

And yes, the right venture capital partners can and do exist. There are venture capitalists who see your value, bring more than just money to the table, and genuinely want to support your growth without controlling it. You are evaluating them just as much as they're evaluating you.

Suelin shares how misalignment can cost everyone, not just the founder. Sometimes investors will act against their own financial interests when ego, bias, or the need for control enters the picture.

> I've had a few incidents where investors behaved in ways that were not best for the business but served their desire for control. These have been hard lessons, but at the end of the day, investors are people too, with the same insecurities and responding to the same incentives.

Founder–investor alignment isn't just about vision or growth trajectory, it's also about values, communication, and how both sides handle power. You can do everything "right" and still find yourself in conflict with someone whose decision-making is driven by comfort and familiarity rather than logic or performance.

There are plenty of positive VC stories out there, especially when values are aligned and expectations are clear from the start. Julie Moir Messervy's experience is one of them:

My COO at the time knew one of the partners at a venture fund. That fund typically invests at a later stage, but they made an exception for us. They were very clear with me that they were investing in *me*, which was a bit scary because I knew what I didn't know, which was still a lot, about building a tech company.

Our venture investor is truly hands-on in a collaborative way. We have an informal check-in every week. If I don't want to meet or they can't make it, no problem. It never feels like I'm reporting to them. It's more like, 'Here's what's happening, here's what we're working on,' and they always add value. Sometimes they join partner calls or help with things like strategy, accounting systems, and infrastructure to support future fundraising. They understand our business, they believe in what we're building, and they've been wise advisors through every step.

VC doesn't have to mean pressure, dilution, or power struggles. When you choose it with intention, and partner with people who respect your leadership, it can look like true partnership, mutual respect, and support that accelerates your path. The same basic principle applies to any money you accept: You need to understand the other person's motivations, and they need to understand yours, so that you can move forward from a place of mutual clarity and alignment.

Venture capital isn't just money; it's a system.
To raise from VC, you have to understand how the system works, who holds the power, and what drives their decisions.

Bias is baked into the process.
Warm intros dominate, networks reflect existing privilege, and most capital is controlled by a narrow demographic. These structural issues aren't *about* you, but they do *affect* you.

VCs manage other people's money.
They manage funds from limited partners and have a fiduciary duty to prioritize financial return above all else. Their decisions are driven by portfolio strategy, not just belief in your business.

Not every *maybe* means yes.
Founders often misinterpret investor enthusiasm as intent. Rejection can come from internal misalignment, portfolio conflicts, or constraints you'll never see.

Strategic investors think differently.
Corporate VCs and strategic partners optimize for alignment with their goals rather than growth trajectory alone. They often move slower but can open valuable doors.

Rejection is often coded.

VC language rarely means what it says. Learn to translate investor speak so you can move on faster and stay grounded in your vision.

Raising VC is a choice, not a requirement.

It's one path and it certainly isn't the only path. VC is best for companies chasing big scale and rapid growth, and it comes with trade-offs.

Alignment is everything.

Whether you're raising from traditional firms, strategic investors, or alternative VCs, focus on partners who believe in your vision, respect your leadership, and bring more than capital to the table.

ANGEL INVESTORS: THE HIDDEN FORCE BEHIND STARTUP FUNDING

Angel investors are one of the most important sources of money for early-stage startups. Many founders don't realize just how many people fall into this category or how much power they hold. In the US alone, there are 24 million households that qualify as "accredited,"[31] which means they meet certain income or asset thresholds set by the government, allowing them to legally invest in private companies. Of those, over 4 million are already investing in startups.[32] That number is almost certainly lower than reality since there's no official list of who's writing checks into private businesses.

Let's put this in perspective.

---

31 According to the US Securities and Exchange Commission (SEC), an accredited investor in the US is someone who meets certain financial requirements set by the SEC. This includes having a net worth over $1 million (not counting their home) or earning more than $200,000 per year ($300,000 with a spouse) for the past two years. Accredited investors are allowed to invest in certain high-risk opportunities, like startups, that aren't open to the general public. See US Securities and Exchange Commission, 2024, https://www.sec.gov/resources-small-businesses/capital-raising-building-blocks/accredited-investors.

32 Angel Capital Association (ACA), https://angelcapitalassociation.org/.

According to the US Bureau of Labor Statistics 2023 Consumer Expenditure Survey, households in the top 20% of earners, which includes all accredited investors, report the following annual averages:

+ Income before taxes: $264,000
+ Income after taxes: $211,000
+ Total spending: $150,000

That leaves $61,000 left over per year, which is the money that is not going toward taxes, daily living expenses, or retirement savings. It's extra. While most people aren't used to thinking of it this way, that surplus could be used to invest in startups.

Now scale that across all 24 million accredited households:

$61,000 × 24 million = **$1.46 trillion in surplus capital every year.**

Let that sink in.

I'm not saying all of that money should go into startups; it shouldn't. But imagine what could happen if even a small fraction of it did:

+ 5% of it = $75 billion per year
+ 10% = $150 billion per year
+ 20% = $300 billion per year invested in new companies

Whoa. That level of investment could completely transform the funding landscape.

It could mean:

+ More bold ideas getting the resources they need to take off,
+ More diverse founders getting their first checks, and
+ More wealth creation flowing not just to select groups, but to *The Rest of Us.*

Angel investing isn't a secret club reserved for finance professionals. In fact, many new angel investors are founders themselves, people like you and me, who want to both get involved and support other builders. As a founder, becoming an angel investor is incredibly valuable. It shifts your mindset to think like the people you're pitching to. You start to notice the signals that spark your interest or raise concerns, and that perspective helps you tell your own story more clearly when you're fundraising. It also sharpens your understanding of what makes a business investable, and where your own pitch might run into challenges. That awareness becomes even more important when you explore other funding paths, like the ones we'll cover in the equity crowdfunding chapter. Often, it just takes an invitation or a story from another founder to open the door to this world for the first time.

Consider this your personal invitation from me. I'll share how I got started.

In February 2022, I made my first angel investment. I honestly can't remember how I met Rachel Cossar, the founder of Virtual Sapiens, but I remember exactly how I felt. I immediately saw what she was building and why it mattered. She was creating AI tools to help professionals strengthen their communication presence, which is becoming increasingly important as video meetings take over our working lives.

Rachel was the kind of founder I wanted to see succeed: thoughtful, visionary, and building from deep personal experience. We had a few conversations, and I reviewed her materials like her pitch deck, cap table, financial projections, and market research. Don't worry if those terms are new to you; I'll break them down later. The point is, it all made sense.

At the same time, Rachel pitched to the angel group (more about angel groups in a minute) I was part of, and it reinforced everything I already believed. I invested $5,000 through that group's private Wefunder page.

That's it. No secret handshake. No finance background required.

It wasn't an amount that would break me if I never saw it again, but it was enough to make a real difference for her, and I genuinely believe I'll see a return. For me, investing is a form of voting. I'm using my dollars to vote for the kind of future I want to see. That's what angel investing can be. That's what it should be.

Derek Ali, a multi-Grammy-award–winning mix engineer, widely known as MixedByAli, shared his experience activating new angels who invested in his startup, EngineEars:

> I knew nobody in the business space, nobody in the venture space. Naturally, me coming from music, I knew a lot of recording artists and producers that were successful. So, I just went to the people that I'm working with on a daily basis. Industry leaders who had been part of my journey from a nobody to becoming one of the biggest creators of music. Now I'm looking to streamline my journey for others in a product and wanted to provide them opportunities to be first-time investors and be part of fixing a broken industry. A lot of them, if not everyone, were first-time investors. Even when you're big and famous and have all this stuff, you still are activating people to invest that haven't before. Looking at your friends like, that is interesting, right?

Derek's story captures what's possible when you expand your view of who an "investor" can be. The next wave of angels won't just come from venture firms or finance backgrounds; they'll come from creators, community leaders, technologists, and professionals across every industry who decide to back innovation they believe in.

HOW ANGELS DIFFER FROM VCs

What sets angels apart from venture capitalists is that they invest their own money, while VCs invest money from other people (limited partners, or LPs). That creates a different kind of motivation.

- VCs have to deliver high returns to their LPs and usually follow strict portfolio strategies.
- Angels don't have LPs to report to, which gives them more flexibility in how and why they invest.

Every angel defines success in their own way. While most hope for good returns, many also invest for reasons that go beyond money and consider other types of returns just as fulfilling as financial ones. They might care deeply about a specific industry or solutions that focus on something impacting their family. They might want to advise early-stage founders, or they might just believe in *you* and your vision.

This flexibility is what makes angel capital so valuable. Unlike institutional investors, angels often care more about long-term potential than short-term hyper-growth. They also bring operational expertise, industry connections, and real-world advice that can be game-changing for early founders beyond their check.

As serial entrepreneur Joel Mutua put it:

> Raising from angels was all about personal connection. I told them my story, and they believed in the mission. VCs were different. It was hype, momentum, and timing. Same company. Totally different approaches.

ANGELS ARE EVERYWHERE

Let's look closer at who angel investors really are, which should help you think through your Ideal Investor Profile (IIP). They're not a homogeneous group. They come from all kinds of backgrounds, and the landscape is constantly changing. Here are a few important trends to understand:

- **More women and diverse investors:** Women now make up 47% of angel investors, a 39% increase since 2021. Female angels are 10 times more likely to care about the gender of the founders they invest in, which helps drive more capital toward diverse teams.[33]

- **Younger investors:** The stereotype of angels being retired executives is fading. More millennials and Gen Z investors are entering the space, often with an impact-first mindset.[34]

- **Geographically distributed:** While most venture capital is still concentrated in San Francisco, New York, and Boston, 63% of angel investors live outside those hubs. That shift helps bring funding to startups in overlooked and under-resourced regions.[35]

- **First-time investors:** Every year, roughly 3,000 people make their very first angel investment. That means the pool of potential

---

[33] Center for Venture Research at the University of New Hampshire, https://paulcollege.unh.edu/center-venture-research.

[34] Kyla Scanlon, "How Millennials and Gen Z Can Reshape U.S. Investing," EQT Group, November 12, 2024, https://eqtgroup.com/thinq/wealth/how-millennials-and-gen-z-can-reshape-us-investing.

[35] Laura Huang et al., *The American Angel: The First Comprehensive Study of the US Angel Investor Market*, Angel Capital Association and Wharton Entrepreneurship, November 2017, https://www.hbs.edu/faculty/Publication%20Files/American%20Angel_50333d06-b332-4221-9919-2c35057ca468.pdf.

capital is growing. You may already know someone who's part of it without realizing it![36]

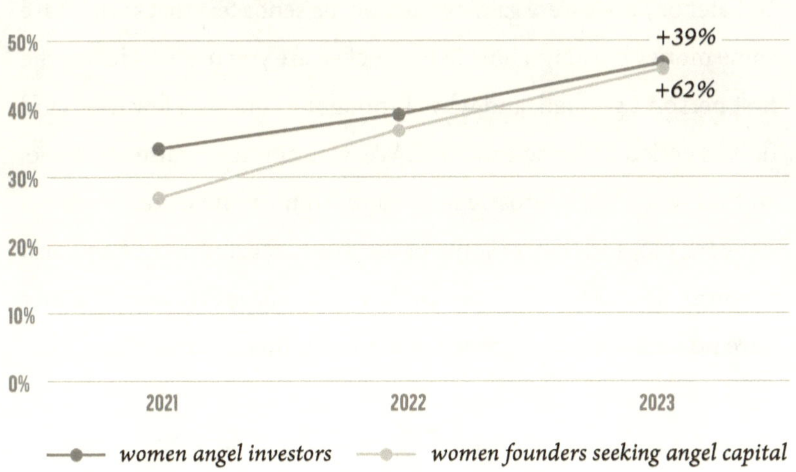

Sources: Center for Venture Research at the University of New Hampshire, https://paulcollege.unh.edu/center-venture-research.

Figure 4.1

Deanna Meador had a similar experience to Derek when it came to finding her early angels:

> 2021 was the first raise we did, and it was from angels. They were mostly people in my network, many that I didn't even know invested in early-stage companies until I said, 'Hey, we're going to raise a round for this company,' and when they expressed interest, I said, 'I didn't

---

36　The Motley Fool, "Everybody Wants to Be an Angel (Investor)," Nasdaq, August 10, 2021, https://www.nasdaq.com/articles/everybody-wants-to-be-an-angel-investor-2021-08-10.

even know you did that!' An example is someone I ran into at a kid's birthday party who I've known forever. He asked what I was doing these days, so I told him about my company, and he said, 'If you ever raise money, please call me.'

Later on, as we were gaining traction, he sent a text that said, 'I have some money burning a hole in my pocket, are you ready?' He was the first person I pitched, and what I thought might be a few thousand dollars ended up being $200,000. We were aiming to raise $600,000, so that was a huge boost. He brought in more investors from his network too, and they're some of the most amazing people and best investors (from a founder's perspective) that I have ever seen. You may have no idea that people you run across do this as part of their life!

This is such an important mindset shift. Angel investors aren't always on social media or speaking at pitch competitions. They might be at your coworking space, your kid's school, your local coffee shop, or a member of one of your affiliations. The key is to talk about what you're building. When you share your progress, passion, and plans, you create opportunities for the right people to raise their hands and say, *I want to be part of that!*

Jen Saxton had a similar experience, but amplified. After building and selling her first company, she launched a second and started fundraising again. She called her strategy her "most unhinged" fundraising move:

I exported every contact I had from Gmail—work, personal, you name it. It was like 15,000 emails. I didn't have time to go through them one by one. So, I just hit send.

She sent a leap-year update on February 29, 2024, after four years without sending anything. It was part life update, part business news. She had a second baby, sold her first company, and launched her second, which has an in-store Target launch. Her husband was still making movies, and yes, the dog was still cute. You can read the full email here: ALLISONBYERS.COM/RESOURCES.

> Some 6,000 emails bounced. About 1,000 people unsubscribed. But 4,000+ people opened it. And within three weeks, $200,000 hit my bank account.

People she hadn't spoken to in years replied. Former classmates. A customer from her earliest pilot (a small-scale test of her original product). A guy whose car seat she cleaned in business school.

> I emailed everyone I've ever met in my whole life, and these people started writing me checks like crazy. I had eight $25,000 checks from people I hadn't talked to since college. It was wild. So, I'm going to send another one next week and see what shakes out.

It worked because Jen was real, bold, and willing to take a risk. Most importantly, she invited people in. Sometimes that's all it takes.

> If you don't have the chutzpah to just email everybody you've ever met—I get it. But for me, it worked.

This dynamic plays out in surprising places. Karen Robinson Cope told me about a friend, a senior executive who ran a $10 billion division, who came to a few angel pitch events and wrote her first check:

> She has this massive 401(k), mostly in public equities and a little in real estate and had never considered investing in a startup before.

But after hearing a few pitches, she turned to me and said, 'Why haven't I done this before?' I realized in that moment that there are so many women like her. High-level leaders, especially from telecom and corporate sectors, with millions of dollars in retirement accounts who just need to be invited in. The women, especially the women in corporate America, they are hungry to get involved and they really feel they can help by opening their Rolodex and some doors for the right entrepreneurs.

Many people with real wealth aren't showing up at startup events or pitch nights. They might be your neighbor, executives, board members, or retirees with portfolios bigger than many held by institutional investors. Nobody is talking to them about startup investing, so they stay on the sidelines. This is a missed opportunity, not just to expand who gets funded, but who gets to fund.

ANGEL MOTIVATION

Angel investing is relationship-driven, not transaction-driven. While returns still matter, most angels say they invest because they:

- **Want to support entrepreneurs:** Many angels are former founders who want to help the next generation succeed.
- **Seek impact:** Unlike many VCs, angels often prioritize startups that align with their personal values.
- **Enjoy the process:** Some see angel investing as a meaningful and exciting way to stay involved in business and innovation.
- **Pursue financial returns:** Of course, financial upside still matters, but it's often not the primary reason they write a check.

Because angel investing is so relational, it's no surprise that most founders meet value-add angels through events (35%) and networking (31%), not cold outreach.

Suelin Chen shared the story of her first investor:

> I was nine months pregnant when I got my first check. I was at a local startup event giving my pitch among four or five other founders and this wonderful angel investor came up to me and offered me $5,000. Prior to that, a few other people had actually offered me money, but I was too shy to take it. I told them I wasn't really ready, but when I put a round together, I'd let them know. Later, I learned the lesson that I didn't have to wait to formalize a round; I could have just taken that money with a flexible financing instrument and put it to work right away.
>
> That first check, while small, gave me confidence. I ended up raising $200,000 when my oldest daughter was maybe just four weeks old. I pitched and closed an investor on the phone in the throes of recovering from a complicated labor where I had hemorrhaged and had two blood transfusions; it was absolutely nuts!

Once connected, angels tend to move quickly. On average, it takes just six weeks from the first meeting to receiving a check, with the median time closer to three weeks.[37]

Karen Robinson Cope shared a story from her network that speaks to this immediacy:

> I just had lunch with a woman who is now an investor in a company that I invested in that's in the femtech space. She had only made one

---

37   Primary data collection from a LinkedIn survey, https://bit.ly/4lsSThD.

other private investment before. We sat down, and she asked me about my investments. I wasn't pitching her, I was just describing what this company does, and she said, 'Oh, I love that!' and wrote a $100,000 check on the spot.

I think it's a great investment, and she's going to profit, but she liked it because of the story and how I described the founder. So many people don't know how to get involved yet. They need a safe space to figure out how they can help, whether with money, time, or expertise.

Karen also shared her own motivation for one of her early investments:

I talk a lot about the importance of failure. Twenty-five years ago, nobody talked about failure, not even in Silicon Valley. I talk about it with founders.

There's one company I invested $10,000 in where I was the first investor. I didn't know if it was going to work or not, but I believed that if this wasn't the deal, the next one with this founder would be a home run. I wanted to be at that table first. Writing that check was like an insurance policy.

The angels who invest in unicorn companies already know the founders. They wrote checks before the company even started, and that's why they were invited in. Women especially need to hear that. We can't expect every investment to return; that's not how it works. You have to let yourself play the game too and think long term versus short term.

The power of personal connection can't be overstated. One warm introduction can open doors that would otherwise stay shut. These relationships can lead to much more than capital and can potentially change the entire trajectory of your company.

Take Rajia Abdelaziz, for example. Through the regional accelerator EforAll, she was matched with a mentor who introduced her to a manufacturing partner, which was a critical connection for developing invisaWear's physical product. That same mentor later became her lead investor.

> He brings me into his office, and he writes a check. I'd never seen so many zeros in my life. He says, 'I'm never going to come back and ask you for this money. The reason I'm doing this is because I've got a twin sister and I've got nieces, and I've witnessed how often they worry about their safety. The statistics are real, and your product will save lives. My only ask is that one day, when you have the luxury of having as much money as I do, that you remember this moment. That you write a check of this size to do something good in the world and to change someone else's life.'
>
> That moment forever changed my life. The moment I'm able to start doing things like that, I really hope to pay it forward to the next person.

These are the kinds of investors you want in your corner. Those who believe in you and your mission as much as your margins.

Catherine Gray, founder of She Angel Investors and executive producer of the award-winning documentary, *Show Her The Money*, also knows firsthand how values-aligned capital can shape a project:

> I asked a woman in my network to put in $125,000 and she agreed if I could find someone else to match it. That was my entrée to reach out to Dawn LaFrieda, who owns 75 Denny's restaurants and is the largest woman franchise owner of restaurants in the country. I told her about the matching investment, and she asked to think about it.

Much later after the film was produced, she told me that while she was considering investing in the film, she was on a plane telling someone about how women receive just 2% of venture capital. As she was getting off the plane, the man sitting next to her said, 'I couldn't help but overhear you. I'm in venture capital, and that 2% stat is true.' Dawn took that as a sign, and in that moment, she decided to invest in the film.

Even though Catherine had secured Dawn's commitment, the original investor backtracked:

When I went back to the original woman, she said, 'I don't think I'm going to do $125,000. Maybe I'll do $25,000 or $50,000.' I never called her back. I only want to take money from people that are trustworthy and have my values. Everyone who invested in this film wanted to make a difference. They saw the opportunity for impact through storytelling and media, even if they'd only ever thought about tech investments before.

One of my investors, Ali Garba, shared how he entered the angel world, and what drew him to Scroobious:

COVID made people do some crazy stuff. I knew I couldn't physically go out, so I started roaming around the internet, and came across the Angel Capital Association. I clicked on it, thought it was interesting, and some time later saw they were having a conference in 2022 in Atlantic City. I signed up, met some fantastic people, and joined a program that teaches you how to start angel investing. Now I have almost 50 startups in my portfolio!

> Scroobious caught my attention because it's very jarring looking at the statistics of who gets venture capital. It's so pitiful. We've got a lot of work ahead of us. I'm a small investor, but I'd like to be by your side and work with you. Those numbers make my blood boil, but we can't just blame people, we have to find a way around that. That's where people like you and I come in.

That program, Milestone Growth Capital Institute, partnered with Scroobious to give cohort members real-world experience discovering and evaluating investment opportunities. Ali used our platform during that program and expressed interest in investing in us, even though we weren't actively fundraising.

Ali's remarks came from a Zoom call where I walked him through my pitch deck. You can feel the connection instantly; we'd found our people in each other.

These stories all highlight how when your vision resonates on a deeply human level—when it feels personal, urgent, and real—angels listen.

FINDING YOUR ANGELS

After I get everyone all excited about angel investors, the next question is always, *Okay, but how do I find them?* Or sometimes, *Do you have a list?*

As the founder of Scroobious, I'm, of course, first going to recommend you join the community to connect with angels in a warm, guided way. Regardless, the reality is that angel investors are everywhere, they just might not call themselves that. The best ones, the ones who will really get what you're building and support you for the long haul, aren't on any list.

This is where we get tactical. Let's walk through how to connect with and earn the trust of angel investors in a way that's both authentic and strategic.

HOW TO REACH OUT

Once you've identified someone who matches your IIP (see the worksheet in Chapter 2), your first instinct might be to send them your deck and ask if they want to invest. Please don't do that. Fundraising is relationship-driven. Your first move should always be building the relationship, not going straight to the ask.

Start with a short note that centers on *them*. Reference something they've shared, published, or invested in and position your outreach as a request for insight, not money. Here's an example:

> *I saw your post about the future of fintech, and I loved your perspective on embedded payments. I'm building something in that space and would value your insight. Would you be open to a 20-minute chat?*

That's it. No mention of investing and no pitch deck attached.

Use that first conversation to genuinely connect. Ask thoughtful questions and listen more than you talk. Take notes. Make the conversation worth their time whether they invest or not. If the vibe is right and the conversation flows, you can follow up later with a note or during a meeting with something like:

> *I have to ask, would you ever consider angel investing? I think you could bring real value to what we're building, and I'd love to work with you. No pressure either way, but I'd be remiss not to ask.*

One of my early investors in Scroobious would never have written a check if I'd opened with a pitch. It was only after a few conversations that he said, "Yeah, I want to invest." He just hadn't thought about it before. After getting to know me, understanding what I was building, and seeing the opportunity, he leaned in.

Sometimes people want to join your party, but they need to be invited.

You'd be surprised how many people don't realize it's okay to ask if they can invest. They might assume that if you wanted their money, you would've brought it up already. In fact, some people think they're overstepping by asking if they can invest. You'll never know unless you have an open, human conversation about it.

If someone says no after you ask, don't shut the door. Keep the valuable relationship alive with something like:

> *I completely understand. I really value our relationship either way and would love to continue our conversations just as we've been having them. If you know anyone else who might be interested in what we're building, please feel free to make an introduction at any time.*

That kind of response keeps the door open, shows maturity, and respects the long game, which is exactly the kind of energy that attracts the right investors. Let people see who you are, what drives you, and why now is the time for them to get involved.

THE MYTHICAL "FRIENDS AND FAMILY" ROUND

Let's take a moment to talk about the so-called "friends and family" round, which is a phrase you'll hear tossed around casually, as if it's a given that every founder has access to a personal network full of financially comfortable people just waiting to invest in their startup. This phrase is really just another way of saying "angel investors you already know or are related to." When people give that advice, they skip over a critical truth.

Wealth is not distributed evenly across racial, gender, or socioeconomic lines. (If you're reading this in a public space, I apologize for the weird looks you're getting after you yelled, "No duh!" at this book.) In the US, the average net worth of a white family is over six times that of a Black family and nearly five times that of a Hispanic family.[38] When startup advice assumes you can access disposable capital through your personal network, it reflects the deep, systemic bias baked into the fundraising world. For many founders, especially *The Rest of Us*, it's not only bad advice, but also deflating. It can stop you before you even start.

Rajia, a founder who turned down a coveted and high-paying job at Google to build her company, shares how these assumptions showed up early in her journey:

> Investors used to tell me they like to see people putting their own money in the game. I had just graduated college, and I couldn't even afford a $14 Domino's pizza. I was like, *What money?* They said, *Friends and family money.*
>
> My dad immigrated to the US in his early 20s, came from nothing, and worked so hard to build the life we have today. When I turned down a job at Google to start invisaWear, I came home to a legitimate intervention from my parents. They simply couldn't understand how I could say no to that much money and told me I was making the biggest mistake of my life. My friends and family don't have money, and even if they did, they thought I had lost my mind.

If you *do* have a personal network that wants to support you financially, that's fantastic, but even then, you may feel uneasy about asking for or accepting money from them. That discomfort is real, and common, especially for founders who haven't worked in venture or investing, because it can be

---

38 Board of Governors of the Federal Reserve System, "Greater Wealth, Greater Uncertainty: Changes in Racial Inequality in the Survey of Consumer Finances," October 2023, https:// dx.doi.org/10.17016/2380-7172.3405. The 2022 SCF reports median net worth of $285,000 (white), $44,900 (Black), and $61,600 (Hispanic).

hard to separate the financial relationship from the emotional one. If you raise money from someone close to you, their investment can start to feel like a test of your worth. If your business struggles, will they regret it? Will it change how they see you?

This emotional weight is particularly heavy for women and other historically marginalized identities. When I facilitate workshops, I often share something from my own lived experience as a woman:

We're taught, sometimes explicitly, often subconsciously, that accepting someone's money means taking responsibility for their outcomes. We don't just see capital as business fuel, but as trust in us personally, and we carry that trust like a moral obligation. This is something we must unlearn. We have to practice separating our personal worth from our company's performance.

I want to highlight a subtle but powerful moment from my conversation with Rajia. She spoke often about her lead investor, the manufacturer and mentor who wrote her first large check, in almost philanthropic terms. But he didn't make a donation, he wrote a check in exchange for equity.

When I pointed this out, it sparked something for her:

> That's such an incredible point, because at the time, we really needed inventory, including chips and components, and his investment made that possible. He made a thoughtful equity investment that supported a critical business milestone. For all the goodness he brought to the table, he was also very intelligent to make a great investment decision, but that being said, as someone with lots of philanthropic effort, the best part is, he gave us much more than money; he gave us mentorship and guidance that ultimately led to us being where we are today.

That moment of reframing matters. People who've spent more time around wealth or investing often learn to separate the business from the personal. If an investment doesn't return, it's understood as part of the risk, not a reflection on the founder. That mindset isn't universal, but it tends to be more common in those circles. For many of us, especially those newer to this world, that emotional separation doesn't come naturally. It takes practice, exposure, and support to build that muscle.

You are not your company. You are building a company, and like any startup, it will hit obstacles. It will iterate, pivot, and it might even wind down. That outcome does not reflect your value as a person. It's a reality of entrepreneurship.

If you're thinking about raising from someone you know, here's a script you can adapt. It balances honesty, confidence, and clarity, and it helps preserve the relationship no matter what:

I'm building a real business with real potential. Most startups don't succeed, and I want to be upfront about that. I can't guarantee I'll return your investment, but I can promise I'll work incredibly hard, make thoughtful decisions, and keep you informed every step of the way. If you choose to support me, I'd love to have you along for the journey, but I'll respect your decision either way.

When you approach people this way, you're modeling what it will be like to work with you. You're building trust from the very beginning. If you do pursue this path, treat it as seriously as any other investment deal:

- Confirm that the person is accredited (if required).
- Communicate clearly about the risks of investing in startups.
- Don't internalize shame about asking, especially if it's rooted in assumptions about how they'll respond.
- Don't decide for them. Give them the full information and let them make their own informed decision.

You're offering an opportunity, not asking for a favor, and you should treat it that way.

ANGELS FOR *THE REST OF US*

Angel investors can be transformational partners. They write early checks, open doors, and often stay with you for the long haul. They're especially valuable for *The Rest of Us* because they often invest based on connection, not just pattern matching.

Jen Saxton sold her first startup to BabyQuip, the world's largest baby gear rental platform, in 2020. Before that acquisition, she was a solo founder grinding to get her idea funded and ultimately raised over $3 million from 88 individual angel investors.

Her path to those angels wasn't quick or easy. She started with small $5,000 and $10,000 checks from classmates, former consulting colleagues, and friends who believed in her enough to bet early. She raised on a convertible note (see Chapter 10) while finishing business school, and even though she won her program's business plan competition, the shared prize money was only $7,000. She put it all right back into the company.

Then she hit the angel group circuit and stayed on it for years. We'll hear more about her experience with groups in the next section of this chapter, and how that process led to having nearly 90 individual investors.

> It was a long, scrappy raise. But it worked. And those angels helped me get to a real outcome.

Finding the right angels takes patience, strategy, and trust. But if you approach it with a clear sense of who you're looking for, lead with authenticity, and treat outreach as relationship-building, not just pitching, you'll create opportunities that go far beyond funding.

Here's how to get started:

- **Expand your view of who angels are:** Don't assume all angel investors follow traditional profiles or openly identify as angels. The landscape is shifting to include more women, younger investors, and mission-driven backers who are actively looking for diverse opportunities. At my first company, a medical device startup, our original angel investors were clinicians, physicians, and professors. They weren't typical investors, but they understood the problem we were solving. At Scroobious, I'm the first investment for some of our angels, because they feel our platform solves a problem they experience personally. You never know unless you ask!

- **Build relationships first:** Angel investing comes from trust and connection, not rigid financial models. You're far more likely to raise money through warm introductions, networking, and targeted outreach than through cold emails or mass messages.

- **Look beyond the check:** The best angel investors bring more than money. They offer strategic guidance, make high-value introductions, and act as real partners throughout your journey. Think of them as an extension of your team, not just a line item on your cap table.

- **Move quickly and stay engaged:** Angel investors typically move faster than VCs, often making decisions within just a few weeks. Be ready to follow up, answer questions, and keep the momentum going.

ANGEL GROUPS

An angel group is a collective of individual angel investors who join forces to invest in startups together. They pool resources, share deal opportunities (known as deal flow), and work as a group to evaluate companies. While many angels invest solo, some prefer to join a group for structure, support, and exposure to more deals. These groups often form around a shared interest like a specific industry, location, university, or mission.

Most groups exist to do three main things:

1. **See more startups:** By working together, angels hear about more companies than they would on their own.
2. **Do better diligence:** They share insights and divide up the work of reviewing a company's business model, finances, team, and risks.
3. **Write bigger checks:** Instead of one person investing $25,000, a group might invest $500,000 or more by combining individual investments.

This team approach can make investing less risky for individual members, and it's helpful for people who are newer to evaluating early-stage companies. However, while angel groups offer many benefits, they also come with challenges, especially when it comes to how decisions get made and how long it takes.

CHALLENGES WITH ANGEL GROUPS

Unlike solo investors who can decide quickly based on personal conviction, angel groups often operate like small venture firms. They have formal processes, internal voting, and decision-making committees. This extra structure can slow things down or block deals altogether.

Here are a few common challenges:

- **Groupthink:** When a group is trying to reach consensus, it's easy for strong opinions to sway the outcome. If one influential person doesn't like a deal, others may follow, even if the startup is strong. On the flip side, if someone is overly excited, the group might ignore red flags. This becomes a problem for founders who don't fit traditional expectations. If your company is outside a major tech hub, led by an underrepresented identity, or uses an unconventional business model, the group might view you as "risky" even when the fundamentals are strong. Because many groups require majority or even unanimous approval to invest, even a small amount of doubt can kill the deal.

- **Slow decision-making:** Most angel groups have multiple layers, including screening committees, diligence teams, and investment committees. That means lots of meetings and lots of waiting. You might be asked to provide business plans, detailed financials, and competitive research just to be considered. If your company needs capital fast to hit a key milestone, this process can be frustrating and even harmful.

- **Risk aversion:** Because members are accountable to one another, they often play it safe. If a previous investment went badly, they may hesitate to support another bold idea. Many groups won't invest in companies in regulated industries, or in founders who don't have Ivy League degrees or Silicon Valley connections. They're also often reluctant to be the first check into a round. If nobody wants to go first, deals stall out.

Rajia's experience illustrates all three of these barriers—groupthink, gatekeeping, and risk aversion—in a single interaction, even with strong traction and prior funding:

> After we secured a $100,000 loan and started getting small angel checks, someone asked if we would pitch an angel group (more on this part of her story in chapter 7). The person in charge of that group ended up being the same woman who had refused to recommend us for the bank loan.
>
> We were pitching out in California, and I had to take a red eye. I was so nervous! I was still so young, and this was the first formal angel group I'd ever pitched. I go in, and again, it's 85% older white men. It was a unanimous vote to fund the company.
>
> We already had a bunch of investments on the same convertible note, with the same terms. This woman was responsible for the diligence and called our valuation outrageous. She refused the group's $50,000 investment, which was so much money to us at the time. The group was furious.
>
> Three different members called me and personally invested outside of the group for triple the amount the group would have done. They started introducing me to their friends, which is how we ended up getting oversubscribed. It was a domino chain of five-minute conversations that went like, 'My friend told me he's investing, and I always invest in the same deals as him.'

NAVIGATING ANGEL GROUPS

Despite the challenges, angel groups can be powerful funding partners if you know how to work with them. Here's how to increase your chances of success:

- **Find aligned groups:** Look for groups that invest in your industry, region, or mission (e.g., healthcare-focused groups for MedTech startups). Prioritize groups that allow members to invest individually rather than commit their money to a pooled fund. That way, you don't need full group approval. Check their portfolio to see if they invest in people who look like you. Have they funded founders from similar backgrounds?

- **Find a champion inside:** You need someone in the group who believes in you. A strong internal advocate can make or break your chances of getting through the process. Identify a member who is excited about your startup and develop a relationship outside of the group.

- **Ask about timelines up front:** Find out how long their process takes before you pitch. If their cycle is 2–3 months and you only have 6 weeks of runway, they may not be a fit right now.

- **Use momentum to your advantage:** Share when another investor has committed. This creates FOMO (fear of missing out) and builds credibility. Show traction, whether it's revenue, users, waitlist sign-ups, or partnerships, to reduce perceived risk.

- **Be ready for tough diligence:** Have your financials, market research, and growth plans ready to go. The process will likely be more formal than with solo angels, so be prepared to answer detailed questions.

ANGEL GROUPS FOR *THE REST OF US*

Angel groups can write larger checks, open powerful networks, and bring deep industry knowledge. BUT they're not always fast or inclusive, and *The Rest of Us* can face uphill battles. The key is understanding how group dynamics work and playing the game strategically.

Let's go back to Rajia's story. After she built the product and gained traction through an Indiegogo campaign (more on that in Chapter 20), her company received national media attention for saving a young woman's life. Revenue was on track to surpass seven figures in year one.

> That's when our manufacturer saw the exponential growth trajectory and knew we'd need capital. Not only did he invest his own money, but he also helped us go to the bank and apply for credit lines.

That traction caught the attention of the same group that had turned her down.

> They were buzzing about our progress within the group, and the same woman who had blocked our deal at a $3 million-dollar valuation cap asked us to pitch again because the group was upset they hadn't joined our pre-seed round. They voted to follow-on in our seed round, and again, she expressed outrage at our valuation. They ended up investing $150,000 at our higher valuation.

That validation should have felt like a victory, but the experience was complicated.

> I felt vindicated, but also sad. So much of the opposition came from a woman, when we should be lifting each other up. I feel sorry for her to an extent because it likely comes from her own lived experience that limits her beliefs. That otherwise could have been such an amazing moment for all of us.

Rajia's experience is a reminder that bias can come from anywhere, sometimes where you least expect it. Progress often happens in spite of the systems we have, not because of them. As a founder, you often need to figure out when to bypass the rules, write new ones, or find the people willing to bet on *you*.

Jen Saxton's story reinforces this. She had 88 angel investors, many of whom came from angel groups. She tried to keep her investor list simple by using a special purpose vehicle (SPV), which is a legal structure that groups multiple investors into one, but that's not how things played out:

> Every single group said they'd use an SPV[39] to consolidate checks. None of them followed through. That's how I ended up with 88 individual investors on my cap table.

Her first check required years of work:

> To get my first angel group check, I had to take four flights to New York, three to San Francisco, and wait two or three years before they actually invested.

After that first check, she was able to syndicate across eight other angel groups, including some lesser-known but highly effective ones. That unlocked access, but only after she figured out how the system really worked.

> I realized it was a voting game. I'd go to breakfast meetings just to work the room and collect business cards. Later, when they saw my name in pre-screening, I'd get votes just because it was familiar. It was low-bar awareness, but it helped.

---

39 *SPV* stands for "special purpose vehicle." It's a legal setup that lets many investors combine their money into one bucket so they show up as a single line on a company's cap table (list of shareholders).

Like Rajia, Jen also encountered objections based on bad information that almost tanked deals:

> One group killed my deal because someone said, 'You don't need this service, the fire station does it for free.' That wasn't even true. But I didn't have someone in the room who could correct it. You need a champion in those meetings, or you won't make it to the next round.

Once her deal was in motion with a recognized leading group name, the process became easier, but the emotional labor and strategic finesse it took to get there were real.

> Now I'm technically a portfolio company of all these groups. One just invited me back to share an update after seeing my Target announcement. I shared my progress and got a check two days later. Then they invited me to pitch something else. But I'm never jumping through all those hoops again. Never playing that game again.

Angel groups can be fantastic partners, but only if you understand the mechanics behind group decisions and learn how to navigate the process effectively. Start early, build relationships, and find champions.

Angel investors are often closer than you think.

They aren't just finance professionals; they're friends, mentors, colleagues, and community members who want to support innovation they believe in.

Connection outweighs credentials.

Angels invest based on trust, alignment, and belief in you. A strong relationship can open the door to capital, mentorship, and strategic support.

You have to talk about what you're building.

Opportunities come when people know what you're working on. Sharing your story creates space for others to raise their hands and say, "I want in."

The "friends and family" round is deeply unequal.

Many founders don't have wealthy networks, and even if they do, asking for money can carry emotional weight. Startup advice that assumes easy access to personal capital ignores systemic inequality and can stop people before they start.

Angel groups have real power and real friction.
They can write big checks and bring influence, but decision-making is slow, political, and often biased. Success depends on navigating the process and finding internal champions.

For *The Rest of Us*, angels are often the gateway.
Early capital, values-aligned backing, and belief from someone who sees your vision can change everything. Don't wait for permission. Build relationships, ask boldly, and open the door for yourself and others.

5

EQUITY CROWDFUNDING & COMMUNITY CAPITAL

Crowdfunding is a newer but increasingly popular way for startups to raise money. Instead of relying on a few wealthy individuals writing big checks, crowdfunding allows you to pool many smaller checks from a wide group of people. Most platforms structure these investments so they roll up into a single line on your cap table, keeping things clean and manageable.

What makes equity crowdfunding different from traditional fundraising is that anyone can participate, including non-accredited investors. That means your customers, supporters, community members, and partners can all become owners in your company, not just cheerleaders. This is why crowdfunding is often called a community round. It invites the people who believe in you to invest in you.

However, raising capital through crowdfunding isn't like pitching VCs or networking with angel investors. It's not relationship-based in the same way. Think of it more like launching a marketing campaign; you need to attract a broad audience and build excitement at scale.

HOW CROWDFUNDING WORKS

When you raise money through a crowdfunding platform, you must follow Securities and Exchange Commission (SEC) rules that govern how private companies can legally accept investments from the public. These rules vary depending on the platform and raise type, but here are some basics you need to know:

- **You can raise up to $5 million per year:** That's the legal cap for equity crowdfunding under current regulations. If you need more than that, you'll need to combine it with other types of capital.
- **You must disclose a lot of information:** Because crowdfunding is regulated, you're required to share company details publicly like financials, risks, team background, and your overall business strategy. This transparency can build trust, but it also means you need to be comfortable putting your numbers out there.
- **Platforms charge fees and set their own rules:** Crowdfunding platforms are businesses. Each has its own process, pricing, support level, and investor audience. Some are more founder-friendly than others. Make sure to research your options and pick the one that aligns with your goals and values.

CROWDFUNDING IS ALL ABOUT MARKETING AND MOMENTUM

A common misconception is that you can launch a campaign and watch the money flow in. That's not how it works. Crowdfunding is not a "set it and forget it" approach—it requires effort, strategy, and real momentum from day one.

Most platforms require you to bring in early commitments before your campaign goes live to the public. This is often done by directing your early angel investors to invest through the platform instead of privately. That activity builds early traction and signals credibility to other potential investors.

You also need a solid marketing strategy. Crowdfunding is all about visibility; if people don't see your campaign, they can't invest. You'll need to promote the raise like you're launching a product. That means email outreach, social media, public relations (PR), and community engagement. Many founders also hire marketing agencies with crowdfunding experience to help drive traffic and conversions.

Lastly, stay engaged once you launch. Investors expect updates, and most platforms have public Q&A sections. If you ignore questions or disappear for a week, people will assume the worst. Engagement drives visibility on the platform itself; campaigns that respond quickly and keep investors informed are more likely to get featured and reach a wider audience. Table 5.1 lists the pros and cons of crowdfunding.

PROS AND CONS OF CROWDFUNDING

PROS	CONS
Access to a wide range of investors	Strict SEC regulations & compliance requirements
Allows non-accredited investors to participate	Investment cap of $5M per year
Creates strong brand advocates & engaged customers	Significant marketing & outreach required
Potentially faster fundraising than VC rounds	Requires early investors to "seed" the campaign
No need to give up board seats or control	May require significant public disclosure of financials

Table 5.1

EVALUATING CROWDFUNDING

Before jumping into a crowdfunding campaign, ask yourself these questions to determine whether it's the right strategy for your business:

+ **Are you comfortable building in public?** Crowdfunding requires a high level of visibility. Your campaign will involve public storytelling, constant updates, and open access to your financial details and fundraising progress. If you're energized by sharing your journey and engaging a wide audience, this can be a strength, not a stressor.

+ **Do you have a community to rally?** Crowdfunding success hinges on community support. You don't need thousands of followers, but you do need a core group of people who believe in you and are willing to spread the word. People won't just stumble across your campaign; you have to drive them to it.

+ **Can you invest time and money in marketing?** This is not a "set it and forget it" process. Campaigns take weeks, if not months, of preparation and active promotion once live. That usually means investing in video production, paid ads, content creation, or hiring help. If you're low on time, budget, or energy, the return might not justify the effort.

+ **Is your business easy to understand or exciting to a broad audience?** Crowdfunding works best for companies that strike an emotional chord or solve a clear, relatable problem. If your business is highly technical, B2B, or very niche, it might be harder to attract widespread interest from the general public.

+ **Do you have early believers lined up?** Momentum is everything. Platforms reward campaigns that get early traction, and nothing kills momentum like a slow start. If you don't have a few people ready to write checks on day one, whether they're friends, angels, or loyal customers, it'll be much harder to convince strangers to jump in. A campaign sitting at 0% funded can be a red flag.

HOW TO SUCCEED WITH CROWDFUNDING

If you've decided to pursue crowdfunding, you need a plan. This isn't a passive process, it's a campaign, and just like any product launch or sales push, it requires intention, preparation, and follow-through.

Here are some things that set successful campaigns apart:

+ **Choose the right platform:** Popular platforms include Wefunder, StartEngine, Republic, iFundWomen,[40] and SeedInvest. Each one has different fees, investor communities, and platform requirements. Take the time to compare your options and choose the one that best aligns with your audience, industry, and fundraising goals.

+ **Line up early commitments:** Before you go live, secure early investors who are ready to contribute on day one. These could be angels, existing customers, friends, family, or anyone who believes in what you're building. That early momentum builds credibility and attracts others; it's much easier to get people excited about a campaign that's already moving.

+ **Create a real marketing plan:** A crowdfunding campaign is a full-on marketing effort. That means planning ahead. Build email sequences, line up social posts, draft announcements, consider

---

40   iFundWomen announced it was acquired by Honeycomb on April 14, 2025, and will be integrated into their platform.

PR outreach, and decide if you'll run paid ads. Treat this like you would any other growth funnel because, in many ways, it is.

+ **Actively engage your audience:** Crowdfunding is interactive. Actively respond to questions and comments on your campaign page and provide frequent updates to keep the momentum going. Invite your audience into the journey so they feel like part of your success.

+ **Leverage FOMO (fear of missing out):** People want to be part of something exciting. Create urgency with time-based perks, matching contributions, or limited investor tiers. Share progress updates often; things like "We just passed 25% of our goal!" or "This campaign already has 50 investors!" are powerful social proof that encourages others to jump in.

CROWDFUNDING FOR *THE REST OF US*

Crowdfunding is an exciting and accessible way to raise capital, but it's not easier than traditional fundraising, it's just different. If you have a strong customer base, a compelling story, and a solid marketing plan, crowdfunding can be a powerful way to turn your supporters into investors and deepen their connection to your company. It democratizes access not just for founders, but for anyone who wants to be part of the startup journey. That said, it takes serious work. You'll need to navigate regulatory requirements, build early momentum, and keep up consistent promotional efforts throughout the campaign. For the right founders, crowdfunding can be both a funding mechanism and a movement.

Crowdfunding unlocks capital from your community.
It's a way to turn customers, fans, and supporters into actual owners and they don't have to be accredited to participate.

It's not easier, just different.
Crowdfunding is more like a product launch than a pitch meeting. Success comes from storytelling, marketing, and early momentum.

You need to show up before you go live.
Most platforms require early checks to seed your raise. Without that traction, campaigns tend to stall fast.

It's a visibility game.
If people don't know your campaign exists, they can't invest. Plan your outreach like a real marketing campaign with email, social, and PR.

It's powerful, but it's work.
Crowdfunding can build brand loyalty and raise real capital, but it requires time, transparency, and ongoing engagement. It's a campaign, not a shortcut.

6

BEYOND THE OBVIOUS: FAMILY OFFICES & PHILANTHROPIC CAPITAL

FAMILY OFFICES

One often-overlooked source of funding is family offices, which are private investment firms that manage the wealth of ultra-high-net-worth families. While they're not as visible as VCs or institutional funds, family offices can be powerful backers for early-stage founders, especially if you align with their values or areas of expertise.

A family office is typically formed by a wealthy family, often after a major liquidity event like selling a company, to manage their finances, investments, philanthropy, and estate planning. Some family offices act as limited partners (LPs) in venture and private equity funds, while others invest directly in startups.

Pitching to a family office is often more like engaging with an angel investor than a VC. It's relationship-driven, strategic, and rooted in long-term alignment, not just short-term returns.

There are an estimated 5,000 family offices worldwide making direct startup investments.[41] But like many angel investors, they can be hard to identify since they rarely advertise or proactively solicit deals. That said, many of them have more liquidity ("dry powder") than traditional VC funds and can move faster because they don't need to coordinate with LPs or operate on rigid fund timelines. Since their horizon is generational, they can afford to be patient.

INVESTING BEHAVIOR

Family offices tend to invest based on a combination of personal connection, strategic relevance, and impact. Unlike most VCs, who focus almost entirely on financial return, family offices often take a more holistic approach.

Here are the three most common types of startup investments family offices pursue:

+ **Strategic investments:** These align with the family's business background or legacy. For example, a family that made its fortune in logistics might be interested in supply chain tech.
+ **Mission-driven investments:** These focus on causes the family cares about, such as education, clean energy, or public health. The family may also have a foundation or philanthropic arm connected to this mission.
+ **Financial growth investments:** These are focused on returns, but with longer time horizons and more flexibility than VC firms typically allow.

---

41   PWC, "How Family Offices Are Investing in a Brighter Future," July 26, 2023, https://www.pwc.ie/reports/family-office-deals-survey.html.

HOW TO FIND AND APPROACH A FAMILY OFFICE

Because family offices rely heavily on trust and personal networks, warm introductions are critical. They don't typically post on social media or sit on demo day panels. Here's how to find and connect with them:

+ **Scan university buildings & hospitals:** Families that donate to institutions often have their names on buildings. That visibility can be a clue to research whether they've set up a family office and what causes or industries they support.

+ **Research industry ties:** If a family built its wealth in retail, real estate, or healthcare, they're likely to be more interested in startups within or adjacent to that sector. Look at interviews, foundations, or past investments to understand their lens.

+ **Mine personal connections:** Start with your network. LinkedIn, alumni associations, founder forums, and even angel investors may have connections to family offices or people who've worked with them.

+ **Personalize your outreach:** Unlike VCs, family offices aren't publicly soliciting deal flow (that's the steady stream of startup investment opportunities they review), and a cold email won't cut it. Your outreach should clearly show how your company aligns with their values, interests, or industry. Keep it personal, thoughtful, and informed.

FACTOR	FAMILY OFFICE	VENTURE CAPITAL FIRM
Capital Source	Family's personal wealth	External LPs (limited partners)
Investment Motive	Financial, strategic, or impact-driven	Primarily financial return
Decision Process	Relationship-based, can be informal	Structured, requires GP & LP approval
Investment Horizon	Long-term (decades, generational)	Short-term (5–10 years)
Risk Appetite	More flexible, can take bigger risks	Portfolio-driven, risk-managed
Fundraising Approach	Relationship-driven, often private	Public, actively deal sourcing

Table 6.1: Family Offices for The Rest of Us

Family offices may not be part of your initial fundraising playbook, but they should be considered. These investors can provide patient capital, deep domain expertise, and access to high-value networks. Because they invest on behalf of a family legacy, they often care just as much about values, relationships, and impact as they do about financial return.

However, they're not checking their inbox for pitch decks. You'll need a thoughtful, relationship-first approach that reflects alignment with and respect for their priorities. If you take the time to understand their motivations and meet them where they are, a family office can be more than just a source of capital; they can be a lifelong partner in your company's journey.

INVESTING WITH PHILANTHROPIC DOLLARS

An innovative and underutilized way to fund a mission-driven business is by tapping into philanthropic capital, specifically, dollars that were originally donated for charitable purposes. Vehicles like donor-advised funds (DAFs) and mission-aligned nonprofits can direct this capital into early-stage, for-profit companies that align with their stated values. For impact-driven founders, this can be transformational.

WHAT IS A DONOR-ADVISED FUND?

A donor-advised fund, or DAF, is like a charitable investment account. Individuals, families, or companies contribute to their fund, often after a windfall or as part of tax planning, and receive an immediate tax deduction. However, they don't need to decide right away how the money will be used. The donor can "advise" the DAF sponsor (the organization managing the fund) to grant the money to nonprofits or, in some cases, invest in mission-aligned for-profit startups.

It's super flexible and popular with wealthy donors because it lets them lock in tax benefits now while figuring out their giving strategy later. The issue is much of that money just sits there. It's technically been given away, but it's not doing any good yet. The donor can't take it back, so if it isn't granted or invested, it has no impact.

In the US alone, over $250 billion is sitting in DAFs, unused.[42] That's capital that has already been set aside for social good and could be redirected into startups building scalable solutions to pressing problems.

---

42   National Philanthropic Trust, "2024 Donor-Advised Fund Report," accessed October 2025, https://www.nptrust.org/reports/daf-report.

WHY THIS MATTERS

Philanthropic capital is especially suited to companies with:

+ A clear social or environmental mission at their core.
+ A longer return timeline, which requires what's often called patient capital, or funding that doesn't demand fast exits or returns.
+ A measurable impact that aligns with a charitable purpose (e.g., improving health outcomes, advancing equity, expanding education access).

It's important to note: **This capital is dilutive**. These are not grants or donations to your company; they are equity investments using charitable dollars. Your cap table will reflect that, just as it would with any other investor.

However, this money often comes with fewer strings attached, more values alignment, and a longer runway to deliver results because the return expectations are often tied to social good rather than personal financial gain.

HOW DAFs WORK

Here's an example from my own company. Scroobious received investment through Inspire Access, a 501(c)(3) nonprofit that serves as a bridge between DAF holders and early-stage, mission-aligned startups. Inspire Access vets a portfolio of founders and presents them to its donor network. Donors can then advise that a portion of their DAF be directed into a specific company.

In our case, I don't know who the original donor was, only that Inspire Access is the entity on our cap table. They conducted diligence, believed in the mission, and made the investment on behalf of the donor. Figure 6.1 shows how this cycle typically works, from donor intent to startup impact.

There are many ways to structure this cycle, and each intermediary in the space has a different operating model, fee structure, and level of involvement.

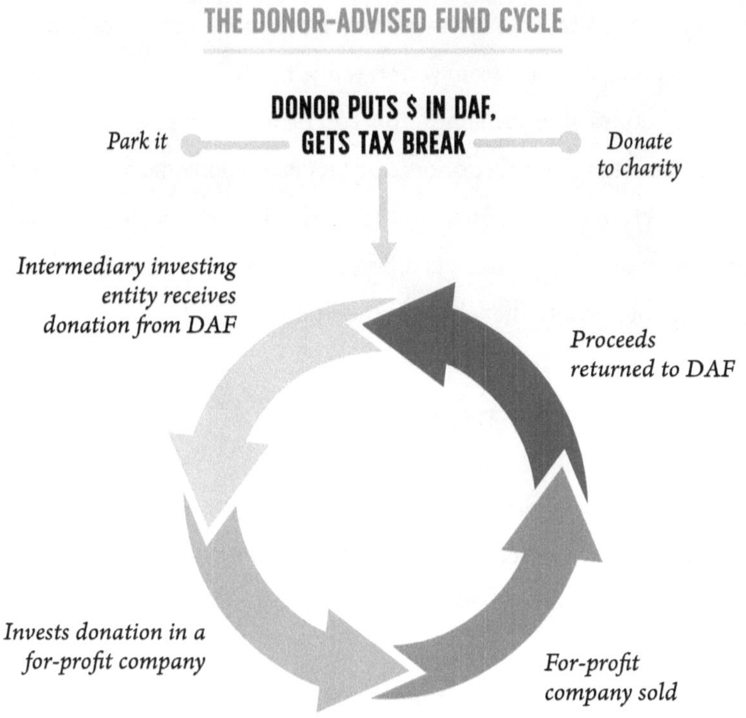

THE DONOR-ADVISED FUND CYCLE

Figure 6.1

Different intermediaries operate in different ways:

+ Inspire Access takes a small percentage of the invested amount to fund its own operations.
+ Others, like CataCap, use a platform-based model that resembles crowdfunding and has a different fee structure.

The key is connecting with the right intermediary who sees alignment with what you're building and is willing to champion your inclusion in their portfolio.

This type of capital isn't for everyone, but if you're building a business where impact is inseparable from your revenue model, and you're comfortable with longer fundraising timelines, this can be a powerful addition to your fundraising strategy. Because donors don't receive a personal financial return, but the satisfaction of doing good and the ability to potentially recycle capital into future impact, the pressure is different. Financial success enables more giving, not more profit. That changes the dynamic.

KEY REGULATIONS AND LIMITATIONS

Using charitable dollars to invest in for-profit businesses is allowed under US law, but it's tightly regulated to ensure the money truly advances a social good. Here are some core rules to keep in mind:

- **No personal benefit:** Donors to a DAF or private foundation cannot receive a personal financial return. If a DAF or foundation invests in a for-profit company, any financial return belongs to the DAF or foundation and must remain dedicated to charitable use.
- **Program-related investments (PRIs):** PRIs are a legally defined type of investment available to private foundations. The primary purpose must be to accomplish one or more of the foundation's exempt (charitable) purposes.[43] PRIs can be made into for-profit or nonprofit entities and are treated differently from traditional, return-seeking investments.

---

43   Program-Related Investments, Internal Revenue Service, https://www.irs.gov/charities-non-profits/private-foundations/program-related-investments.

They are a separate vehicle from DAFs, which can also make mission-aligned or impact investments in for-profit companies, as long as those investments clearly further a charitable purpose and do not provide personal benefit to the donor.

+ **Due diligence required:** Whether a private foundation is making a PRI or a DAF sponsor is making a mission-aligned investment, the charitable entity must document how the investment advances its charitable purpose. When the recipient is a for-profit company, this typically involves enhanced due diligence and ongoing oversight.

Not all DAF providers or nonprofits are set up to do this kind of work. That's why founders usually access this capital through specialized intermediaries that understand the rules and are willing to do the extra diligence.

PHILANTHROPIC CAPITAL FOR *THE REST OF US*

This kind of funding is still off the radar for many founders, but it's growing. It won't be your fastest check, and it requires mission alignment and transparency, but if you're building something with purpose and social meaning at the center, philanthropic capital can help you scale with values-aligned funding that sees your impact as the return.

Family offices are hidden but powerful funders.

They invest personal wealth, often with more flexibility, longer timelines, and values-driven goals than traditional VC firms.

Relationships matter more than pitch decks.

These investors don't advertise. You'll need warm intros, strategic alignment, and thoughtful outreach tailored to their interests.

Philanthropic capital is untapped and mission-aligned.

Vehicles like donor-advised funds (DAFs) can direct charitable dollars into for-profit startups that drive measurable social or environmental impact.

Impact-first doesn't mean grant-only.

These are equity investments that are dilutive, but often patient and purpose-driven, with different return expectations.

Both sources require alignment over urgency.

These aren't fast checks, but they can become long-term, mission-aligned partners, especially if your business is built to drive meaningful change.

NON-DILUTIVE CAPITAL OPTIONS

Equity funding, whether through venture capital, angel investors, or crowdfunding, requires giving up ownership in your company. But not all capital requires dilution. Non-dilutive funding refers to money you can raise without giving away equity, allowing you to grow while maintaining full control of your business.

Many founders, especially first-time founders and *The Rest of Us*, overlook non-dilutive options or assume we're not eligible. There's a wide variety of possibilities, including grants, revenue-based financing, community development funding, and other creative approaches that can provide the capital you need without sacrificing ownership.

James Valencia, the founder and CEO of Radical Shoots, an urban microgreens company, has yet to take outside investment. Instead, he's bootstrapped his business through sweat equity, trades, personal loans, and grants to get his venture off the ground.

To fund my first little 100-square-foot maker space room, I used to sweep all the wood shops throughout college to trade for membership. When they moved to a big warehouse, the director let me try it rent-free for two months. At my other farming job, I offered to give one of our partners a tour of the new space, just so I could chat more with him. Not as a pitch, but in regular conversation, I blurted out my vision for what I could build and he gifted me six more months of that space, which allowed me to wean myself off my other job and work for myself full-time.

His big break came from a mix of hustle and timing. While selling at a local farmers market, he noticed an abandoned city-owned greenhouse and saw an opportunity to expand. Around the same time, a veteran grower in town approached him about buying his business, which included 35 active restaurant accounts. James knew it was a rare chance to accelerate growth, but he didn't have the cash.

So, he got creative again:

- He built a green roof for a local hotel bringing, in ~$25,000 revenue.
- He secured a $10,000 bank loan.
- He borrowed $15,000 from his sister.

That patchwork of funds allowed him to acquire the business, expand into the greenhouse, and absorb the customer base, all without giving up equity. Since then, he's continued to grow without dilution, primarily through grant funding.

> We won a $75,000 grant from Walmart Foundation, and two $50,000
> grants from USDA and the Tennessee Department of Ag.

For James, grants were a growth strategy. They let him stay focused on long-term vision and mission alignment, and kept his business rooted in the community.

> I can't imagine anything worse than taking a ton of investment and
> then having to rush or pivot just to satisfy that. That kind of pressure
> keeps me up at night.

His story shows that raising capital doesn't have to mean giving up control. Sometimes it means trading time and effort instead of equity, and when you do it well, the result is a stronger foundation that's aligned with your values and vision.

Now let's explore some of the most effective non-dilutive funding options.

GRANTS

Grants are a powerful form of non-dilutive capital because they provide free money that doesn't have to be repaid and doesn't require giving up ownership. That said, grants are not easy money. They are competitive, often time-consuming to apply for, and may come with strict usage or reporting requirements.

My former business partner gave me advice I still use as a filter today: only apply for grant money for something you'd do anyway, even without the grant. That keeps you focused and prevents you from chasing funding that doesn't truly serve your core business. When you find a grant that aligns with your goals and meets the criteria, it can be transformational, especially in the early stages when capital is scarce.

WHERE TO FIND GRANTS

There are several categories of grants available to startups and small businesses:

+ **Government grants:**[44] Agencies like the Small Business Administration (SBA), National Science Foundation (NSF), and Department of Energy (DOE) offer funding for startups in specific sectors.
  * Small Business Innovation Research (SBIR) and Small Business Technology Transfer (STTR) grants provide millions of dollars annually to innovative early-stage companies, particularly in tech, healthcare, and energy.

+ **Corporate & foundation grants:** Many large companies and philanthropic organizations offer funding for startups aligned with their mission.
  * Example: Google for Startups Black Founders Fund provides non-dilutive capital to Black entrepreneurs.

+ **Local & industry-specific grants:** States, cities, and trade associations often offer grants targeted at local economic development or specific industries. These can be easier to access and more relationship-based than federal programs.

---

44 As of this writing in 2025, the current US administration has proposed and/or enacted significant budget cuts to federal innovation programs, including the Small Business Innovation Research (SBIR) and Small Business Technology Transfer (STTR) grants. These programs have historically provided non-dilutive capital to thousands of early-stage startups, particularly in tech, healthcare, and energy, and have been a vital source of funding for founders from marginalized backgrounds. While some funding still exists, the future of these programs is uncertain, and founders should monitor policy developments closely. Reduced federal support may increase competition for remaining grants and underscore the importance of diversifying capital strategies.

THINGS TO KNOW ABOUT GRANTS

While grants can be an excellent source of funding, here are five key considerations:

1. **Competitive and onerous process:** Grants often require detailed applications, financial disclosures, supporting materials, and sometimes third-party validation. You may need to demonstrate traction, impact, or alignment with the grant's goals. For the most sought-after programs, success rates can be below 10%. Winning the grant isn't the end because compliance and reporting requirements can be extensive and long-term, especially with government funding.

2. **Limits on scale:** Grants are often for smaller amounts like $5,000, $25,000, maybe $100,000, depending on the source. That's incredibly helpful for early-stage growth but may not be sufficient for scaling fast or covering ongoing operating costs.

3. **Eligibility restrictions:** Not every grant is available to every founder. Some are limited by:
   - **Demographics** (e.g., grants for women, veterans, or underrepresented founders)
   - **Geography** (city/state-specific programs)
   - **Industry** (e.g., biotech, cleantech, education)
   - **Entity type** (some are for nonprofits or hybrid models)

Always review eligibility before spending significant time on an application.

4. **Alternatives and complements:** In addition to traditional grants, consider:

   - **University incubators** that offer stipends or grants for student/alumni startups.
   - **Non-equity accelerators** that provide capital, mentorship, and support without taking equity.
   - **Government innovation vouchers** that fund product development, research, or prototyping with academic or institutional partners.

   These options often come with less red tape and more hands-on support.

5. **Fraud and scams:** Legitimate grants never require upfront payment to apply. If someone asks for large fees to "guarantee" grant funding, it's a red flag. You should be able to access most information through official government websites, community organizations, or startup support networks. At most, a small fee might be charged by trusted consultants or grant writers, but don't pay thousands for access to something that should be public.

Grants aren't easy, but they can be worth the work. They're especially valuable for mission-driven founders, technical innovation, or founders who want to stay scrappy and self-directed without giving up ownership early. Grants can extend your runway, de-risk product development, and unlock credibility for future fundraising.

REVENUE-BASED FINANCING

Revenue-based financing (RBF) allows startups to raise capital without giving up equity by agreeing to repay investors through a percentage of future revenue. Unlike traditional loans, there's no fixed repayment schedule and payments adjust based on your actual earnings. This can be especially useful for businesses with seasonal or uneven revenue.

Best for:

+ Companies with predictable revenue streams, such as SaaS businesses or e-commerce brands.
+ Startups that need growth capital but don't want to take on long-term debt or dilution.

Popular RBF providers:

+ **Pipe:** Provides upfront cash for SaaS companies based on recurring revenue.
+ **Clearco:** Offers funding for e-commerce and direct-to-consumer (DTC) brands to support marketing and inventory spend.
+ **Capchase:** Delivers flexible capital to companies with subscription-based business models.
+ **Local funds:** There are regional RBF funds like RevUp Capital, Sage Growth Capital, Flexible Capital Fund, and many more.

RBF can be a smart middle ground between equity and debt. Just make sure the repayment structure works with your projected revenue growth; otherwise it could strain cash flow at the wrong time.

LOANS AND ALTERNATIVE DEBT FINANCING

Traditional bank loans aren't always accessible to early-stage startups, but a growing number of alternative lenders and specialized loan programs offer debt-based capital without requiring collateral or personal guarantees.

Startup-friendly loan options:

+ **SBA loans:** The Small Business Administration backs loans through partner lenders with lower interest rates and flexible terms.
+ **Microloans:** Programs like Kiva, Accion, and Grameen America offer smaller-dollar loans to startups that may not qualify for traditional financing.
+ **Revenue-based loans:** Unlike traditional loans, these are repaid through a percentage of revenue rather than fixed payments.

On paper, these loan programs are designed to expand access to capital. In practice, though, many founders, particularly *The Rest of Us*, still encounter gatekeeping and bias, even when they check every box.

Rajia Abdelaziz's experience illustrates this dual reality with striking clarity:

Once we got the critique that we needed to put our own money into this, which we didn't have, we also applied for a $100,000 loan from the university. We needed $150,000 to develop the technology. We figured if we could first secure $100,000, it would make it easier to raise the final $50,000 from investors. We'd have a prototype and our own skin in the game, because my co-founder and I were personally guaranteeing that $100,000.

They did secure that loan as the first capital into their company, but not without navigating extreme bias in the process.

> We were blindsided when a gatekeeper at the university, who had promised to write a positive recommendation, sent a letter to the bank saying she didn't recommend us for the loan. Our manufacturer, who was also an advisor, was shocked. He went over her head at the university asking for an explanation. After that, we were summoned to her office and received a furious tirade.
>
> She looked me dead in the eyes and asked, 'Do you understand you're cosigning the loan? Do you know what that means? Can you repeat to me what that means, that you would be liable? Who's going to pay back that money? Do you have $50,000 in your bank account? Does your dad have $50,000 in his bank account?'
>
> I have two engineering degrees, one in electrical engineering and one in computer science. I was making $90,000 as a software engineer at Amazon. I was more than qualified to understand that I would be paying back that $50,000.

Despite meeting every eligibility requirement, they almost lost it because one person didn't believe a 21-year-old woman understood financial responsibility.

This is a story that may feel painfully familiar. It's a reminder to always dig deeper when you're met with an unexpected rejection and to recognize when bias, not merit, is the real reason behind a no.

Rajia also demonstrates the power in owning your identity and your agency because the bias didn't stop there.

We were scheduled to pitch the bank panel, and nearly everyone was an older white man. People in my network were telling me not to wear makeup, to put my hair in a tight ponytail or bun, don't wear a skirt, don't wear pink, don't look too girly. I did the opposite, and I gave them a very simple, clear-cut pitch:

'Your sister, your mom, your daughter, your wife. One of those four women will, statistically, be sexually assaulted at one point in her life. Today, I'm giving you the opportunity to do something about it and help save her life. I almost became part of those statistics. I saw firsthand how hard it is to take out your phone in a scary situation. We all protect our loved ones with home security. We should all protect them with personal security.'

It was a unanimous vote to loan the company its first $100,000. From there, armed with a working prototype and real funding, every investor they approached said yes. They were oversubscribed.

WHEN LOANS FEEL PERSONAL

For many founders, especially those from communities historically excluded from wealth-building opportunities, taking on debt can feel deeply personal and risky. Melissa Wood shared how her discomfort with debt was shaped by lived experience:

The risk is huge. What if something happens and I can't pay it off? I just don't like the idea of taking money and not being able to pay it back. I couldn't be comfortable with myself.

It's not just about financial mechanics; it's about integrity, ethics, dignity, and the emotional weight of responsibility. Melissa had been through financial hardship that left lasting marks:

> We went through a financial mess when I was younger. I had cancer, we
> had a new baby, and it all hit at once. We had to settle some debts, and I
> hated that. I hated that we couldn't pay people back who had provided
> a service. But we had to do what we had to do.

Her story reveals something often left out of startup playbooks, which
is that the fear of debt isn't always about risk tolerance. Sometimes it's the
memory of what it costs, emotionally and relationally, when things go wrong.
This mindset is especially prevalent among women and founders of color,
who are statistically more likely to have faced financial insecurity and less
likely to have access to generational wealth or safety nets.[45]

As Melissa's business matured, her perspective shifted, but her core values
didn't:

> My mindset has shifted. I know the value I bring, and I'm confident
> that anyone who backs me isn't just taking a chance; they're making
> a smart investment that will pay off many times over.

That shift, from debt as danger to capital as confidence, is one many founders experience over time. But it doesn't erase the trauma behind it. When
you've lived through financial instability, "risk" doesn't live in a spreadsheet,
it lives in your body, your relationships, and your memories.

For *The Rest of Us*, building with integrity is nonnegotiable. That means
rethinking how we use capital; not avoiding it, but approaching it with clarity,
alignment, and a deep respect for what's at stake.

---

45   Hwang, V., Desai, S., and Baird, R. (2019) "Access to Capital for Entrepreneurs: Removing
     Barriers," Ewing Marion Kauffman Foundation: Kansas City. https://www.kauffman.org/
     wp-content/uploads/2019/12/CapitalReport_042519.pdf

TAX CREDITS AND GOVERNMENT INCENTIVES

Governments at the federal, state, and local levels offer a range of tax credits and incentives to support small businesses, especially those investing in innovation, sustainability, or job creation. These programs can reduce your tax burden and free up cash flow when capital is tight.

Some of the most valuable programs include:

- **R&D tax credits:** This federal program allows startups to offset payroll taxes if they're investing in research and development, such as building new technology or improving products. You can potentially save thousands per year, even if you're not yet profitable.
- **Work opportunity tax credit (WOTC):** If you hire employees from certain underrepresented or historically disadvantaged groups (e.g., veterans, formerly incarcerated individuals, long-term unemployed), you may qualify for federal tax credits.[46]
- **State-specific incentives:** Many states offer their own tax breaks, cash grants, or matching programs for startups in high-priority sectors like clean energy, artificial intelligence, life sciences, and advanced manufacturing. These incentives vary widely by region and are often underutilized.

If you're spending money on R&D or growing your team, it's worth consulting with a qualified accountant or tax advisor to explore which credits apply. Even if the dollar amounts aren't massive, these programs can unlock non-dilutive funding that helps extend your runway and reinvest in growth.

---

46   While the WOTC is authorized through the end of 2025, its future beyond that date will depend on legislative action. Employers interested in leveraging this credit should stay informed about any changes to the program.

STRATEGIC PARTNERSHIPS AND CORPORATE SPONSORSHIPS

Some startups can raise capital through strategic partnerships, corporate sponsorships, or revenue-sharing agreements with larger companies that see value in the startup's product, mission, or market access.

For example:

+ A healthtech startup might partner with a hospital system to co-develop a solution, with the hospital funding part of the development in exchange for early access or exclusivity.
+ A sustainability-focused brand could secure a sponsorship from a corporation looking to support environmental, social, and governance (ESG) initiatives and reach socially conscious customers.

These relationships often require careful negotiation and clear alignment with the corporation's goals. They have the potential to provide capital, distribution, operational support, and brand credibility without giving up equity.

CROWDFUNDING BEYOND EQUITY

While equity crowdfunding involves selling shares, there are also non-dilutive crowdfunding models that allow you to raise capital without giving up ownership:

+ **Rewards-based crowdfunding:** Platforms like Kickstarter and Indiegogo let startups raise funds by offering early access to products, limited-edition items, or other perks instead of equity.

+ **Debt crowdfunding:** Sometimes called peer-to-peer lending, this approach allows founders to borrow money from individual backers who are repaid with interest, often through platforms like Kiva, Honeycomb Credit, Funding Circle, and others.

These models work best for consumer-facing businesses that can rally a community around their product or mission. Success depends on storytelling, trust, and a compelling reason for people to support you early.

BOOTSTRAPPING (OR REVENUE-FUNDED GROWTH)

One option often discussed with a halo of nobility is bootstrapping. Let's reframe that. I prefer the term revenue-funded growth because it reflects strategic discipline and intentionality. Revenue-funded growth means you're building a company by reinvesting the money your business earns. It's not dependent on outside capital; it's powered by your customers. That can be incredibly empowering because you retain full ownership and control, and you're not beholden to investor expectations or timelines.

Of course, no source of capital is truly "free." Revenue-funded growth still comes at a cost, which is often your own savings, your time, your health, or the ability to pay yourself. It may mean slower growth, limited investment in R&D, or tough choices about when and how to hire. It's not always feasible, especially for capital-intensive or highly regulated industries like hardware, life sciences, or manufacturing.

Still, for many founders, revenue-funded growth isn't a fallback. This is a smart, values-aligned choice. In today's market where more investors are placing greater emphasis on burn rates and a path to profitability, a track record of sustainable, customer-funded growth can actually make you more attractive to the right kind of capital down the line.

NON-DILUTIVE FUNDING FOR *THE REST OF US*

Non-dilutive funding can be a game-changer for founders who want to grow without giving up ownership. While these options require research, preparation, and sometimes longer timelines, they preserve equity and allow founders to stay in control of their company's future.

If you're considering non-dilutive funding, ask yourself:

+ Does my business align with a grantmaker's mission?
+ Do I have recurring revenue that could support revenue-based financing?
+ Can I leverage tax credits or incentives to free up cash?
+ Would a corporate partnership accelerate my growth without requiring equity?

Exploring these options allows you to build a diversified capital strategy that supports your company's growth while preserving your ownership, values, and long-term vision.

Not all money is created equal, and not all money is meant for you.
VC may be the loudest voice in the room, but it's not the only, or best, fit for many businesses. Choosing the right type of capital is how you protect your vision, your values, and your ownership.

Access ≠ optionality.
Many founders end up on limited funding paths because they're the only ones they can see or reach. This chapter breaks down your options so you can choose from a place of strategy, not scarcity.

The rules were written for others, but you still get to play.
Understanding how each capital source thinks (venture firms, angels, family offices, CDFIs,[47] grantmakers, etc.) helps you frame your story in a way that resonates, even if their models weren't built with you in mind.

Dilution isn't inherently bad, but it isn't always worth it.
Giving up equity can be the right move at the right time, but if it's not aligned with your goals or the stage of your business, choosing a non-dilutive path might be the best direction.

---

47 A CDFI (Community Development Financial Institution) is a mission-driven financial institution, certified by the U.S. Treasury, that provides loans and other capital to underserved entrepreneurs and communities. In the startup context, CDFIs often offer early-stage or growth capital, sometimes paired with technical assistance, to founders who may not qualify for traditional bank financing, with the goal of advancing community and economic development rather than maximizing profit.

Community capital is real capital.

Crowdfunding, grant funding, and ecosystem-aligned capital sources may not carry prestige, but they often come with deeper alignment, trust, and long-term support, especially for *The Rest of Us.*

ACCELERATORS, INCUBATORS, AND STUDIOS—OH MY!

An entire industry has developed to support founders. Accelerators, incubators, and venture studios offer mentorship, resources, networks, and sometimes funding. For many founders, especially *The Rest of Us*, these programs can seem like a path to visibility, community, and early traction. To be clear, some of these programs *are* transformational. I've seen founders walk away with lifelong mentors, strategic introductions, and critical early support.

But, like most things in fundraising, the picture is more nuanced. Not every program delivers on its promises. Some are genuinely helpful, others just aren't the right fit, and a few talk a good game but don't help in meaningful ways, or at worst, can take advantage of founders. This chapter will help you understand the landscape so you can evaluate programs with clarity rather than hope alone. We'll break down what these programs are, how they differ, how to assess fit, and how to protect your time, energy, and equity in the process.

THE BIAS BEFORE THE PROGRAM

Before you even get into an accelerator, incubator, or venture studio, there's a gate to get through, and it's influenced by the same biases found across the whole fundraising system. This doesn't mean every program is biased or harmful; far from it. Many are actively working to level the playing field, but it's important to understand the structural dynamics so you don't internalize a no as a reflection of your worth or your company's potential.

Most programs require an application that includes a pitch deck, financial projections, a competitive landscape, and sometimes product demos. On the surface, this seems straightforward. But creating those materials requires having enough exposure to know what "good" looks like, understanding investor norms, and having the time to produce polished documents. So, you need to include many of the elements the program is designed to teach you in the application to get into the program!

There's also a time cost. Preparing pitch materials, practicing your narrative, tracking down customer research, and building a deck can take dozens of hours. For founders who are working full-time jobs, managing caregiving responsibilities, or simply bootstrapping every minute of their runway, that investment of time can be prohibitive. If you're coming from a nontraditional background, didn't go to business school, or haven't had exposure to venture norms, you may not even know what's expected or how much weight something like a polished deck or investor-style financial model carries in the application process.

Even once you apply, human bias shows up. Review committees, no matter how well-intentioned, bring their own assumptions. Research consistently shows that identical pitches are judged differently depending on the perceived gender, race, or accent of the founder. One study showed that investors were more likely to fund a pitch narrated by a man than the exact same pitch narrated by a woman.[48] The same pattern appears when names "sound" white versus non-white.

Networks also play a major role. Many programs rely heavily on referrals. That means if someone in your existing network has been through the program, or knows the selection team, you're more likely to receive serious consideration. Founders without inherited networks or warm introductions often find themselves at a disadvantage before anyone even opens their application.

This doesn't mean the program is bad. It means the system is imperfect.

If you weren't accepted into a program, that doesn't automatically mean your idea wasn't strong. You may not have spoken the insider language yet, known the preferred deck format, had the right referral, or simply weren't the "pattern" reviewers are used to seeing.

Yulkendy Valdez, a founder who later joined the programming side, described how her perspective shifted once she saw the inside:

> As a founder, I used to think, 'I'm already doing all the things—why wouldn't this accelerator want me?' But once I took on a programming role, I realized I had become a gatekeeper. I saw how the process often feels more like playing the lottery than making decisions based on talent or traction. When you're reviewing hundreds, sometimes thousands, of applications, it becomes impossible to deeply know every founder or community. Even with the best intentions, bias creeps in … You really see the bias when the cohort is announced.

---

48   A. W. Brooks et al., "Investors Prefer Entrepreneurial Ventures Pitched by Attractive Men," *Proceedings of the National Academy of Sciences*, 111, no. 12 (2014): 4427–4431, https://doi.org/10.1073/pnas.1321202111.

> I'd look at the list and think, 'Wait a minute, this startup doesn't even have a product yet, and they got in?' Meanwhile, someone else with real traction was passed over. It comes down to what signals of 'credibility' are easily recognized. If you're a second- or third-time founder, or you have an Ivy League degree or a big tech company on your résumé, you get more deliberation time. Founders without that pedigree? They're often dismissed in minutes.

Programs that truly prioritize equity work hard to correct for these dynamics. They build clear, transparent selection criteria, train reviewers, and invest in outreach to *The Rest of Us* by partnering with ecosystem leaders who understand diverse communities. It's a green flag if you see that level of intentionality from program design to alumni outcomes.

Let's start by defining each one in plain terms.

ACCELERATORS

Accelerators are designed to do what the name suggests: help startups move faster. Think of them like pressure cookers. They're short-term, high-intensity programs built to rapidly push you from early idea to a sharper, more investable business.

They usually offer a structured curriculum, mentorship, co-founder networking, and a "demo day," which is a pitch event in front of potential investors.

When accelerators are well run, founders walk away with a clearer story, tighter operations, early customer insights, and a support network they can lean on long after graduation.

Some programs are truly transformative. Others, however, can burn your time, take your equity, and send you on your way with a hoodie and a few generic slide templates. It's a broad landscape, and like any industry, quality varies.

+ There are over 3,000 accelerators globally, including more than 1,000 in the US.[49]

+ The accelerator market was valued at over $5.3 billion in 2024 and is projected to reach $9.5 billion by 2033.[50]

That second number is the accelerators' revenue, not the founders' revenue. Accelerators are businesses, too, and their incentives don't always align perfectly with yours.

UNDERSTAND THE BUSINESS MODEL

There's no one-size-fits-all model for accelerators. Before joining one, ask a simple question: How do they make money? The answer will tell you a lot about how they operate and what they'll prioritize.

Common models include:

+ **Equity for cash:** You give up 5–10% of your company in exchange for ~$100,000–$150,000.

+ **Equity for services:** They take equity in exchange for access to a network, mentors, or support services. The value here varies widely.

+ **Fee-based:** These programs charge upfront fees instead of taking equity. You'll often hear them referred to as "non-dilutive" accelerators.

+ **Sponsored or grant-funded:** Some accelerators, especially those run by nonprofits, universities, or government-backed groups,

---

49   BetaBoom, "Best Startup Accelerators in the United States," updated November 11, 2025, https://www.betaboom.com/magazine/article/best-startup-accelerators.

50   Business Research Insights, *Startup Accelerator Market Size, Share, Growth,* 2025, https://www.businessresearchinsights.com/market-reports/startup-accelerator-market-115518.

don't take equity at all. These can be great fits when they have strong support, clear outcomes, and aligned missions.

Accelerators were originally positioned as founder-friendly stepping stones. But many now operate more like pre-VC firms with pressure to produce big outcomes quickly. That doesn't make them bad, it just means you need to understand their incentives and make sure they match what you need at your stage.

Yulkendy shared this shift from firsthand experience:

> Accelerators were supposed to be that friendly, supportive extension before you're ready for a formal institutional round, like an angel investor who doesn't care about your metrics yet. That's just not true anymore. These programs have funders, corporate sponsors, and they're under pressure to produce companies that raise seed, Series A, Series B. It's a huge industry now. Some even make you pay to be part of it. The vibe has changed. They're not patient capital; they're chasing outcomes.

This isn't universal. Many accelerators still prioritize founder development, community, and patient support. Keep an eye out for the ones that align with your goals.

THE TRAP OF ACCELERATOR-HOPPING

Some founders, especially *The Rest of Us*, end up cycling through program after program. They join accelerators for visibility, credibility, connections, or simply because it feels like the only door that's open. Without a clear purpose for participating, this can backfire.

Investors may start to wonder why multiple programs didn't lead to traction or capital. Founders sometimes tell me they collected badges and logos but didn't see real growth.

Too many accelerators can send a signal that you're always preparing but not progressing.

Yulkendy explained:

> My co-founder and I did something like 20 programs. Not all accelerators, some were fellowships or incubators, but that's what we had to do to even be seen. Founders like me, from marginalized communities, get pushed into a cycle of pitch competitions and demo days because traditional investors won't return our emails. You're out here stacking logos, trying to get noticed, and you're not building your business. I've seen founders stuck in that loop for years.

Not every founder's story looks like this. Modjossorica (Rica) Elysée, a serial entrepreneur, flips the script and shows the upside of using accelerators with intention. She participated in 11 accelerators, each chosen for a specific strategic reason like regional access, customer introductions, corporate partners, or visibility in markets she couldn't reach alone.

> Look, I've done a few of these programs. Boston, LA, Tulsa, New York—you name it, I've probably had the free snacks and the matching swag hoodie. But here's the thing: I never did them for the curriculum. Everybody's teaching the same "how to pitch" slides and the same "what's your TAM?" speeches. I did them for access. Each city had its own flavor. One opened doors to tech partners, another plugged me into the beauty world, another gave me mentors I still text when I'm

spiraling. None of them magically moved my business forward—I did. But each one gave me a different kind of fuel.

If I didn't show up early, stay late, ask the 'dumb' questions, and make myself known, it didn't matter. These programs aren't cheat codes—they're treadmills. You only move if you walk.

Rica's experience highlights the positive potential when you're clear about why you're saying yes. The right accelerator at the right time can be a true unlock.

DEMO DAY ISN'T THE FINISH LINE

Most accelerators culminate in a demo day, which is a polished pitch event for investors. These events matter for the program. Their funders and sponsors are in the audience, and their credibility is on the line.

That pressure can shape your pitch more for performance than for real fundraising. Founders often graduate with a stunning deck that wins applause but doesn't withstand deeper investor conversations. They realize they need more clarity on their numbers, go-to-market plan, and operational details. Demo day can be valuable for exposure and confidence-building, but it's not a guarantee of capital.

Rica shared:

Let's be real—not every investor who shows up is there for you. Some are just checking the 'community engagement' box. You can feel it. But you still show up. You still pitch. You still learn how to read a room—and a term sheet.

Demo days can still be really useful. They can open doors, create momentum, and build your pitch stamina. Just make sure you walk away with the skills and understanding you need for real fundraising conversations, not just the stage version.

CHECKLIST: HOW TO EVALUATE AN ACCELERATOR

Use these criteria to decide whether an accelerator program is a fit:

PROGRAM STRUCTURE	☐ What does the curriculum cover? Is it tactical or fluffy? ☐ Will you get real support on go-to-market, financials, and investor readiness? ☐ Is it virtual, in person, or hybrid? ☐ Who are the mentors and workshop leaders?
EQUITY & FUNDING	☐ What is their business model? Do they take equity, charge fees, or offer grants? ☐ Do they provide direct cash or only services? ☐ Do they have follow-on rights or expectations?
OUTCOMES	☐ How many alumni in your stage and industry raised capital afterward? ☐ What does their investor network really look like? ☐ What support exists after graduation?
CULTURE FIT	☐ Do they have a track record of supporting founders like you? ☐ Are solo founders, women, people of color, or nontechnical teams represented in alumni?
TRANSPARENCY	☐ Are the terms clear and in writing? ☐ Is the selection and decision process transparent?

Table 8.1

I strongly encourage talking to alumni. Ask the program for warm introductions to at least two or three founders. Or search the accelerator on LinkedIn and reach out directly.

When you speak to alumni, ask:

+ What did you actually get out of it?
+ Would you do it again?
+ Did it help you raise money?
+ What should I watch out for?

INCUBATORS

Incubators are slower, steadier, and more flexible than accelerators. Think of them like greenhouses. They're designed to give early-stage ideas a place to grow before being exposed to the outside world.

An incubator can be:

+ a physical space (like a university innovation center or coworking hub)
+ an organization offering resources and support (often nonprofit or university-affiliated)
+ a hybrid program that provides both space and structured programming

Unlike accelerators, incubators typically focus on education, community-building, and early validation, rather than rapid growth or investor readiness. They are especially helpful for first-time founders or people exploring an idea before they're ready for high-pressure fundraising environments.

Most incubators offer:

+ Coworking or lab space (sometimes free or subsidized)
+ Light mentorship and advisor access
+ Workshops or events
+ Occasional small grants, stipends, or non-dilutive support

Many incubators do not take equity. Some offer free services funded by grants or universities, while others charge small fees or rent. The quality varies widely, though. Some are deeply supportive communities, while others are under-resourced rooms with vague programming.

AS ALWAYS, BUSINESS MODELS MATTER

Incubators come in many forms, and understanding who funds them will tell you what they're designed to deliver.

Common models include:

+ **Grant-funded or nonprofit-backed:** Community-driven, often free to founders, and focused on local impact or early education.
+ **University-affiliated:** Often offer space, mentorship, and a structured path to early validation. These can be especially valuable if you're new to entrepreneurship.
+ **Corporate-sponsored:** Funded by a company with a strategic interest in certain markets or technologies. Helpful if aligned, limiting if not.
+ **Equity- or fee-based:** Some incubators take small equity stakes or charge for membership or coworking. This isn't inherently bad; it just means you're paying for the support.

Always ask: Who is this incubator really built to serve? Founders, sponsors, or the institution?

James Valencia had a transformative experience with Vanderbilt's Wond'ry and the National Science Foundation Innovation Corps (I-Corps) program:

> When I went to talk to the women who ran the Wond'ry, Vanderbilt's innovation center, it totally changed my course. They told me about a new incubator program for founders, and to qualify, I had to either do some pre-programming or go through the NSF I-Corps. I did I-Corps and they taught me the customer discovery process, which if I hadn't learned, I think I would have ended up as a flop. Wond'ry provided me with a mentor that I still meet with weekly.
>
> I don't come from an entrepreneur family, so I didn't have any support for starting a business, and that's what those programs provided. I also now have a network of alumni and other mentors to talk with. They've set up countless pitches for me when before I had literally no idea what the fundraising scene was. I didn't know what venture capital was, or the difference between private equity and a family office. Now I understand all of that.

This is the best version of what an incubator can be: a bridge between your idea and your understanding of how to build it.

IP AND LICENSING CONCERNS

If an incubator is connected to a university, research institution, or corporate partner, always read the fine print on intellectual property (IP). I mean, do this all the time anyway, but read it an extra time over in this case.

Some university-affiliated incubators may claim rights to inventions you develop using their space, equipment, or resources. Others may require you to license your own IP from them if it originated on their campus or in their offices. This is very common in life sciences, biotech, and deep tech spaces.

Before joining, ask about IP policies. If you're in a technical field, consult a lawyer familiar with university or institutional spinouts. Confirm that you own what you build.

THE VALUE OF COMMUNITY

One of the most powerful parts of incubators isn't the programming; it's the people.

Founders often say the biggest benefit was the peer group they built. For *The Rest of Us*, especially those who haven't been surrounded by entrepreneurs before, that community can be grounding, motivating, and validating. Sometimes the incubator becomes the first place where you feel like you belong.

As with accelerators, marketing won't tell you the whole story, but alumni will. Ask to speak with people who have completed the program.

GEOGRAPHY AND SECTORS

Incubators often reflect the strengths and priorities of their local ecosystem. A biotech incubator in Boston may not be the right fit for a fintech founder in Atlanta. Some incubators are tailored to women, people of color, or local founders, while others unintentionally exclude them. Make sure the incubator is aligned with your sector, stage, and identity.

CHECKLIST: HOW TO EVALUATE AN INCUBATOR

- ☐ What is their business model? Who benefits?
- ☐ Do they take equity, fees, rent, or nothing?
- ☐ What are their IP policies? Do you own what you build?
- ☐ What is the time commitment? Can you realistically meet it?
- ☐ Is the community diverse, supportive, and active?
- ☐ What does the alumni network look like?
- ☐ What support, if any, continues after you leave?

VENTURE STUDIOS

Venture studios are a different beast. Think of them like production companies for startups; they actively help *create* companies. Some studios generate ideas in-house, validate them, and then recruit founders to build those companies. Others partner with external founders, often nontechnical ones, to help develop early-stage ideas and bring them to life. In both cases, the studios provide resources, team capacity, and capital in exchange for a significant ownership stake.

This model has exploded in popularity. There are now more than 720 venture studios worldwide (some estimates put the number closer to 800+), up from just 130 a decade ago.[51] That growth signals that venture studios are becoming a mainstream path to building high-growth startups.

Studios typically offer:

---

51 Future Ventures, "Venture Studio vs. Incubator: Which Model Suits Your Startup Best?" August 19, 2025, https://www.futureventures.ca/insights/venture-studio-vs-incubator-which-model-suits-your-startup-best.

- **Pre-developed ideas:** For studio-originated startups, they generate and test the concept before building a team around it.
- **Hands-on operational support:** For founder-originated startups, they provide hands-on product, engineering, design, and marketing support to build on early ideas.
- **Initial funding:** Early capital plus access to their investor network.
- **A structured launch plan:** Shortens the time from concept to market.

For founders, working with a studio can be incredibly powerful, especially if you have a compelling idea but need help building product, hiring talent, or accessing capital. But like any partnership, it involves trade-offs. Studios usually take a larger equity stake and may expect a tighter alignment with their process, vision, and team. When aligned well, a studio can feel like having a co-founder with expertise, funding, and speed. When misaligned, it can feel like giving up more control than you intended.

Julie Moir Messervy's story shows how studios can play a targeted, supportive role when paired with mentorship and a clear understanding of what you need:

When I started hitting limits in knowledge and experience building a tech company, I sought education. I joined incubators including LaunchVT, The Capital Network, and MassChallenge. Early on, I went to MIT's Venture Mentor Service since I'm an alum. There, I kept finding mentors to help us, and one of those people eventually became our first COO. It started with watching how he worked with us through the mentoring process. About four meetings in, I took him aside and said, would you be open to this?

> We didn't have the funds to pay him at the time, but he brought
> in an investor and found a venture studio to help us build the tech,
> which was exactly what we needed. They're still my tech company
> today and invested in us.

Julie didn't come to the studio with a finished product. She showed up
with traction, clarity, and a specific gap. The venture studio filled that gap with
technical support, operational strength, and capital, which was exactly what
she needed. This is the best-case scenario. The studio acted like smart, aligned
capital, meeting her where she was and helping her build what came next.

THE EQUITY TRADE

Venture studios typically take much more equity than accelerators or incubators, often 30–60% in exchange for their support. This can make founders feel
more like partners or operators than traditional owners. That's not inherently
bad, especially if you're a nontechnical founder who needs a full product team,
you want to de-risk at the earliest stages, or you're optimizing for speed and
build capacity rather than maximum ownership.

The question to ask yourself is if you're comfortable with that level of
shared control for the value you get in return. There's no right answer; it all
depends on your goals, skills, and stage.

SERVICE CONTRACTS AND STRINGS ATTACHED

One thing founders don't always realize is that many studios require ongoing
service contracts as part of the partnership.

That can mean:

+ You must continue using their engineers or product team post-spinout.
+ You may need permission to hire your own team.
+ You might be locked into specific pricing or scopes of work.

For studios, it creates recurring revenue and alignment. It might feel limiting for founders, especially if the support becomes too generic, slow, or expensive relative to your needs. Ask early on:

+ Do I have freedom to hire my own team?
+ If I outgrow the studio's services, can I leave?
+ What happens if I want to rebuild the product?

Those questions are all aimed at understanding expectations so you can set the right ones for yourself.

CHECKLIST: HOW TO EVALUATE A VENTURE STUDIO

As with accelerators and incubators, I encourage you to ask a lot of questions of the studio's leadership and alumni. Some key questions for alumni include:

- [ ] What did you gain that you couldn't have done alone?
- [ ] How did the studio handle disagreements or pivots?
- [ ] Were the in-house teams high-quality and responsive?
- [ ] Would you work with them again?
- [ ] How did equity and service contracts feel over time?
- [ ] Did they help you raise? Introduce investors? Build product?

COMPARING ALL THREE

CATEGORY	ACCELERATORS	INCUBATORS	VENTURE STUDIOS
MAIN PURPOSE	Speed up growth in a short, intensive period ("pressure cooker")	Provide space, time, and support for early ideas to develop ("greenhouse")	Create or co-build startups with shared resources ("production company")
TYPICAL DURATION	2–4 months	Flexible or ongoing	Ongoing until spinout, often 12–24 months
EQUITY/FEES	5–10% equity typical; some charge fees	Often free or low-cost; sometimes rent or small equity	30–60% equity common; may include service contracts
FUNDING PROVIDED	Modest checks ($50K–$150K typical)	Occasional small grants or none	Larger upfront capital plus access to studio-backed investors
PROGRAMMING	Structured curriculum, workshops, and demo day	Light mentorship, community events, optional workshops	In-house product, engineering, design, legal, finance, and concept validation

CATEGORY	ACCELERATORS	INCUBATORS	VENTURE STUDIOS
FOUNDER ROLE	Visionary + day-to-day executor	Visionary exploring and testing concepts	Visionary + operator, often co-building with the studio's team and process
BIGGEST BENEFITS	Investor exposure, structure, momentum	Community, education, early validation	Deep support, team capacity, faster time to build
BIGGEST RISKS	Focusing too much on demo day; joining too many programs	Weak programming; unclear IP or licensing terms	Significant equity trade; long-term service obligations; reduced control
BEST FOR	Founders ready to refine their pitch, accelerate growth, and seek investors	Early-stage founders seeking learning, community, or a low-pressure build environment	Founders who want strong operational support, non-technical founders, or those open to co-owning an idea

Table 8.2

Richard Millunchick, a startup coach and advisor, shared some sage advice about choosing a program:

Selecting an accelerator program is not much different from selecting a startup to invest in (or, if you are a founder, selecting your investor partners). There are many accelerator programs out there, and each has a different focus and set of goals. With this in mind, what are your goals as a founder/business, and are you prepared to do your due diligence? In addition, are you also committed to the program? As an advisor or investor, I have been invited to observe and participate in the GrowthX revenue accelerator program multiple times. Most founders are not salespeople and need to focus on identifying the ideal customer profile, developing a culture of consistently building a quality pipeline, and driving revenue. The most fabulous idea in the world means nothing if there are no revenue-generating clients. So, the companies I have observed that participated in the GrowthX program that commit build a real pipeline and drive revenue progress. But we all know that not every founder commits, and their results reflect that, as there are no shortcuts to success.

In short, the founder needs to work for it, as the adage from *Field of Dreams*—"Build it and they will come"—is really just stuff for the movies.

LEGAL TERMS AND NEGOTIATING

Many founders assume big-name programs like a bank's accelerator automatically come with founder-friendly terms. Sometimes that's true; many programs are fair, transparent, and genuinely aligned with supporting early-stage companies, but not always. Even household name programs can include terms that are surprisingly aggressive or simply misaligned with what an early-stage founder should accept.

Rica learned this firsthand:

Let's just say … I've seen some clauses that made me clutch my pearls. Founders signing deals that looked good on paper until you realized the paper owned you. You live, you learn, and you lawyer up early next time.

Sometimes a program is trying to secure upside, sometimes they're using a template that was built for later-stage companies, and sometimes the team running the program simply hasn't adjusted their legal documents to match the spirit of what they advertise. Where founders get into trouble is if they ignore red flags because the opportunity feels prestigious or rare. For *The Rest of Us*, there's a real psychological pressure to "be grateful," and that pressure can make unfair terms feel like the cost of entry.

The lesson here isn't to avoid these programs or distrust everything. Many of them offer excellent, aligned terms that genuinely help you grow. I do recommend that no matter how shiny the brand is, you should always have an attorney or expert review an agreement document before signing.

VALIDATION THROUGH PARTICIPATION

For *The Rest of Us*, getting accepted into an accelerator, incubator, or venture studio often carries weight far beyond the program itself. These programs usually have an application and vetting process. Someone, often investors, mentors, or experienced entrepreneurs, looked at your idea, your team, and your potential and said, *Yes, you belong here.*

That validation matters.

+ It can boost your confidence when you're used to hearing no.
+ It signals to future investors that others have already put eyes on your business.

+ It helps you communicate credibility to customers, partners, or even your own family.

There's real value in that! For many founders, especially those who have been underestimated or under-resourced, that acceptance can be the first external affirmation that their work is seen, understood, and worth backing. BUT there are a few grounding reminders to keep in mind:

+ **It's a starting point, not a finish line:** Participation doesn't automatically lead to funding, traction, or guaranteed success.
+ **Not all validations are equal:** Some programs have rigorous screening; others accept almost everyone who applies.
+ **You still need to deliver:** Investors will ultimately care about your traction, your model, and your ability to execute, not just the logos on your website.

If being selected gives you momentum, confidence, or connection, use it. Just don't confuse the credibility of the program with the long-term credibility of your business. That comes from the work you put in every day.

These programs are businesses, too.

Accelerators, incubators, and venture studios each have their own incentives and revenue models. Understand who they're built to serve: you, their funders, their sponsors, or their own investment pipeline.

Validation matters, but it isn't everything.

Being accepted into a program can feel like proof that you belong in the startup world. Use that credibility as fuel, but remember it's only one part of the much larger journey you're on.

Equity and control come at a cost.

Accelerators often take 5–10% equity, incubators sometimes claim IP, and venture studios may take 30–60% ownership and require long-term service contracts. Make sure you understand what you're trading and that the trade makes sense for your goals.

Community can be the hidden value.

For *The Rest of Us*, the peer network of fellow founders who understand your journey may be more valuable than the curriculum itself. Don't underestimate the power of belonging and shared experience.

Red flags are real.

High fees, vague benefits, unclear terms, forced service contracts, or reluctance to connect you with alumni should all give you pause. A good program welcomes questions, transparency, and informed decision-making.

9

DEVELOPING A COMPREHENSIVE FUNDRAISING STRATEGY

Everything we're covering here in Part I, including capital types, strategy, timing, and investor fit, is the foundation your pitch depends on. In Part II, we'll build your pitch deck step-by-step, but before you can tell a compelling story, you need to understand what story you're actually telling and whom it's for. The next two chapters set you up for that.

Up to this point, we've explored the full menu of ways to fund a business, including non-dilutive capital, crowdfunding, philanthropic dollars, loans, revenue-based financing, angels, family offices, and more. You now understand the broader capital landscape far better than most founders ever do.

But at some stage, many startups, especially those aiming for meaningful scale, will raise an equity round. That's where the stakes get higher, the expectations shift, and the strategy becomes even more important. For *The Rest of Us*, this is the part of the journey that feels the most intimidating. That's exactly why we're going to break it down here together.

So many founders start fundraising by jumping straight into pitching. I'm the first to support the idea that making your deck is a critical part of fundraising, but that's not where it starts. If you don't begin with a strategy, you risk wasting time, burning out, or chasing capital that doesn't align with your business.

This chapter will help you build an equity fundraising strategy that is intentional, aligned, and built for your path forward.

FUNDRAISING TAKES TIME

Fundraising takes time. It's one of the most inefficient parts of building a company, even though investors often back startups that make other systems more efficient. Let's walk through what the time commitment looks like on both sides.

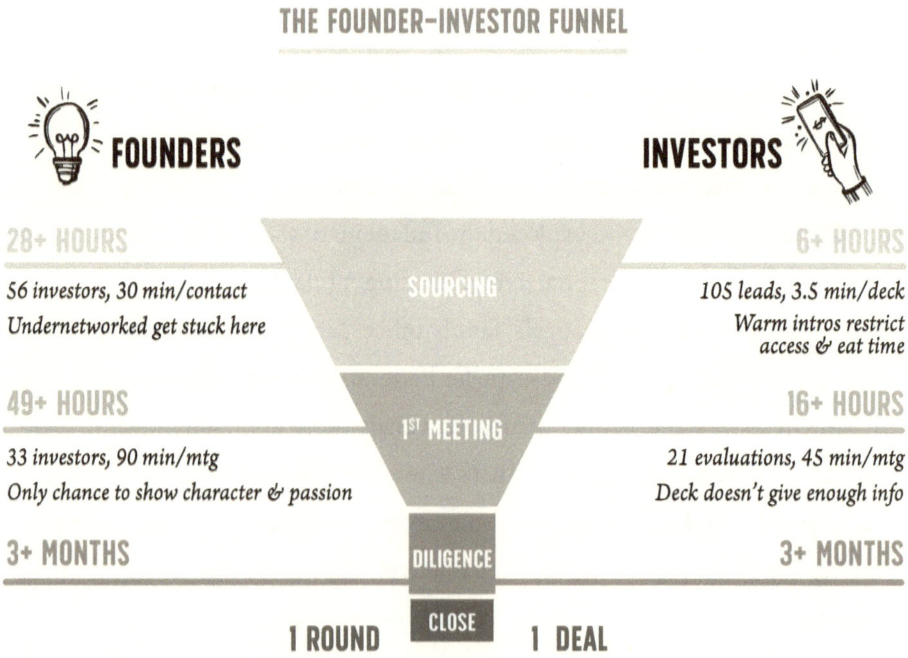

Figure 9.1

Before we break down what fundraising time actually looks like, take a moment to look at the infographic in figure 9.1. It shows the average time founders and investors spend moving through a single round from sourcing to close. Here's what the timeline means in practice:

Sourcing Investors (Founders)

Founders who successfully close a round reach out to an average of 56 investors. The "who successfully close a round" bit is important context. This dataset comes from those who made it through, and as we've covered, those founders are disproportionately white and male. So, if you're part of *The Rest of Us*, expect higher numbers: more outreach, more meetings, and more scrutiny.

First Meetings

Of those 56 investors, founders typically secure 33 first meetings. Prep time, the meeting itself, and post-meeting follow-up add up to roughly 90 minutes per investor, or another 49+ hours. These meetings are often your one chance to show who you are beyond the deck.

Diligence

If an investor decides to move forward, due diligence takes, on average, three months. Some rounds move faster, and many take longer. This includes deeper conversations, customer calls, financial review, team interviews, internal approvals, and legal work.

Angel investors can sometimes compress this timeline because they don't have committees or institutional processes, but diligence still takes time, even if it's days or weeks instead of months.

Investors face inefficiency too, though of a different kind.

Sourcing Founders (Investors)

Venture investors spend an average of 3.5 minutes per deck reviewing roughly 100 decks just to get to a single deal. That's over 6 hours of initial screening. (This includes mostly warm introductions, which limits who gets seen, but we'll unpack that dynamic later.) Angel investors often spend more time looking at a deck because they don't receive as many to review.

First Meetings

Investors run about 21 meetings, spending 45 minutes each, totaling ~16 hours evaluating potential fits.

Diligence

Their diligence timeline generally mirrors yours, with another three months on average.

Fundraising is slow and labor-intensive on both sides. Founders who underestimate the time involved risk burning out or losing momentum as a result. Having a plan before you start, one that accounts for the volume of outreach, meeting load, and diligence runway, makes the entire process more manageable and dramatically increases your odds of success.

PREPARE YOUR CAMPAIGN BEFORE YOU START

STEPS TO PREPARE YOUR FUNDRAISING CAMPAIGN

DO YOU NEED TO FUNDRAISE?	INVESTOR PERSONAS	INSTRUMENT	TIMEFRAME	MATERIALS	TRACKING	OUTREACH	FOLLOW UP
Revenue or grants instead?	Realistic capital source(s)	SAFE, Convertible Note, Priced Round	Tight ship or rolling raise	Pitch presentation, data room	Workbook or CRM	Start with bottom of list for practice	Consistent and personalized

Figure 9.2

Before you commit to raising equity capital, pause and ask yourself one essential question: *Is this really the right path for me and my business?* Working through your pitch is often the fastest way to get that clarity. As you pressure-test your story, your numbers, your model, and your long-term vision, you may discover that your company doesn't naturally align with traditional VC expectations, and that is absolutely okay. You can build a thriving, profitable company without raising a single dollar of venture capital. See figure 9.2 for a step-by-step view of how to prepare your fundraising campaign.

Equity fundraising, particularly from venture capital, has been overly romanticized. It's often portrayed as the standard route to success, when in reality, it's just one tool among many. What matters most is building something sustainable and aligned with your goals. One of the most valuable things you can do for yourself, and your business, is to get honest about what kind of growth you want, the kind of capital that supports that growth, and the trade-offs you're willing, or not willing, to make.

Julie Moir Messervy's experience is a perfect example of designing a funding strategy around your reality, not someone else's blueprint. She built her tech startup alongside her services-based landscape design business:

> That was a conscious decision in response to the 2008 downturn, being in a small town in Vermont and having four people who worked for me. I was well-known in the field through my previous work, books, and lectures, so I kept getting exciting projects that earned revenue while we built our apps to scale our value for a broader clientele. And my design team loved the new challenges posed by the tech we were building together. Having the two businesses at the same time—our well-known landscape design firm and our fledgling startup—enabled me to keep everyone employed and help pay for our tech development as we worked on finding partnerships.

Julie didn't choose between "bootstrap" and "venture." She blended revenue, existing strengths, and hiring intentionality to build on her own terms.

You can mix and match capital strategies.

It doesn't have to be all VC or all bootstrapping. You can combine funding sources based on your goals, your timing, your risk tolerance, and your life circumstances. These decisions will likely evolve as your business grows.

Suelin Chen described her early fundraising as more organic than orchestrated:

> Things rarely go as planned. I always struggled to strictly timebox and orchestrate the kind of canonical fundraise that people talk about where you get all your ducks in a row and just pitch everyone within a couple weeks. I had plenty of experience doing that when my job was managing client transactions before I founded Cake, but I was never quite able to make it work like that for my own company.
>
> If I had to critique myself, I was sometimes overly opportunistic with things that came our way. It's a balancing act of being flexible and responsive to signals from the market while not getting pulled in too many directions.

Her story is common. Very few founders run a perfectly timed, perfectly controlled fundraising motion, especially *The Rest of Us*. Life, customers, opportunities, forces outside of your control, and survival all shape your path.

One hybrid model gaining traction is called seed-strapping. It's a cross between bootstrapping and traditional equity fundraising. The idea is that you raise a small seed round to get things off the ground, then focus on building a revenue-generating business that doesn't require ongoing equity raises.

This approach gives you early capital without forcing you into the high-growth, high-burn VC playbook. In today's environment with AI, no-code tools, automation, and fractional talent, many founders can scale leaner and faster. If you're questioning whether you're "VC-backable," or simply don't want that path, seed-strapping is an appealing alternative because it prioritizes control, sustainability, disciplined growth, and a business that doesn't depend on perpetual fundraising.

TAKING YOUR FIRST STEPS

If, after reflection, you decide that raising capital is the right path for you, the next step is to prepare your campaign before you send a single email. This preparation is what makes your pitch effective later. Everything you line up now—like your investor targets, instrument, materials, and timeline—becomes the foundation for a compelling, coherent story when you're in the room with an investor.

1. **Define your ideal investor personas (IIP):** Who are the right types of investors for your business and your round? What are they looking for, and how can you best align with that? (See Chapter 2.)

2. **Choose your fundraising instrument:** Decide whether you'll raise using a SAFE, convertible note, or priced round (these are simply different legal structures for how investors give you money; we'll walk through each in Chapter 10). Your instrument affects your timeline, valuation conversation, and the types of investors who will participate.

3. **Set your timeline:** Are you committing to a tight fundraising window, or doing a rolling raise (raising gradually as conversations

unfold)? Neither approach is "right." It depends on your urgency, cash runway, and willingness to manage a longer process.

4. **Build your data room:** A data room is a folder (Dropbox, Drive, Notion, etc.) that contains everything an investor will eventually need: pitch deck, financials, cap table, product screenshots, customer lists, legal documents, and so on. Preparing this early shows professionalism and prevents bottlenecks when investors request information.

5. **Practice your pitch—out loud:** Before you meet with a single investor, get reps in. Say the pitch **out loud**. Record yourself. Practice with peers, advisors, or friendly founders. Speaking it in your head is not the same. Your pacing, tone, confidence, and clarity only show up when you actually articulate it. If this part feels overwhelming right now, don't worry. Part II of this book walks you through your pitch deck, slide by slide. You'll build and refine it step-by-step. You're not meant to have it ready yet.

Fundraising can get chaotic quickly. You will be emailing, scheduling, tracking investor feedback, updating materials, and following up all at once. Decide ahead of time how you plan to stay organized. This could be a spreadsheet, a CRM tool (HubSpot, Streak, Pipedrive, etc.), or even a Trello/Asana-style kanban board. The tool doesn't matter as much as consistently using it.

When you're ready to begin outreach, start with your lower-priority investors. By that, I mean investors who *might* be a fit but aren't your dream partners. The people where a misstep or a less-polished pitch won't seem like as big a deal. These could be:

+ Investors who are outside your ideal stage or sector.

+ People who invest occasionally but not consistently.

+ Funds that are interesting but not your top choice.

+ Angels who don't have strong pull in your market.

+ Anyone you're less emotionally attached to impressing.

Think of them as your practice lane: real conversations with real investors, but without the pressure of risking your most important relationships right away. Begin with this group to refine your story, gather feedback, and identify patterns in the questions you're asked. Once your pitch feels sharper and you're more comfortable in meetings, then move to your high-priority investors.

Personalization is key here. It takes more effort, but it's worth it. Generic copy-paste emails rarely work. A thoughtful message that shows you understand who the investor is and why you're reaching out has a MUCH higher chance of landing. If they don't reply, follow up. Don't assume silence means no interest; it often just means your message fell below the inbox fold (am I dating myself with that expression?).[52] I can have 200+ emails from real people in my inbox at any given time. If someone nudges me again, I'm grateful. So, follow up weekly. Be polite, be personal, and get yourself back to the top of the inbox.

FUNDRAISING TIMING

When we talk about timing, I want you to think about it in two ways: your internal timeline between raises and the external fundraising calendar. Both

---

52   We used to say "below the fold" in reference to a print newspaper, now it's your email. Make sure you're "above the fold."

shape your process, and being intentional about each one can make your raise far smoother.

YOUR INTERNAL TIMELINE

If you're raising a pre-seed or angel round, you're typically raising somewhere between $100,000 to $1 million. Yes, that's a wide range because pre-seed varies enormously by sector and geography. Whatever your number is, target three to nine months of runway. That means enough time to build, test, and show some early traction before you raise again.

At this stage, investors aren't expecting perfection. They're looking for signs that you've got a compelling idea, a working MVP (minimum viable product, which is a basic version of your product that shows it works), an experienced team (or the self-awareness to know what you still need), and early indicators of revenue potential. They're betting on progress and promise.

By the time you're raising a seed round, typical amounts jump to $500,000 to $5 million and should fund 12 to 18 months of growth. Every round after that tends to follow a similar cadence. So, if you close a seed round in April, for example, plan for your next raise around the following spring.

THE EXTERNAL CALENDAR

Fundraising is surprisingly seasonal. Investors are people too, and just like *The Rest of Us*, they're influenced by school schedules, holidays, and vacation plans. Here's the general rhythm of the year:

+ **Fall (September to mid-December):** Peak season. Kids are back in school, people are back from summer break, and investors are re-engaged. If you can, align your raise with this window when capital is freer flowing and meetings are happening.

+ **Holidays (end of December through early January):** Avoid. It's hectic, filled with holidays and travel, and people just aren't focused on taking calls or making deals.

+ **Winter (mid-January through February):** Things start picking back up. It's a decent time to fundraise as it's less crowded than the fall, but still productive. Investors are resetting their goals and looking ahead.

+ **Spring (March through May):** Another strong window. There's a push to wrap things up before summer, and people are generally more optimistic and available.

+ **Summer (June through August):** Tough. Many people are traveling, on vacation, or mentally checked out. It's not impossible to raise, but it's an uphill climb.

To be clear, these patterns are tendencies, not laws. As Suelin shared:

> I remember clearly, I got a term sheet on July 4th because I called one of my advisors right after receiving it and I could hear fireworks in the background. He said to me, 'Um, I'm watching the fireworks right now, what do you mean you got a term sheet?' I thought investments didn't happen in the summer, so it felt unexpected.

A CREATIVE APPROACH TO TIMING

Deanna Meador took a uniquely bold approach to her raise, and it paid off in a big way.

> We decided to raise on International Women's Day and only allow investors from Tennessee because we wanted to show other entrepreneurs that there's capital here.

We were already talking to large customers and needed to ramp quickly. A traditional raise didn't fit our timeline; we were a small team, and the thought of spending months fundraising wasn't appealing. All the stats about lack of funding for women were hitting me daily, and we thought, 'Let's try something different.'

Instead of a months-long campaign, Deanna launched a one-day raise. The original goal was $1 million in 24 hours, but to align with a planned celebration that evening, she shortened it to just eight hours.

> We didn't show the pitch deck or reveal the raise amount in advance. We told people to stay by their phones on International Women's Day because an opportunity was coming, and they'd have to make a decision that same day. I sent the deck, terms, and answered diligence questions all in real time.

She worked her list from 7:00 a.m. until 2:43 p.m., closing the last commitment minutes before needing to be at the event venue for the 4:00 p.m. celebration. The total amount raised ended up being $1.5 million.

> I sent and received 193 messages including calls, texts, and emails, all from my living room. I didn't want my team making those calls because that's my responsibility as CEO. Every investor came in on the same SAFE note and terms. It was a lot of work, but also a lot of fun, and it made for a great story.

The day itself was dramatic, but the real magic came from Deanna's months of prep work behind the scenes. Identifying her target list, estimating check sizes, keeping potential investors warm, and having a backup plan in case things didn't go as expected.

> For anyone considering this kind of raise, prep is everything. Have your legal lined up, know who you're calling, send regular updates so you stay top of mind, and if you fall short, be ready to reframe it. Share what you learned and keep building.

This story is a reminder that while there are fundraising norms and patterns, there are no rules. If a traditional raise doesn't fit your needs, timeline, or values, you can find another way!

WHEN TIMING WORKS AGAINST YOU

While you can and should be strategic with your timing, the reality is that even the best-laid plans can get upended by forces outside your control.

Take Jen Saxton, founder of Tot Squad, who had not one but two major term sheets, one for $4 million and another for $5 million, fall apart at the last minute. The global climate shifted overnight, and investors did too.

> I had two big term sheets in 2022 with post-money valuations of $17 and $28 million. It all fell apart because Russia invaded Ukraine the day of my Walmart launch. Walmart called and said they were pulling the press release because the war just broke out. Then came inflation, recession, formula shortage, supply chain chaos, and all the investment money went away, so I had to go back to bootstrapping.

I've lived this too. I incorporated Scroobious in January 2020 with a clear plan to raise capital, hire a team, and grow quickly. Two months later, COVID hit, my kids' schools closed, everything went virtual, and the world shut down. That strategy I spent over a year planning went straight into the trash. I shifted into a slow, sustainable survival mode. Burn rate didn't matter as much because I was focused on bandwidth, a global pandemic, and just getting through the day. I slowed way down, proved out the product by working directly with founders, built our customized educational content without needing capital, and eventually did a slow, rolling raise from angels.

This is why it's so important to be aware of all your funding options, which you're doing by reading this book. We've all heard about the need to pivot your business model or product strategy, and sometimes you need to pivot your fundraising strategy. When you experience a setback, the real test is how you decide to move forward.

For Jen, that meant bootstrapping her way back to life and focusing on revenue-driven growth.

> I basically ran out of money by the end of 2022. I had to stop paying myself, lay off my whole team, move everybody to 1099 part-time, and go back into mega-bootstrapping mode. But I kept going because I knew if I stayed alive long enough, I could close one of these deals. In May of this year [2025], I signed this megadeal with Target, and now I'm off to the races again.

Sometimes, survival *is* the strategy. Staying in the game gives you a chance to win it later.

HOW MUCH MONEY DO I NEED TO RAISE?

This is one of the trickiest questions for any founder because the answer isn't one-size-fits-all. Every business is different, every market is different, and every team has its own pace. In a perfect world, you'd raise enough capital to reach profitability and never fundraise again. But let's be honest, that's rarely how it works. Most startups raise in stages, securing just enough to hit the milestones that will unlock the next round of funding. So instead of trying to guess the "right" number, ask yourself this: What is my next fundable milestone?

Investors don't fund companies just to help them survive; they fund momentum. Your job is to raise enough capital to create meaningful progress.

Your next fundable milestone might be:

+ Launching your MVP.
+ Hitting a specific revenue target or margin improvement.
+ Proving demand through strong user or customer growth.
+ Securing a major partnership.
+ Demonstrating technical feasibility.
+ Expanding into a second market.

Whatever it is, that milestone should increase the value of your company and make it more compelling than it is today.

BURN RATE MATTERS, ESPECIALLY HIRING

A major driver of how much you should raise is your burn rate, and for most early-stage companies, salary is the biggest expense. If hitting your milestone requires hiring or contracting talent, estimate the actual cost of that team, including salaries, taxes, benefits, and the time it will take them to deliver.

Ask for too little and you risk running out of runway before reaching the milestone, which can put you in a far weaker negotiating position. Ask for too much and investors may question whether you understand your business model, your hiring plan, or your timeline. This is why a thoughtful financial model—not a spreadsheet full of guesswork, but a grounded mapping of resources to outcomes—makes all the difference.

BRIDGE, NOT A CUSHION

Before you settle on a number, map the concrete steps between where you are now and where you need to be for the next round. Which actions move the needle the most? Which investments unlock the most value? Your raise should be the bridge that gets you from Point A to the next fundable Point B, not an emergency buffer, and not a wish list.

Up next, we'll get into the mechanics of how you raise, specifically the different types of fundraising vehicles available to you like SAFEs, convertible notes, and priced equity rounds. Choosing the right structure is just as important as choosing the right amount, and understanding the trade-offs is key to staying in control of your business.

Strategy protects your time and energy.
Without a plan, fundraising turns into "spray and pray." A thoughtful strategy helps you stay focused and conserve the time and bandwidth that are often most scarce for founders without deep networks or built-in safety nets.

Lead with your "why," not the pressure to fundraise.
Raising capital because "that's what startups do" can pull you off course. Anchor your plan in milestones that matter for *your* business, not in trends or investor hype cycles.

Build for the reality, not the myth, of fundraising.
The Rest of Us are often asked for more traction, more proof, and more time. When you plan for a longer road, the process feels less like a personal failing and more like a strategic journey you're prepared to navigate.

Your raise is about more than the money.
It's also about whom you invite onto your cap table, the expectations that come with that capital, and how well those partners align with your values and long-term vision. The right money accelerates you. The wrong money complicates everything.

10

FUNDRAISING VEHICLES

When you raise capital, you're essentially exchanging ownership in your company, your equity, for money. But figuring out how much that equity is worth can be tricky, especially in the early stages. You may not have revenue, customers, or even a finished product. So how do you assign a dollar value to your company when there isn't much data yet?

This is where many founders get stuck. Investors base early valuations on traction, which simply means evidence that your business is working. Traction can be anything that signals real progress like early users, letters of intent, a growing waitlist, a working minimal viable product (MVP), pilot results, partnerships, or even a strong growth curve in engagement. The more traction you have, the easier it is to justify a higher valuation.

If you try to set a valuation before you have enough traction to support it, you risk undervaluing your company and giving away more equity than necessary. Investors may also push for a larger stake because the perceived risk is higher. Once that equity is gone, it's gone.

To avoid this, early-stage startups often use fundraising instruments that let them bring in capital now without locking in a valuation yet. Instead of selling shares at a fixed price (also known as a strike price), you're giving investors the right to receive shares later, after your company grows and its value becomes clearer. The two most common tools for this are:

+ SAFEs (Simple Agreements for Future Equity)
+ Convertible notes

Both let you to raise money today while deferring the valuation until a future round, typically when a larger investment sets a clearer price. This gives you time to hit milestones, build more traction, and improve your valuation before issuing shares.

Let's walk through how each of these works, their pros and cons, and how to think about which structure fits your situation.

SAFEs: SIMPLE AGREEMENTS FOR FUTURE EQUITY

SAFEs (Simple Agreements for Future Equity) were introduced by Y Combinator and have quickly become the most common way for early-stage startups to raise money. They were created to be fast, simple, and founder-friendly. A SAFE lets you bring in capital now without setting a valuation or taking on debt.

A SAFE is not a loan. There's no interest, no monthly payments, and no deadline to repay anything. Instead, it's a promise that the investor's money will turn into equity (ownership in your company) later, usually during your first priced equity round, such as a Series A, when an official valuation is established.

One important difference between a SAFE and a convertible note is that a SAFE does not have a maturity date. That means it can stay on your books indefinitely if you never raise a priced round. This is part of what makes

SAFEs higher-risk for investors, but it's also why they're simpler and faster for founders.

Why investors like SAFEs:

* When the SAFE converts, investors usually get extra benefits, like a valuation cap or a discount, that reward them for taking early risk.
* They require less negotiation and simpler paperwork, which means deals get done more quickly.

Why founders like SAFEs:

* You can raise money quickly without setting a valuation too early, which protects you from pricing your company too low.
* No maturity date means no countdown clock, and no interest means one less financial burden as you grow.

HOW SAFES CONVERT INTO EQUITY

Since SAFEs don't set a price per share up front, most include terms that shape how the SAFE converts later. The two most common tools are:

* **Valuation cap:** A ceiling on the valuation at which the SAFE converts. A lower cap = more shares for the investor. A higher cap = more founder-friendly because it causes less dilution.
* **Discount rate:** A percentage (often 10–25%) that lets SAFE investors buy shares at a cheaper price than new investors in the

next round. For example, if new investors pay $1.00 per share and the SAFE includes a 20% discount, the SAFE investor pays $0.80 per share instead.

Both of these are ways to reward early believers while still letting you delay the valuation conversation until you have more traction and a clearer sense of your company's worth.

WHY SOME INVESTORS CHOOSE SAFES

Many investors, especially early-stage angels, mission-driven funds, and accelerator programs, actively prefer SAFEs because they reduce friction for early-stage founders and keep the focus on partnership. Not all investors want the protections or leverage that come with debt instruments like convertible notes.

+ **Fewer Strings Attached:** SAFEs are cleaner and simpler. There's no interest, no maturity date, and no risk of forcing a founder into repayment. Investors who care about supporting innovation without adding pressure often see this simplicity as a feature, not a drawback.

+ **Faster and Simple to Close:** SAFEs are standardized and quick, which helps investors participate in rounds efficiently, especially at the pre-seed stage where speed matters. Notes usually require more legal work and negotiation.

+ **Standard in Early-Stage Startups:** SAFEs have become the dominant early-stage instrument across accelerators, angel groups, and startup programs. Many investors choose them simply because they're familiar and align with early-stage norms.

- **Equity-First Mindset:** Some investors don't want to act like lenders. They want to support a founder's vision and share in the upside, not collect interest like a bank. SAFEs let them lean into that philosophy.

For values-driven or relationship-first investors, SAFEs can actually feel less risky because they reduce founder stress, keep the cap table cleaner, and speed up execution. In contrast, more traditional or risk-averse investors may still prefer convertible notes because they offer interest, deadlines, and clearer recourse.

THE RISK OF STACKING SAFES: UNDERSTANDING DILUTION

SAFEs are incredibly useful, especially in the early days when you need capital quickly and don't want to set a valuation too soon, but they come with a dilution trade-off that's easy to miss.

Every time you raise money through a SAFE, you're promising future equity, usually at a discount or based on a valuation cap. Because those shares don't exist yet, they don't show up on your cap table today. On paper, it looks like nothing has changed. In reality, you've already given away a portion of your future ownership.

It's common to raise SAFEs in small chunks over time—$25,000 here, $50,000 there—as money becomes available. This is often called a "rolling SAFE." It can be a practical and flexible way to get capital in the door, but it also creates a blind spot because it's easy to lose track of how much equity you've promised once everything converts. Then, when you finally do your first priced round and all those SAFEs convert at once, the cumulative dilution can be shocking. You might suddenly realize you own far less of your company than you expected.

Rolling SAFEs are especially common among *The Rest of Us* because the fundraising process is rarely linear. When you're not getting large, institutional checks, you make progress however you can using smaller checks, longer timelines, lots of individual angels, and constant momentum-building. This approach is resourceful and often necessary. It's not sloppy planning; it's adapting to a system that doesn't give you the same access or speed that others get, which makes it even more important to stay ahead of the dilution math.

OWNERSHIP CALCULATION FORMULA

$$\frac{\text{ROUND SIZE (\$)}}{\text{POST-MONEY CAP (\$)}} = \text{\% OF COMPANY OWNERSHIP IN ROUND}$$

Figure 10.1

EXAMPLE (DON'T BE SCARED BY THE MATH—YOU CAN DO IT!)

Let's walk through a simple, real-world example to show how ownership can change from company formation through multiple SAFE rounds and a priced round. This is exactly the kind of modeling most founders don't do early on, so you're already ahead by learning it now.

Here's how it unfolds:

Starting Point

+ Founders own 90%.
+ 10% is set aside for an employee stock option plan (ESOP).

SAFE #1

+ You raise $1M using a SAFE with a $5M post-money valuation cap
+ Ownership for this SAFE: $1M ÷ $5M = 20%
+ That means SAFE investors now own 20% of the company.

Important: SAFEs don't get diluted over time. Their percentage stays fixed, which means the founders and ESOP take on all the dilution.

+ Founder ownership: 90% × (remaining 80%) = 72%
+ ESOP: 10% × 80% = 8%

SAFE #2

You raise another $1M, this time with a $10M post-money cap because you've built more value into the company.

+ Ownership for this SAFE: $1M ÷ $10M = 10%
+ Now the company cap table has:
  · 20% from SAFE #1
  · 10% from SAFE #2
  · Leaving 70% for everyone else
+ Founder ownership: 90% × 70% = 63%
+ ESOP: 10% × 70% = 7%

Series A Priced Round

+ You raise $3M at a $20M post-money valuation
+ Ownership for new Series A investors: $3M ÷ $20M = 15%

- Now we have:
    - 20% (SAFE #1)
    - 10% (SAFE #2)
    - 15% (Series A)
    - Remaining for founders + ESOP: 55%
- Final founder ownership: 90% × 55% = 49.5%
- Final ESOP: 10% × 55% = 5.5%

This example shows how easy it is to unintentionally give away a large portion of your company, even when each individual raise feels small or manageable. If you're not modeling dilution from the start, it's hard to see how the pieces add up over time. That's why understanding these dynamics early on is so important. SAFEs can be an excellent tool to raise capital quickly, but without careful planning, they can seriously eat into your ownership.

By tracking your caps and conversions, setting realistic terms, and modeling ahead, you can protect your equity and build a healthy cap table that supports long-term growth.

HOW OWNERSHIP CHANGES ACROSS ROUNDS

SAFE 1

Raised: $1M

Post-Money Cap: $5M

SAFE 2

Raised: $1M

Post-Money Cap: $10M

SERIES A

Raised: $3M

Post-Money Val: $20M

	INITIAL SPLIT	POST-SAFE 1	POST-SAFE 2	POST SERIES A
FOUNDERS	90%	72%	63%	49.5%
ESOP*	10%	8%	7%	5.5%
SAFE 1		20%	20%	20%
SAFE 2			10%	10%
SERIES A				15%
TOTAL	100%	100%	100%	100%

* Employees Stock Option Program (ISOP): Equity reserved to compensate early employees.

Figure 10.2

CONVERTIBLE NOTES

A convertible note is another common early-stage fundraising tool. On the surface, it behaves a lot like a SAFE in that you get money now, and the investor gets equity later when your next priced round happens. But there's one major difference:

A convertible note is debt.

That means a few things:

- It has a maturity date (a deadline).
- It accrues interest over time.
- If it doesn't convert into equity before the maturity date, the company technically owes the investor the principal plus interest, just like a loan.

That may sound stressful, but don't panic. Many convertible notes convert well before they ever reach maturity. Still, you need to understand how they work so you're not caught off guard like I was.

At my last company, the medical device startup, revenue didn't come until years down the road. Medtech is capital-intensive with a regulatory process, clinical trials, partnerships with pharma, practitioner pathways ... everything takes extra time and extra money. Large institutional rounds are often necessary just to survive long enough to get to market.

During our push to raise our Series B, we missed a rapidly approaching maturity date on a sizable convertible note from a venture capital firm. When the date hit, I got a call from the general partner who was our lead. It was not a friendly call, nor a short one. He had every right to demand repayment of the full note plus interest, an amount that would have bankrupted us. I drew on every negotiation skill I had to convince him not to call the note.

This is the real risk behind convertible notes: they work beautifully *until they don't.*

WHY INVESTORS LIKE CONVERTIBLE NOTES

Convertible notes give investors more protection than SAFEs because:

+ If a priced round happens, the note converts into equity (often with a discount or valuation cap, similar to a SAFE).
+ If a priced round doesn't happen by the maturity date, the investor can demand repayment.
+ Because there's interest, their investment grows over time.

That added security is why some institutional investors prefer notes.

WHY FOUNDERS NEED TO BE CAREFUL

The maturity date is what you have to keep your eye on. If you don't raise a priced round in time:

+ Investors can demand repayment (which most early-stage startups cannot afford).
+ You may need to renegotiate terms, sometimes with multiple note holders.
+ You may feel pressured to raise a round before you're ready, simply to trigger conversion.

Convertible notes can be an excellent tool, but they come with built-in timers. As long as you track those timers carefully and plan your fundraising strategy around them, you can use notes effectively without getting backed into a corner.

YOUR LEVERAGE

You've already heard my cautionary tale about how convertible notes can create pressure when they get close to maturity. But there's another side to them, one that gives you more power than you may realize.

Unlike equity, which is permanent once issued and cannot be taken back, a convertible note begins its life as debt. Until it converts, that debt creates optionality for you. When a note reaches its maturity date and hasn't yet converted into equity, both you and the investor have choices. Depending on the specific terms of the note, the options may include:

- Repaying the principal and interest
- Renegotiating (extending the maturity date or adjusting terms)
- Converting the note if both parties agree
- Automatic conversion (if your note includes that clause)
- Other terms that kick in automatically, such as penalties or forced conversion, depending on how the note is written

Not all notes allow simple repayment, so it's critical to read the fine print. Some include automatic conversion provisions or penalties if you haven't closed a "qualified financing" by the maturity date. Always know exactly how your particular note behaves at maturity.

Jen Saxton learned this firsthand. When she pivoted her company and started raising for a new direction, she still had a few noteholders from her early days. Most rolled into the next phase easily, but a couple became increasingly demanding. They dragged out discussions, asked for repeated financial updates, and generally slowed Jen down at a moment when speed mattered. She didn't want the emotional or operational drag, so she made a choice: she paid them back.

Even though she was nearly out of cash, Jen used a portion of her remaining runway to write those investors a check and close out the relationship. As soon as she did, the tone shifted. The same investors who were pushing back suddenly panicked:

Wait, wait, we don't want our money back! Are you about to hit a big milestone?

Too late. As the founder, Jen had full discretion to pay off the note and walk away. No more updates. No more energy drain. No more power struggles.

KEY DIFFERENCES BETWEEN SAFES AND CONVERTIBLE NOTES

SAFES VS. CONVERTIBLE NOTES

FACTOR	SAFE	CONVERTIBLE NOTE
IS IT DEBT?	No obligation to repay	Yes, it behaves like a loan if it doesn't convert
AGREEMENT TYPE	A promise to issue shares later	A loan that can turn into shares later
INTEREST ACCRUAL	None	Typically 2–8% per year[53]

---

53   Typical interest rates on convertible notes range from 2–8% annually, depending on stage, investor type, and market conditions. This range is supported by: Y Combinator and startup accelerator guidance recommending low interest to reduce founder burden (Y Combinator SAFE primer); Cooley GO and Wilson Sonsini deal data, showing standard convertible note rates of 4–6%, occasionally extending up to 8%; Angel Capital Association resources, which identify 5% as a common midpoint for early-stage notes.

FACTOR	SAFE	CONVERTIBLE NOTE
DEADLINE TO CONVERT	No maturity date, waits for a future fundraise or sale	Has a maturity date, usually 1–2 years
RISK FOR FOUNDERS	Can give away more of the company than expected in later rounds	May need to repay principal + interest if conversion doesn't happen
RISK FOR INVESTORS	If no fundraising or sale occurs, they may never get shares	If the company can't repay or raise, renegotiation is needed and repayment isn't guaranteed
LEGAL INVOLVEMENT	Minimal, usually a standard template	More legal setup required, it's a debt instrument

Table 10.1

PRICED ROUNDS (TERM SHEETS)

Up until now, the fundraising tools we've talked about, SAFEs and convertible notes, let you raise money without putting a firm dollar value on your company. Those instruments delay the question of "What is my company worth?" until later, when you have more traction and a clearer picture of growth. A priced round is the moment that question finally gets answered.

Instead of promising future equity, you're now selling actual shares at a negotiated price. That price is based on a formal valuation of your company, and reaching this point is a real milestone. In short, it means investors are ready to assign a specific dollar value to your business, and that's a big deal.

This stage can feel intimidating. The legal and financial language in a term sheet might be unfamiliar or even overwhelming at first. You wouldn't be the first or the last person to have their eyes go fuzzy trying to read all the legalese. Take a breath because you don't need to understand everything at once. What matters is learning the basics so you can make informed decisions, negotiate with confidence, and protect your vision for the company you're building.

A term sheet is the document that outlines the deal. Think of it as a road map. It spells out:

- How much money investors are putting in
- What type and amount of equity they're getting in return
- The rights and preferences they'll have as shareholders

A term sheet is not a final contract. It's a negotiation starting point. You'll likely go back and forth before landing on terms that work for both you and the investor. If your previous raises were through SAFEs or convertible notes, this will be your first time dealing with these kinds of rights and protections. That's completely normal. What matters now is understanding how these terms shape your ownership, control, and future fundraising options.

BREAKING DOWN A TERM SHEET: WHAT FOUNDERS NEED TO KNOW

A term sheet might look intimidating, but it's really just a document that outlines the key terms of your investment deal. When you raise a priced round, this is where you and your investors agree on what each party is getting and what rights come with the investment.

Most term sheets are built around five key areas:

- Valuation & Economics
- Governance & Control
- Monitoring
- Ownership & Dilution
- Liquidity & Exit Terms

Let's break each one down so you know what to expect and where to focus.

VALUATION AND ECONOMICS: SETTING THE PRICE OF YOUR COMPANY

This section defines how much your company is worth and how much ownership investors receive:

+ **Pre-money valuation** = your company's value *before* the investment
+ **Post-money valuation** = pre-money valuation + the amount raised

The higher your valuation, the less equity you give up. Founders naturally aim for a higher valuation to minimize dilution, while investors push for a lower one to increase their ownership. Stock option pools for future hires are typically included in the pre-money valuation, which means dilution comes from the founders, not the new investors. That's why this is a key negotiation point.

GOVERNANCE AND CONTROL: WHO MAKES THE DECISIONS?

This section determines how decisions are made and who has influence at the board level.

+ **Board seats:** Lead investors often request a seat on the board to stay involved in major decisions.
+ **Protective provisions:** These are rights that require investor approval for certain actions like selling the company, raising more money, or issuing new shares.

Investors want a say in protecting their investment. You want the flexibility to run your business. A balanced term sheet gives investors oversight without creating bottlenecks.

MONITORING: INVESTOR RIGHTS TO INFORMATION AND OVERSIGHT

Investors expect regular updates on your progress, which is where information rights come into play.

+ These define how often you must share financial reports or company updates.
+ You can negotiate to provide reports quarterly instead of monthly, and limit access to major investors.

The goal is to provide transparency without overwhelming your team with reporting requirements.

OWNERSHIP AND DILUTION: PROTECTING INVESTOR STAKES

Most investors want the ability to maintain their ownership percentage in future rounds. That's where pro rata rights (or right of first offer) come in.

+ **Pro rata rights:** Let investors maintain their stake by investing again in future rounds.
+ **Super pro rata rights:** Let them buy *more* than their share, which can crowd out new investors.
+ You'll also encounter **anti-dilution provisions**, which protect investors if a future round happens at a lower valuation (a "down round").
+ **Weighted average anti-dilution:** The most common and founder-friendly, it adjusts ownership proportionally.

+ **Full ratchet anti-dilution:** More aggressive where investors get the best price offered to anyone, which can drastically dilute founders and employees.

LIQUIDITY: WHO GETS PAID AND WHEN?

This section covers how funds are distributed in an exit or liquidation.

+ **Liquidation preference:** Preferred shareholders get paid before common shareholders. A **1x preference** (they get their money back) is standard.
+ **Participating preferred:** Investors get their money back *and* share in the remaining distribution. This is less favorable to founders.
+ **Nonparticipating preferred:** Investors get the greater of their money back or their share of the exit, but not both.

Other liquidity-related terms to look out for:

+ **Drag-along rights:** Let majority shareholders force a sale, including minority shareholders.
+ **Co-sale (tag-along) rights:** Let investors sell their shares alongside founders in a secondary sale.
+ **Redemption rights:** Allow investors to force the company to buy back their shares after a set period.
+ **Registration rights:** Allow investors to require the company to go public under certain conditions.

HOW TO APPROACH A PRICED ROUND WITHOUT FEAR

A priced round is a big step, but it doesn't have to be intimidating. Yes, it marks a more complex phase in your fundraising journey, but with the right support and a solid understanding of the basics, it's completely manageable. Most of the terms you'll encounter are standard, and nearly all of them are negotiable. You don't have to navigate this alone; experienced lawyers, advisors, and even founder peers can help you interpret the terms and advocate for yourself.

Here's how to approach it with confidence:

- **Understand the basics:** You don't need to memorize every legal detail, but you should feel grounded in the fundamentals. Know how valuation, equity ownership, governance, and payout rights affect you and your company's future. That knowledge gives you the power to ask smart questions and make informed choices.

- **Focus on what matters most:** Not all terms carry the same weight. Prioritize the ones that shape your long-term ownership and control the most, like valuation, board composition, liquidation preferences, and anti-dilution protections. These are the levers that most directly influence your outcome.

- **Work with trusted legal and financial advisors:** A strong startup attorney you trust is worth every dollar. They've seen hundreds of term sheets and can help you spot red flags, negotiate fair terms, and avoid costly mistakes. If you don't have this support in your network, look for accelerators, community groups, or nonprofit organizations that offer low-cost legal help for founders.

- **Choose investors wisely:** Capital is important, but it's not the only thing that matters. The right investors bring mentorship, networks, and partnership. Look for people who share your values and are in it for the long term. A fair, straightforward term sheet is only valuable if the relationship behind it is strong.

- **Think beyond this round:** The terms you negotiate today will set the tone for future fundraising. Be mindful of how things like liquidation preferences and pro rata rights will play out in the next round. Think strategically about your cap table—your future self will thank you.

If you're a first-time founder or part of *The Rest of Us*, here's something important: Some investors may assume you're less experienced and try to include terms that are more aggressive than necessary. This isn't about fear; it's about awareness and power.

You may encounter things like:

+ Excessive liquidation preferences that limit your payout in an exit
+ Full-ratchet anti-dilution, which can dramatically reduce your ownership if your next round is valued lower than your last one (a "down round")
+ Aggressive board control that gives investors outsized decision-making power
+ Overreaching pro rata rights that make it harder to bring in new investors later

These clauses are sometimes presented as "standard," but standard doesn't mean fair or aligned with your long-term goals. Ask questions. Loop in an advisor. Push back when something feels off. That's not being difficult, it's being a responsible steward of your company.

Fundraising tools shape your ownership and control.

Each instrument, including SAFEs, convertible notes, and term sheets, determines who owns what and when. Understanding how they work is how you protect your equity and your ability to make decisions down the road.

SAFEs are simple, not harmless.

They're fast and founder-friendly, but easy to misuse. Stacking multiple SAFEs without modeling dilution can quietly erode your ownership before you realize it.

Convertible notes carry time pressure.

They add structure but introduce maturity dates, interest, and repayment risk. Keep track of when notes come due and don't let deadlines force you into a round before you're ready.

Priced rounds bring clarity and complexity.

They signal growth and seriousness but introduce negotiation over valuation, control, and economic rights. Know which terms affect your future the most before you sign.

***The Rest of Us* raise differently, not poorly.**

Smaller checks, rolling rounds, or creative structures aren't a weakness; they're often a reflection of systemic barriers. What matters is understanding how each choice affects dilution and keeping your fundraising intentional.

Protect your future self.
Every agreement you sign today becomes part of the company you'll be leading tomorrow. Keep ownership, agency, and alignment at the center of every decision.

PART II

The Pitch

Now that you understand the landscape of early-stage capital, including where it comes from, how it works, and what trade-offs to expect, you're already ahead of the game. Too many founders jump into fundraising without a clear picture of their options. You've taken the time to understand how to fund your business on *your* terms.

But knowing what kinds of capital exist is only half the battle. To actually raise money, you need to tell a compelling story. You need to communicate your vision in a way that makes people feel excited, confident, and ready to join you.

That's where *Part II* comes in!

In this second half of the book, we'll walk through how to craft and deliver a pitch that's clear, persuasive, and grounded in strategy. Whether you're speaking to angels, VCs, or any other type of funder, your pitch needs to speak to the motivations of the other person. You don't need to be flashy or charismatic to do that, you just need the right structure and genuine confidence.

We'll start with a framework I developed while working directly with hundreds of founders and investors: **The Core 10 Pitch Framework**. It's a proven structure that helps you organize your story, speak with confidence, and tailor your message to the right audience. Everything you need to craft a strong pitch is in this book, but if you want more guidance beyond these pages, the Scroobious platform walks you through each element of the framework step-by-step, with examples and explanations that make the process feel manageable. Many of the founders you're hearing from in this book have built their pitches using this framework on Scroobious, which helped me see what worked across a wide range of industries and identities.

Let's build your pitch—step-by-step.

11

THINK LIKE AN INVESTOR

*Figure 11.1: Parents' view of my
daughter's 3rd grade band performance*

The photo in figure 11.1 is a perfect example of what happens when a presentation is created without considering the audience's point of view. If the teachers had envisioned the performance through a parent's eyes, they would have immediately noticed the problem: Parents couldn't see their kids' faces. A quick perspective shift from having the teachers sit in the audience seats viewing students on the stage would've solved the issue instantly.

The same thing happens in fundraising.

It's incredibly common for entrepreneurs to have deep clarity on their customer, but far less visibility into how investors think. Founders who have never been shown the investor's perspective often create pitch decks that start out as marketing material. You know how to talk about your product, your solution, and your value to customers. That part is intuitive.

What's less intuitive is how to communicate the value of your *company as an investment*—how you'll turn someone's dollars today into more dollars later. You're not pitching them on becoming a user; you're pitching them on becoming an owner. They may never be your customer, but they might be your ideal investor.

Suelin Chen, who raised roughly $9 million for her startup, Cake, and successfully sold it, captures this distinction:

> The skills to fundraise are not the same as the skills to run a company. There are many people who would be good at running companies and building things, but because they aren't as good at fundraising, they are resource-constrained and can't accomplish what they could. On the flip side, I also see all these people who are really good at fundraising and kind of suck at running their companies.

Melissa Wood, founder of Formus, echoed this learning curve:

> Why don't more investors just shoot straight with you? Over the past two years, I've had to learn so many things the hard way, piecing together insights bit by bit. I'm naturally a researcher and a learner, and I've spoken with more than 100 investors so far. But I haven't accepted any outside capital yet. We're getting close to being ready, but until now, I've turned down every offer. I'm not a shy person; I'm out there networking, meeting people, and learning everything I can.

What both Suelin and Melissa highlight is that thinking like an investor isn't instinctive unless you've been inside that world. Once someone explains it to you clearly, it becomes far less mysterious, and far more doable.

That's exactly what Part II is here to do.

UNDERSTANDING RISK: HOW INVESTORS THINK AND WHAT THAT MEANS FOR YOUR PITCH

Pitching is all about two things: telling a clear story and reducing the risks people see in your business. Different types of investors have different motivations. Some care most about financial return, others care about impact, innovation, identity, or strategic alignment. No matter who you're talking to, they all have one thing in common: They want to feel confident that giving you money today will lead to something meaningful tomorrow.

If you were getting a bank loan, that "meaningful tomorrow" is guaranteed through interest. With investors, especially early-stage ones, the return comes through equity, which is their ownership stake in your company. Because early-stage investing is so risky, they're looking for signs that you can grow the business enough to make their investment worthwhile.

This means your job in a pitch is not just to explain what your business does. Your job is to systematically remove reasons for someone to say no. Every section of your pitch deck exists to lower a specific kind of risk they're evaluating, whether that's financial risk, market risk, team risk, product risk, or simply uncertainty about where you're headed. Once you understand the types of risk investors pay attention to and how they interpret the information you share, you can shape your story in a way that feels natural to you and compelling to them.

FAMILIARITY FEELS SAFE

Investors don't just evaluate your business; they evaluate their own comfort with you. That comfort has far more to do with familiarity than with financial logic. Even the most sophisticated investors subconsciously gravitate toward people who look like them, move in their circles, or remind them of others they've backed before.

Humans don't see risk clearly. We see it through the lens of who feels familiar. So even when investors believe they're making purely objective decisions, much of what shapes their confidence happens below the surface. Our brains are wired to equate *familiarity* with *safety*, and *difference* with *uncertainty*.

Several well-documented psychological principles explain why investors tend to gravitate toward "people like them":

+ **Similarity-attraction bias:** We feel more comfortable with people who share our background, interests, or identity.
+ **Ingroup bias:** We favor people in our social or professional circles and tend to see outsiders as less trustworthy or more risky.
+ **Familiarity heuristic:** We subconsciously assume that what we've seen before is safer or more likely to succeed.
+ **Affinity bias:** Decision-makers often connect more easily with people who remind them of themselves.

These biases aren't always conscious, but they're powerful. We see them influencing who gets access to positions of power and resources everywhere we look.

SYSTEMIC PATTERNS OF HOMOGENEITY

Let's take a moment to look at some numbers.

LEADERSHIP AND BOARDS

- 98% of Fortune 500 board seats are not held by women of color.[54]

- 96% of US executives are not Black.[55]

- 91% of Fortune 500 CEOs are men.[56]

CAPITAL ALLOCATION

- 99.6% of US venture funding goes to non-Black founders.[57]

- 99% goes to male-led startups.[58]

- 93% of venture capitalists are white men.[59]

---

54 Alliance for Board Diversity and Deloitte, *Missing Pieces Report: A Board Diversity Census of Women and Minorities on Fortune 500 Boards,* June 2023, https://www2.deloitte.com/us/en/pages/center-for-board-effectiveness/articles/board-diversity-census-missing-pieces.html.

55 Coqual, *Being Black in Corporate America: An Intersectional Exploration,* 2019, https://coqual.org/reports/being-black-in-corporate-america-an-intersectional-exploration/.

56 Hinchliffe, E., & Abrams, J. (2024, March 25). S&P 500 boards have hit a tipping point that may lead to more female CEOs. Fortune. https://fortune.com/2024/03/25/female-women-ceos-diverse-boards-sp-500/.

57 Glasner, Joanna. "Share Of Startup Funding For Black Founders Hits Multiyear Low." Crunchbase News, February 6, 2025. https://news.crunchbase.com/diversity/startup-funding-share-black-founders-down-cleantech-healthcare/.

58 PitchBook, *US All In: Female Founders in the VC Ecosystem,* 2023, https://pitchbook.com/news/reports/2023-us-all-in-female-founders-in-the-vc-ecosystem.

59 Edwards, Elizabeth. "Check Your Stats: The Lack Of Diversity In Venture Capital Is Worse Than It Looks." Forbes, February 25, 2021. https://www.forbes.com/sites/elizabethedwards/2021/02/24/check-your-stats-the-lack-of-diversity-in-venture-capital-is-worse-than-it-looks/.

- 89% of law firm partners are white.[60]
- 77% of newsroom leaders are white.[61]
- 70% of referral hires are white men.[62]

This level of homogeneity doesn't happen by accident. It's the result of repeated decisions made through the lens of familiarity. People investing in or elevating others who look like them, went to the same schools, or move in the same social circles.

Founders who don't match the existing pattern are often seen as riskier, even when they've done everything "right." That's the core challenge *The Rest of Us* face: We're not evaluated on merit alone but through the filter of unfamiliarity. That's why democratizing access matters so much. When I talk about *The Rest of Us* this is what I mean.

A system designed for the few can't serve the future.

The more people we empower to participate, as founders, investors, mentors, advisors, board members, and connectors, the more reference points decision-makers have. The more reference points they have, the more likely they are to see someone different as familiar, as safe, and ultimately, as fundable.

As movie producer, founder, and investor Catherine Gray put it:

---

60 National Association for Law Placement. *2022 Report on Diversity in U.S. Law Firms.* Washington, DC: NALP, January 2023. https://www.alanet.org/docs/default-source/diversity/2022nalpreportondiversity_final.pdf.

61 Craig T. Robertson, Meera Selva, and Rasmus Kleis Nielsen, "Race and Leadership in the News Media 2021: Evidence from Five Markets," Reuters Institute, March 2021, https://reutersinstitute.politics.ox.ac.uk/race-and-leadership-news-media-2021.

62 PayScale's 2018 report, *The Impact of Job Referrals on Employee Engagement and Workforce Diversity,* is cited in PayScale blog posts and a contemporaneous press release, but the original downloadable report is no longer available on PayScale's public site as of 2026.

> Fundraising is all about relationships. Anybody who thinks otherwise probably is not going to be able to raise money because it is absolutely based on that and about finding like-minded people who believe in what you do. If a friend calls me up and says, 'Hey, this is really important. I think it's of interest to you, you're probably going to want to invest in this,' I will listen more than if someone randomly reaches out to me.

Sometimes, familiarity can be built through proxy when someone inside a homogeneous group publicly supports you.

Karen Robinson Cope, a multi-exited founder who has raised over $100 million and is a prolific angel investor, shared one of her early fundraising stories:

> When I first started raising money, I was a young woman in a room of primarily white men, and, of course, no other women. Most of them were between 45 and 70 years old. I remember them talking, saying, 'Yeah, yeah, yeah, great idea, great idea' with no talk of investing. Then, I'll never forget, one man stood up and said, 'Karen, here's a $100,000 check,' and all of a sudden, they all pulled out their checkbooks. That first man to write a check was an entrepreneur; he was one of the original founders of Synchologic. The rest of them were professional investors like money managers, fund managers, or VCs, but had never been entrepreneurs.
>
> Follow-on investors are a dime a dozen. You've got to get that one person who believes enough that they're willing to write that first check.

When you understand how powerful familiarity is in shaping investor behavior, the next piece naturally falls into place. Investors aren't just choosing what feels familiar, but also what feels least risky. Whether or not they articulate it this way, investors spend most of their time scanning for signals that help them answer a single question: "How risky is this bet?"

This is where many first-time founders get tripped up. They build their pitch as if they're talking to a customer by highlighting features, benefits, usability, or mission. But investors are evaluating the probability that your company can produce a strong return.

THE INVESTOR MINDSET: WHY RISK MATTERS

Investors look at your company very differently from how a customer looks at your product. A customer buys because they like what you've built. It solves a problem for them, feels trustworthy, or simply makes their life better. An investor, on the other hand, is evaluating the likelihood that their money will grow if they give it to you, which is something much less tangible.

They're constantly weighing risk and reward. Their mental math sounds something like this:

+ How likely is this company to succeed?
+ How big could the return be?
+ What are the chances I'll lose my money?

Remember, investors already know that most startups fail. They've seen companies that looked amazing on paper disappear within months. So, when they look at you, they're measuring the unknown of your company against the known safety of their current alternatives of other founders they understand, markets they've bet on before, or business models they already trust. Familiarity feels safe. The unknown feels risky. This is why risk assessment sits at the heart of the investor mindset. Every part of your pitch becomes a clue that helps them decide whether your opportunity is worth taking a chance on.

HOW INVESTORS SEE YOUR PITCH: STORY VS. RISK

Figure 11.2

Figure 11.2 shows how each section of your pitch tells a story while also addressing the risks investors are actively evaluating. A strong investor narrative communicates both the opportunity and how you're de-risking it.

One of the most important mindset shifts for new founders is understanding that investors don't invest out of charity or enthusiasm; they invest because they believe they will make money. You don't need to focus on persuading them to "support" you; show them, clearly and convincingly, that their money will be in good hands and has a real chance to generate meaningful returns with you.

PITCH DECKS SERVE AN IMPORTANT PURPOSE

Pitch decks aren't going away anytime soon, and honestly, they do serve a purpose, both for investors and for you as a founder. If I had the choice, I'd take a real, personal conversation over a slide presentation every single time, but a deck is still one of the fastest, clearest ways to help someone understand what you're building and why it matters.

At its core, a pitch deck is both a communication tool and a strategic exercise. It forces you to make choices about what matters most, prepare for the questions investors will inevitably ask, and get crisp about your story. That's something especially important for *The Rest of Us* navigating a biased system.

Here's why pitch decks matter:

+ **It's your first impression:** For many investors, your deck is their introduction to you. Before you ever get a meeting, your deck tells them who you are, what problem you're solving, and why you're uniquely suited to solve it. It's your chance to spark curiosity and pull someone into your story.

+ **It helps investors understand your business quickly:** Investors think in patterns and probabilities. A structured deck makes it easier for them to evaluate you using the mental frameworks they already rely on. It keeps them oriented and helps them follow your logic without getting lost in the details.

+ **It clarifies your business model and strategy (sometimes for the first time):** Putting a deck together forces you to articulate how your business actually works: how you make money, how you reach customers, and why now is the right time. This clarity is enormously helpful for you, in addition to potential investors.

+ **It signals preparation and credibility:** A thoughtful deck shows investors you've done the work. It tells them you're serious, capable, and thinking about the right things. For *The Rest of Us*, this matters even more.

+ **It gives you a clean, efficient way to show traction and potential:** You don't have much time to make your case. A deck lets you put your strongest proof points like market size, early traction, revenue projections, and team strengths front and center in a way that's easy to digest.

+ **Most importantly, every slide helps you de-risk the business:** Investors are constantly scanning for risk. Your deck gives you a structured way to address the risks they care about before they even voice them.

Now that you understand *why* pitch decks matter, the next step is learning *how to build one that works*. Over the years, working with hundreds of founders and listening to thousands of investor conversations, I developed a practical structure called the **Core 10 Pitch Framework**. It's a simple, intuitive way to organize your story so investors can understand it quickly and so you can speak about your business with clarity and confidence.

Before we dive into each pitch section, we'll start with a high-level overview of the Core 10 and how it maps to the way investors think and evaluate risk. This will become your roadmap for crafting a pitch that resonates.

You are not the problem, bias is.

If you've felt dismissed, underestimated, or scrutinized more than your peers, it's not your imagination. Traditional investing frameworks were built by and for a narrow group. This chapter helped you decode those frameworks, not to contort yourself to fit them, but so you can navigate them with clear vision and steady footing.

Investors are managing risk, and identity bias is part of that equation.

Perceived "risk" often has more to do with familiarity than facts. That's why your lived experience and market insight are qualifications, not liabilities. When you articulate those strengths clearly, you help investors see what they would otherwise miss.

You don't have to think like an investor, you need to show you understand how they think.

You can stay grounded in your values and still present your opportunity in terms investors recognize. Translating your story into the language of capital doesn't mean changing who you are.

They're not doing you a favor.

Fundraising can feel like asking for permission, especially for those of us who've been excluded from these rooms. But capital is a tool, not validation. You are offering investors the chance to participate in your vision, your community, your impact, and your upside.

You belong in the room, and you bring value they may not yet have the lens to see.
When you lead with clarity, data, and the distinctive insight only you can offer, you reshape the room just by being in it.

12

THE CORE 10 PITCH FRAMEWORK

Figure 12.1

We're going to shift from understanding the game to playing it with confidence. Creating your pitch deck can feel like a full-time job you never asked for. You tweak one slide, then another, then get a flood of (often conflicting) feedback, and suddenly the whole thing starts to feel like quicksand. Many founders wonder, *Can't I just skip this and get to the conversation?*

The short answer is not really. Pitch decks are still a standard part of the fundraising process. Investors expect them, and they rely on them as a fast way to understand who you are and what you're building. A helpful way to reframe this exercise is that your pitch deck is more than just a fundraising tool, it clarifies your thinking. Creating your pitch deck forces you to distill your story, your traction, your strategy, and your vision into clean, digestible pieces. That's not easy work, but it's incredibly valuable.

As Catherine Gray puts it plainly:

> Most of pitching is in the conversation, but it is absolutely necessary to have a good deck. Investors want to know where their money's going, so yeah, you need a great deck.

James Valencia shared how transformative the process was for him:

> I'm very passionate about what I do, and it took a while to understand that a pitch is supposed to have a pretty set structure. It's helped me frame what we're doing specifically for whoever I'm talking to. I have a pitch deck for the Food is Medicine grant applications, I have one for a space accelerator for biomedical manufacturing because they need high-quality food that can be exposed to radiation, and I have one for hospitality customers. While these are different audiences, most of the deck is the same, but we change out the ask, the financials, etc.
>
> The process of creating my pitch deck helped me envision what I want out of the business because it makes me think about the exit.

> What's my goal, what do I want? Putting it together helped me nail down my value props [propositions], which was really important.

Part of what makes pitching so hard is that there's no single "right" way to do it. Every investor has a different opinion. You will get conflicting advice, often from well-meaning people, and yes, it will be frustrating. For *The Rest of Us*, feedback can be even more intense. We often get comments about tone, confidence, or delivery instead of substance. That noise makes it even more important to have a clear structure you can rely on, a framework that keeps you grounded in your story rather than pulled in a hundred directions by other people's biases.

Your job is to listen, consider the source and the context, and then decide what aligns with your vision and what you can confidently leave behind. The most effective pitch is one that feels authentic to you, your voice, your company, your vision, and that you can present with confidence and clarity.

A good pitch deck shows investors that:

* You deeply understand the problem and the opportunity.
* You have a strategy and path to execution.
* You can communicate your value clearly.
* You are someone worth spending more time with.

The goal isn't to say everything, but to earn the next conversation.

BEYOND FUNDRAISING: WHY YOUR PITCH POWERS EVERYTHING

The same clarity that helps you fundraise also powers everything else you do as a founder. Building your pitch sharpens your business because it forces you to define the essentials of what you do, who you do it for, and why it matters.

Equity investors aren't the only audience that needs your story. The work you do to build a clear, compelling pitch pays off everywhere else you need belief, trust, or buy-in.

- **Grants:** Reviewers skim fast. A crisp narrative that ties problem → solution → outcomes captures attention and increases your chances of being funded. Many grants also want to see that you understand the business side well enough to build something sustainable that strengthens the economy.
- **Accelerators & incubators:** Most ask for a short deck and/or video. The same structure you use for investors translates directly into getting past their first filter and into interviews.
- **Recruiting & advisors:** High-caliber people join clear stories. Your pitch helps them see both the opportunity and their role in it.
- **Partnerships & customers:** Your investor pitch easily adapts into a business-facing story that helps partners see the value of working with you.
- **Media & speaking:** A tight narrative becomes your default talk track for interviews, panels, and keynotes.

Working on your pitch *is* working on your business. It surfaces gaps, sharpens your vision, and helps you communicate what others need to hear before they'll join you, whether they're investors, partners, or your next great hire. The real return on investment (ROI) of working on your pitch is clarity, confidence, and connection.

Julie Moir Messervy's story is an example of how this clarity emerges. When she decided to launch a tech company, she didn't come from the world of venture capital, accelerators, or even software. She came from gardens.

> I'd spent my whole career designing public parks and landscapes for institutions and high-end homes. I'd created many wonderful things, but there was always this question nagging at me: Why should beauty and good design only be for the wealthy? Why couldn't I help more people have the garden of their dreams?

That impulse, to democratize what had once been accessible to only a few, became the seed for her company. But entering the startup world was a shock.

> I came in as a designer, not a businessperson. I was thrown into a situation where it was sort of sink or swim, repeated a million times. There must be so many people in that position where you start from what you know, and suddenly you're in a whole new world trying to figure it out.

Her experience mirrors that of so many founders who come from domain expertise. They understand a problem better than anyone, but they have to learn a whole new language to build and grow a company around it.

As Julie put it, "The business of startups is not the common path."

Julie had written eight books and spent decades teaching through lectures and publications, and designing private and public spaces. Technology offered her a way to scale that mission. "It felt like the tech world was finally ready to support what we were doing," she said. "It gave me a new way to share knowledge that I'd been trying to explain for years."

Her transition wasn't simply about adopting new tools; she was translating a lifetime of expertise into a system that could reach more people. Every time you explain your idea more clearly, you strengthen how you build, how you lead, and how others understand where they fit into your vision.

When you can see your business story clearly, others can too.

FUNDRAISING IS A PROCESS AND SO IS PITCHING

Fundraising almost never comes down to a single pitch meeting. It's a relationship-building process where trust accumulates over time. Your pitch materials should reflect that reality. Instead of creating a single, static deck, think in terms of flexible tools you can pull from, depending on the moment.

You'll want:

+ A **core deck** for cold outreach and send-ahead emails
+ **Modular content** you can swap in or out depending on the format, time, or audience

I developed the Core 10 Framework as a recommended structure for pre-seed and seed-stage decks based on years of experience, research, founder education, and hundreds of investor interviews. There is no single "correct" way to pitch, and you definitely don't need to follow this structure slide by slide, but I strongly recommend covering each of these ten topics somewhere in your pitch, even if you change the order.

This narrative structure works for both pre-seed and seed-stage companies because the investor questions are the same. The difference is in how much evidence you're expected to show. Pre-seed investors expect clarity of thought, founder-market fit, early signals of demand, and a credible plan. You're still de-risking the idea. Seed investors expect more proof points like traction, revenue experiments, stronger customer validation, early partnerships, or technical milestones. You're now de-risking execution. The story is the same, but the information available and level of detail deepens.

The Core 10 Pitch Framework:

1. Mission
2. Problem
3. Solution
4. Business Model
5. Market Size
6. Competition
7. Why Now?
8. Go-To-Market
9. Team
10. Thank You

These ten sections help you tell a compelling, credible story that connects with how early-stage investors make decisions. They also give you a repeatable structure you can modify for any audience, including investors, accelerators, grants, partners, or recruits.

SECTION GOALS

We're about to go deep into each section of the Core 10, one chapter at a time. Before we zoom in, it helps to understand the big-picture goal of each part of your pitch. At a high level, here's what you're aiming to communicate:

+ **Mission, Problem, and Solution:** These first three sections carry the most weight. If investors don't understand why you started this company, what problem you're solving, and how your solution works, nothing else in your deck matters. This is the emotional and strategic foundation of your story. Once investors believe in the why and what, they're ready to evaluate the how.

+ **Business Model:** Show how you make money. You don't need every operational detail, just a clear and simple explanation of how revenue happens. Investors want to see that you've thought through the basics of how value turns into dollars.

+ **Market Size:** Investors need to know the opportunity is big enough to justify the risk. A bottom-up market size based on your specific pricing and target customers is best. If you've never done this before, don't worry. You can absolutely learn it, and I'll guide you through it step-by-step.

+ **Competition, Why Now, and Go-To-Market:** These sections show you understand the landscape, why this moment is the right time, and how you plan to reach your customers. This is about demonstrating clarity of thought, not perfection. No one expects you to have every detail figured out at the early stage.

+ **Team:** Investors back people. Use this section to show why you, and anyone supporting you, are the right ones to build this. If you're solo or still assembling your team, that's completely fine. We'll talk about how to frame that honestly and strategically.

+ **Thank You:** Close with gratitude and clear next steps. Include your contact information and any specific asks, like introductions to customers or category experts.

The goal of your pitch isn't to close the deal in one meeting, just to earn the next conversation. You're telling a story that says: *Here's what I'm building, here's why it matters, and here's how I plan to make it real.*

Each of the upcoming chapters breaks down one section of the Core 10 Pitch Framework at a time. You'll see real-world examples of how founders have told their stories and reduced risk, across different identities, industries, and lived experiences. First we'll quickly talk about how to bring your story and strategy to life visually and practically because what you say matters, and how you show it matters just as much.

SLIDE DESIGN TIPS THAT WORK

You don't need to be a graphic designer, or hire one, to make clear, compelling slides. Your goal isn't to wow anyone with fancy visuals, but knowing how people absorb information will help make your story easy to understand.

Here's the big insight most people miss with any presentation: **Humans cannot both read words and hear words at the same time and process them both.** Think about the last time you were reading something, and someone started talking to you. You probably had to stop reading or ask them to wait. Our brains simply don't multitask well between written and spoken information.

That dynamic shows up in your pitch, and how it shows up depends on the setting:

In Person: Your voice leads; your slides follow. When you're in the room with someone, the natural instinct is to look at the person speaking. That means investors will listen to you first and glance at the slide second. Your slides should support what you're saying, not compete with it. In this setting, clean, simple slides work best. Think of them as visual anchors that reinforce your message.

Remote: Your slides lead; your voice follows: On Zoom or any virtual meeting platform, the dynamic flips. Even when you look directly at the camera, which still creates a sense of eye contact, the investor doesn't feel pressure to stare back. They'll naturally look at your slides first. That means your slides need to carry the weight. They should communicate the key point clearly even before you say a word, and you need to pause long enough for people to read them before you start talking. Otherwise, the audience will read while you talk, and they'll miss half of both.

I am absolutely not suggesting you make separate versions for each scenario. I strongly advocate for making one flexible deck that works in both contexts. We'll walk through how to design the kind of deck that's simple, readable, and effective, no matter the format.

A good slide supports your narrative.

A great one helps your audience absorb what matters without overwhelming them or pulling focus away from you.

THE ANATOMY OF A SLIDE

Your goal with every slide is simple: make your point quickly and clearly so the investor can focus on you. Think of a slide like valuable real estate; if something on it doesn't help the viewer understand your story, it doesn't belong. Good slide design isn't about making things pretty. It's about making your story easy to follow and hard to forget. You don't need a design background or fancy tools. You just need a clear point and respect for your audience's attention.

Quick design principles:

+ Make your slides glanceable. An investor should grasp the main idea in a few seconds.

- Use header statements that tell the investor the key point of the slide.
- Keep text sparse, language simple, and layouts clean.
- Use high-contrast and readable fonts. Don't make people work to understand you.
- Use white space intentionally to reduce cognitive overload.
- Only include visuals that enhance understanding, not distract from it.
- Always include slide numbers and cite your sources in small text at the bottom.

SLIDE HEADER STATEMENTS

One of the simplest, most powerful improvements you can make is upgrading your slide headers. Too many headings are really just labels like "Problem," "Competition," or "Team." These don't tell the investor anything, they just name the category. I cannot encourage you enough to use header statements. They can fundamentally change the impact of your pitch.

A header statement tells the investor the point of the slide. For example:

LABEL (DON'T DO THIS)	HEADER STATEMENT (DO THIS)
Solution	Gen Z job seekers get hired 3x faster through gamified skill-building
Market Size	Our target market represents $1.2B in annual revenue potential and is growing 18% YoY.
Competition	Our approach fills the trust gap competitors overlook by focusing on verified employer skills data.

LABEL (DON'T DO THIS)	HEADER STATEMENT (DO THIS)
Team	Our team has deep domain expertise with lived experience of the problem.
Why Now	Recent regulation changes make our solution possible for the first time.

Table 12.1

I kid you not, investors will skim header statements first to decide whether to keep reading. Clear headers do the work for them by lifting the main take-away to the top of the slide and making your story flow logically. A simple trick is to pretend your headers are the first sentence in a paragraph. Everything else on the slide should support that one idea. If something doesn't fit, move it to another slide or to the appendix.

Another trick I give founders is to paste all your headers into a document and read them straight through. If it reads like a clear, cohesive story, you're on the right track. If it reads like a list of disconnected labels, you need to revise. It won't read like a continuous paragraph, but it should make logical sense and walk someone through the core narrative of your business from start to finish.

If you've ever felt pressure to over-explain or over-prove as someone who doesn't pattern match, clear headers can actually be one of your strongest tools. They let investors see your insight and traction without getting lost in unnecessary detail.

KEEP LANGUAGE SIMPLE AND SPARSE

Complex language doesn't make you sound smarter, it just makes your pitch harder to understand. Even if you're building cutting-edge tech, you can and should explain it simply.

Instead of: "A comprehensive platform for customer engagement revolutionizing social media for niche creators."

Try: "The easiest way for writers to share their social media posts."

Use bullet points or short phrases. It's totally fine to break up sentences or use fragments if they clearly convey your point.

FONT TIPS (BECAUSE INVESTORS SQUINT)

Assume someone is viewing your deck on a laptop, across a conference table, or even on their phone.

- Use 16-point or larger for body text.
- Use legible fonts (no scripts or decorative styles).
- Keep font size and weight consistent (larger for headers, smaller for body text).
- Use bold text or color sparingly to highlight key numbers or phrases.
- Avoid low-contrast color combinations that make text hard to read.

Try to lay out content horizontally, not vertically. Slides are landscape-oriented for a reason; make use of that width and keep the reader's eye moving left to right.

MAKE ALIGNMENT WORK FOR YOU

Neatness matters more than most people think. Poor alignment creates mental friction and makes slides feel messy or amateurish.

* Use alignment guides, grouping, and distribution features in your slide software.
* Tools like Canva, Gamma, Pitch.com, and Beautiful.ai handle most of this automatically—use them!
* Don't manually eyeball placements. Let the software do the work for you.

CHARTS, TABLES, AND VISUALS

Charts and tables can be great if they simplify, not complicate. If you're using a chart:

* Label your axes clearly. Don't make investors guess what Y represents.
* Use a short, specific title that explains the takeaway.
* If your table is too detailed for a quick read, pull out the key insight and show *that* instead. Put the full table in the appendix if needed.

If you've ever seen a founder flash a complex table and say, *Don't try to understand this, it's just proving the point that this is complicated,* or something to that effect, you probably remember the eye rolls. It's even worse if you expect the investor to read and understand the table!

DITCH THE STOCK PHOTOS

Unless you're showing off your actual product, team, or customers, avoid generic imagery (especially smiling stock people). These images draw attention without adding any meaning. Every element on your slide should either add information or make information easier to understand. If it doesn't, it's a distraction.

CITATIONS AND SECTIONS

Three final polish moves that instantly increase your credibility:

- Use section breaks in your slide deck to visually organize your content and guide your pacing (e.g., "The Problem," "Business Model," "Why Now"). The breaks are for you; they won't show up during the presentation.
- ALWAYS cite your sources. Use small font at the bottom of each slide. This builds credibility, saves time during due diligence, and helps investors trust the data you're showing.
- Spell-check and proofread. Typos and grammar errors distract from your message and can make an investor question your attention to detail. Run a spell-check, read it out loud, and, if possible, have someone else review it. This tiny step makes a disproportionately strong impression.

CORE DECK VS. APPENDIX

Once you've built your core deck, anything that goes into more detail than you have time to present, or anything that doesn't quite fit the main narrative, belongs in your appendix. Your appendix is your expanded universe. You can pull from it during longer meetings or bring up slides live during Q&A. It's a power move when an investor asks a tough question and you can say, *Great question, I actually have a slide on that.*

Don't feel pressure to delete good content just because it slows down the main story. If a slide is useful, detailed, or addresses a frequent investor concern, park it in the appendix and keep it organized. Think of it as your personal pitch toolbox.

SENDING YOUR DECK

If you're sending your deck ahead of time, include a short note like:

This is my core deck, but I'm happy to share an extended version with a detailed appendix if helpful.

This shows you're prepared and respectful of their time without overwhelming them.

VERSION CONTROL = SANITY CONTROL

You may hear advice to create multiple versions of your deck—one for presenting, one for sending, one with extra text, and so on. While that might sound smart in theory . . . in practice, it's a mess. I've seen so many founders drive themselves crazy trying to keep multiple versions updated. You forget which one you changed. You send the wrong one. You pitch from an outdated version and it throws you off. Don't do that to yourself.

Here's what I recommend:

- Create one master deck.
- Use a balanced level of text that's enough to make sense on its own as a send-ahead, but not so much that it's overwhelming in a live pitch. This is where header statements help A LOT.
- Use your appendix slides like modular blocks you can move in or out depending on the meeting.
- Maintain one file that's always current. Your future self will thank you.

You never know when or where your deck will be forwarded without your knowledge. If your traction or revenue is changing quickly, as it often does at the early stage, date-stamp openly. Many founders put a date on the cover slide and the file name. Some even add a tiny date in the footer of each slide. Do whatever helps you stay consistent and avoid confusion.

INTRODUCING THE CORE 10 VISUAL GUIDES

As we dive into the Core 10 Pitch Framework, each chapter will start with a simple graphic showing you:

+ What's going through an investor's mind on that slide
+ What risks you're mitigating by including it
+ What questions you should be answering

Think of these visuals as your pitch cheat sheets. They're not prescriptive templates, but they ground you in a world full of conflicting opinions and "must do" playbooks. They're useful whether you're starting from scratch or refining your 64th version.

My goal is to help you feel confident and in control of your story. You don't have to be flashy; you just have to be clear. These guides will help you do that. Now, let's start with your why—your mission.

Your pitch deck is a thinking tool, not just an investor requirement. Building it forces you to clarify your story, tighten your strategy, and see your business the way an investor will. That clarity is valuable for fundraising and every other part of your company.

A pitch doesn't close the deal; it starts the relationship. The real goal of a deck is to earn the next conversation. Each section reduces a different kind of perceived risk and helps investors understand why you're worth more of their time.

The Core 10 Pitch Framework gives you a reliable foundation. There's no single "right way" to pitch, but the Core 10 ensures you cover the essentials investors need to see, while still letting your personality, mission, and lived experience come through.

Clean, simple slide design makes your story easier to absorb and harder to dismiss. Glanceable headers, sparse text, consistent formatting, and visuals that clarify without cluttering help every investor understand your value quickly. Good design is about reducing cognitive load so your message lands.

13

MISSION

· **ALIGNMENT AND COMMITMENT** – How meaningful is this company's mission to the founder (you!), and how dedicated will they be to it long term?

· **CLARITY** – Is the company's mission understandable and logical?

We've arrived at the first of the Core 10 pitch sections: your mission. Why are you doing this?

This is typically a single slide in your deck, but it's one of the most emotionally important. This is where you ground the audience in who you are, what drives you, and why anyone should believe you're the right person to build this business.

YOUR ORIGIN STORY

The strongest way to open your pitch is with your origin story. While creating the Core 10, I interviewed hundreds of investors and dug through every scholarly and corporate study I could find on pitch structure. One theme showed up over and over again: **investors want to know why the founder started the company**.

After conducting or sitting in on literally thousands of pitch reviews, I can tell you the same thing firsthand. Investors consistently say, *I wish I knew more about the founder's story.* Founders often feel pressure to skip the personal stuff and jump straight to traction. Yes, numbers matter, but at the pre-seed or seed stage, investors are really investing in—*you.* They know building a company will get really, really, really, *really* hard. Your mission section helps them answer two foundational questions:

+ Will this person still be here when things *do* get hard?
+ Are they driven by something deeper than the potential financial upside?

A clear, honest origin story builds credibility faster than any metric can. Ask yourself:

+ Did you experience this problem firsthand?
+ Did it impact someone you care about?
+ Do you have insight or domain knowledge others don't?

You don't need drama to be compelling. Tell the honest story about what motivated you to start your company. Even the most polished investors are still people, and people connect through story. I started this book with my origin story for the same reason: Emotional connection builds trust. If I had skipped that part, would you be reading these words with the same openness?

Joel Mutua's story illustrates this beautifully:

> My mom was widowed with seven kids, and she fed us by delivering groceries to schools, even the one I went to. I saw all the gaps in that process, even as a kid. That's why I wanted to solve last-mile delivery. My first company, Quick Cart, was born from that. I had saved $15,000 from my job and I invested it all into starting the company. My family chipped in some too, but they thought I was crazy. I had a clear trajectory to be a CEO at the company I was working for, but I couldn't stay. I had to solve this problem.

The Rest of Us tend to solve problems we have experienced or witnessed. That lived experience brings a kind of insight and advantage that traditional investors don't always know how to see. Real fundraising isn't TV, but let's go ahead and talk about *Shark Tank* for a second. The editors always cut to a Shark asking, *What's your background?* or *Why did you start this?* Then the founder tells their story, there's a moment of connection and emotion, and suddenly a deal is on the table. It might be TV magic, but it's rooted in real human psychology. Emotional connection grabs attention. It makes people lean in.

James Valencia's story is another example:

> My mom is a pediatrician and super into Western medicine. My dad's side is Hispanic, plagued by diabetes and heart disease. I started doing vertical and hydroponic farming as my first step into sustainable technology and learning about how important food is for culture and can be used to prevent chronic illnesses. I didn't come from farming,

and it was a big revelation for me to consider contributing to what's on my plate.

If you heard his pitch without that context, the hydroponic farming piece likely wouldn't seem as interesting. So, use real photos of yourself (please, no stock imagery) and tell investors what made you care enough to build this thing from scratch. It also lets you weave your expertise into the story without needing a separate "credibility" section.

Figure 13.1

On the slide, this would look like a picture of you doing something relevant to your business, not just your professional headshot, and a short description or three to five bullet points explaining what led you to start your company—not your entire life story, but the key events or experiences that make your mission unmistakably yours.

Lindsay Kuhn, founder of Wingspans, had a fantastic origin story slide. The image (see figure 13.1) was striking, and the short text was both resonant and funny. When I reached out to ask her permission to include it, she shared how, like everything in entrepreneurship, even her own understanding of her mission evolved over time:

> As a woman in engineering, I know that representation matters and see career exploration as an equity issue.

This is exactly why I talk about the pitch deck as a living, breathing document. Building a startup is unpredictable, not only in how you execute your business vision, but in how your understanding of your own motivations deepens with experience.

HOW IT'S DIFFERENT FOR *THE REST OF US*

Our why often carries more weight, and more scrutiny. For many of us, our mission isn't just about solving a market inefficiency, it's addressing unmet needs we have experienced firsthand in our spaces and communities. That kind of origin story is powerful, and your lived experience is an enormous advantage. However, it often means many of the investors you pitch won't understand how large the market opportunity is, which can lead to tougher questions.

We're also the ones most likely to have been told to "stay professional," "be objective," or "don't make it personal," so we underplay the very thing that gives us a competitive edge. You might be used to minimizing parts of your identity in an effort to be taken seriously in spaces that unjustly and unfairly doubt you.

Your lived experience is expertise. It is a legitimate business driver. It is not a liability.

Please know that your story is your edge, your competitive advantage, and the emotional connection. Investors want mission-driven founders because they are less risky, and they are compelling. You *are* that founder. Don't bury it.

However, you do need to be mindful of how you tell your story, particularly if it tends to make you feel emotional yourself. We are often asked to perform our pain by overexplaining, reliving trauma, or providing more proof than others would be asked for. You do not owe your trauma to anyone. Share what's *real* and what's *relevant* to your business but keep your boundaries intact. Vulnerability and professionalism can coexist.

Your origin story might be where implicit bias first shows up in a pitch. Investors often won't give you the benefit of the doubt that your lived experience is enough to validate a business idea. So, here's your tactic: anchor your story in insight. Tie your experience to data, market opportunity, or domain expertise.

Not just: "This happened to me."

But: "This experience revealed a pattern. Here's the data, the market, and why I see something others miss."

You are both passionate and positioned.

FULL-CIRCLE STORYTELLING

As you build this section, focus on the essentials: what you do, who it's for, and why you started it. This section is about you as the founder and CEO. It sets the emotional stakes and positions you as the person who will carry this vision forward. Later, when you close the deck with your Team slide, you create a powerful arc from the moment the idea sparked to the people joining you to bring it to life.

This section often transitions naturally into the next one, The Problem, because most companies are born out of someone experiencing something hard or frustrating and saying, "Why isn't there a better way?"

So now that we've explored your *why*, let's talk about the *what*.

Your Mission slide is your emotional anchor.

It shows what drives you, what you couldn't ignore, and why you're uniquely equipped to build this.

Your story is strategic, not sentimental.

At the earliest stages, investors are betting on you. Your origin story answers their most important question.

Emotion creates connection; clarity creates confidence.

Explain your mission simply enough that anyone, inside or outside your industry, can repeat it back accurately.

Your lived experience is an asset, not an obstacle.

For *The Rest of Us*, experience *is* expertise. Own it without minimizing yourself.

You don't owe anyone your trauma.

Authenticity and boundaries can coexist. Share what informs the business, not what exploits your pain.

Anchor passion in insight.

Tie your story to data, market understanding, or unique access. Show that you're motivated and informed.

Start with why, end with who.

Opening with your mission and closing with your team creates a narrative arc that reinforces purpose and people.

14

THE PROBLEM

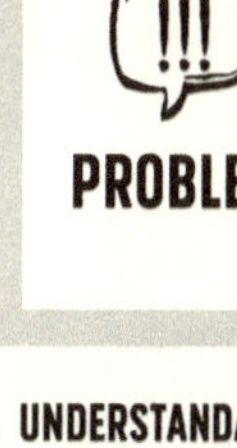

- **UNDERSTANDABLE**—Has the problem been communicated clearly?
- **VALID**—Is the problem proven (ideally with data)?
- **ACUTE**—Is the problem significant enough to incentivize new behavior/payment for a solution?
- **SOLVABLE**—Is a solution to the problem possible?

Now that you've shared your mission and origin story, it's time to show that there's a real problem behind your "why." This section is usually two to four slides, and its entire purpose is to answer one question: Is this a meaningful, painful problem for a large number of people that's worth solving?

Before you say a word about your solution, investors need to believe the problem is real and independent of how you plan to fix it. Investors don't just want to hear a problem exists; they want to know it's painful, proven, and profitable to solve. They approach this section through four core questions:

+ **Understandable:** Can I grasp the issue quickly, without needing industry expertise?
+ **Valid:** Is there credible evidence this problem exists (ideally data, not anecdotes)?
+ **Acute:** Is the pain strong enough that people will change behavior or pay for relief?
+ **Solvable:** Is this a problem that can be solved, or is it an entrenched, immovable reality?

In other words, you're removing the risk that:

+ There's no real problem.
+ The pain isn't felt strongly enough.
+ The problem isn't realistically solvable.

If an investor doesn't believe the problem is real, they won't care about your solution, no matter how elegant, innovative, or technically impressive it is. This section isn't about selling a product or service to a customer. You're showing an investor why this problem is big enough, painful enough, and urgent enough to justify a bet on you, and why solving it creates an opportunity where their capital can grow.

A solution is only as valuable as the problem it addresses. Your job here is to make that problem undeniable.

NARROW BROAD PROBLEMS INTO SOLVABLE ONES

It's completely normal to start with a big vision. You might be motivated by a massive systemic issue like climate change, inequitable access to education, the racial wealth gap, healthcare disparities, you name it. But in your pitch, the problem section needs to drill down into a version of the problem that is specific, concrete, and solvable by your company.

Investors don't back abstract missions. They back clear, well-defined problems that affect identifiable groups of people in meaningful ways. That means you need to answer:

+ Who exactly is experiencing the pain?
+ How often or how intensely do they feel it?
+ What's the measurable impact—money lost, time wasted, frustration, risk, missed opportunity?

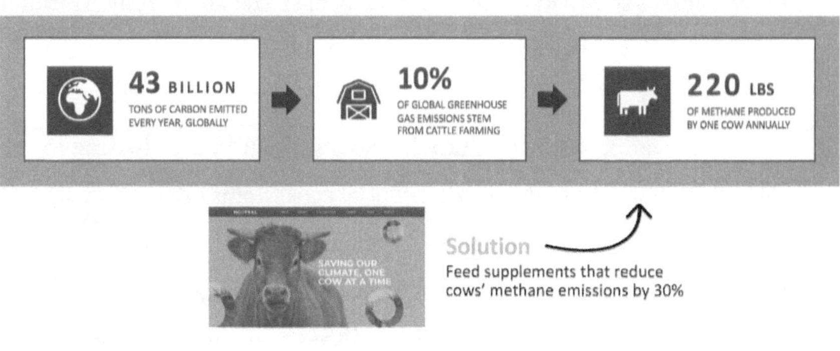

Figure 14.1: Example Slide

For example, if your mission is fighting climate change, your first instinct might be to lead with the global carbon emissions problem. That's fine as a starting point, but it's way too broad for one company to solve.

A sharper approach looks like this (see figure 14.1):

1. Global carbon emissions (too big to solve directly)
2. A subset: greenhouse gases from cattle farming
3. A smaller subset: methane produced by each cow
4. A solvable pain point: reducing methane through feed supplements

You're still tackling a meaningful part of a global issue, but now you've landed on a problem that has clear boundaries, a defined customer, and a path to a solution. That's what investors need to see.

Jennifer Kushell's path with Exploring Your Potential (EYP) is a great illustration of how founders can move from a giant mission to a solvable, high-impact problem. Jennifer had spent years working globally on youth, workforce development, and entrepreneurship. Everywhere she went, she saw the same giant issue: Young people were unprepared for their futures.

That problem is so broad it's almost impossible to tackle directly. Through deeper conversations, Jennifer pinpointed the solvable pain point:

> I started traveling with the State Department and participating in global delegations to build entrepreneurial ecosystems internationally. Students would wait in line for hours to talk to me. Then, Bloomberg called and asked me to build some tools for kids in business schools learning about careers. They explained these kids weren't reading business publications, so we built a program for them, and [they] asked us to build even more and create a curriculum.

That request pushed her to dig deeper. She met with the dean of the University of Central Florida, who told her, "I have 8,000 business school students and 8 career counselors." When she asked how much of their time was spent on actual counseling versus administrative work, he said: "Maybe 25%." Jennifer reflected:

> So, two people are counseling 8,000 students as they go through college about their life. And that was like, boom.

That insight helped her pinpoint the specific pain point that universities are unequipped to guide students at scale, leaving students unsupported and overwhelmed. Instead of trying to solve "career readiness for all youth," she built a curriculum and scalable platform that schools could implement immediately. When she debuted the program at the Dean's Conference, over 100 schools expressed interest on the spot.

This is what it looks like to move from a mission to a solvable problem. Find the systemic issue that motivates you, then anchor your work in a specific, solvable pain point.

USE DATA TO MAKE THE PROBLEM REAL

Data is one of the fastest ways to move an investor from "interesting" to "I see it." When you quantify the problem, you shift the conversation from opinion to evidence, which is something investors rely on heavily when assessing risk.

Two examples illustrate this well:

DeepCharge, co-founded by Yousof Naderi, tackles device downtime in logistics operations (see figure 14.2). Rather than saying, "Downtime is expensive," Yousof shows exactly how expensive: $6,000 lost every minute per facility, which is a $3.2 billion hidden problem across logistics. In one glance, the investor understands the scale, the urgency, and the business case. There's no abstraction, just a clear, painful, measurable problem.

Figure 14.2

Kura, founded by Stéphanie Joseph, focuses on cross-border infrastructure for small and medium-sized businesses (SMBs). Instead of talking broadly about remittance challenges, Stéphanie shows the precise friction points: Merchants in receiving countries cannot directly capture digital remittances or aid payments at the point of sale (POS). There's a less than 20% POS digital acceptance, 70% of recipients have no bank account, and 85% have no access to a card product. These datapoints make the systemic problem instantly concrete (see figure 14.3). Investors don't have to imagine the barriers because they can see them.

When you talk about the problem, speak in everyday language with phrasing that a nonexpert would immediately understand, then support it with numbers. Sometimes the strongest framing highlights not only the pain, but the opportunity. For example, I often talk about how *The Rest of Us* are underfunded and overdeliver, which makes us an undervalued asset class and creates the potential for outsized returns.

Whenever you include data or a stat, make sure it's from a credible source and that you cite the source on the slide.

ALWAYS cite your sources; investors will notice. Just tuck the citation in small text at the bottom of the slide so they're clean, unobtrusive, and professional.

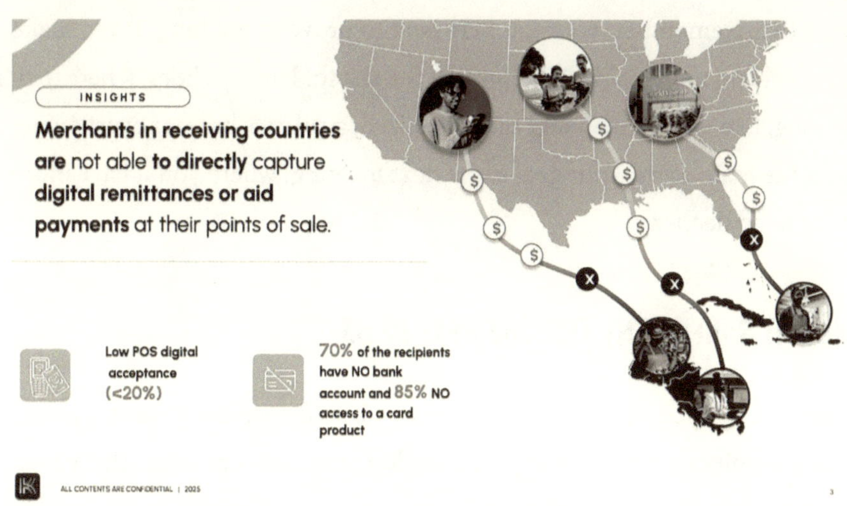

Figure 14.3

BE SPECIFIC AND BRIEF

This can't be overstated: specificity is everything.

Instead of: *This is a problem for every working professional.*

Try: *Mid-career women in hybrid roles lose 15 hours a week managing duplicate tools.*

The broader you are, the harder it is for investors to believe you've found a real customer base. If your product or service is "for everyone," it will end up being for no one. Even Dolly Parton doesn't appeal to everyone … and she's Dolly.

When the problem feels deeply personal, especially for *The Rest of Us*, it's easy to want to share every data point you've spent months gathering. I've been there. There's a mountain of research about the funding gap for underrepresented founders and the opportunity that creates for investors. Early on, I overwhelmed people with all of it, and the impact got lost.

One powerful statement plus a few carefully chosen data points is far more effective. Remember, your job here isn't to prove everything, it's to make the problem undeniable. You can save the rest for backup slides, where they belong, like well-packed luggage: organized, available, but not overflowing into the main story. Your goal is the next meeting, where you'll have more time to go deeper.

HOW IT'S DIFFERENT FOR *THE REST OF US*

Proving a problem exists can feel like an uphill battle, especially when it affects a community investors aren't part of or don't naturally consider. That gap in perspective often puts you in a defensive position, where you're expected to prove *both* that the problem is real *and* that it matters. What feels intuitively obvious to those with lived experience may feel invisible, unfamiliar, or "too niche" to someone outside it.

If your problem ties to systemic inequities like funding gaps, access barriers, or representation issues, you might run into subtle (or not-so-subtle) resistance. Naming the problem sometimes requires naming the system that created it, and that can feel uncomfortable for people who benefit from the status quo.

This is why *The Rest of Us* often feel the urge to overprove, overexplain, or over validate. But there are ways to reframe the conversation so you're not fighting uphill and you're moving the investor toward seeing what you already know to be true.

Here's how to tilt the odds back in your favor:

- **Translate lived experience into data:** Lead with insight and validate with evidence. Your personal story is powerful, but if an investor doesn't share your background, they may dismiss it as anecdotal. Pair your story with external data like studies, surveys, trend reports, or market benchmarks. This shifts the burden from "trust me" to "here's what the market is telling us," transforming lived experience into market insight.

- **Reframe the problem as an undervalued opportunity:** Underserved markets = undervalued markets. This shifts from a deficit-based frame to an opportunity-based one. Underserved focuses on who isn't getting enough, which can lead investors to view these markets as risky, difficult, or burdened by challenges. Undervalued tells a different story of hidden potential that others have missed. It reframes the narrative to match what investors are ultimately seeking, opportunities with financial upside, and shows there are paying customers waiting in the market.

- **Tie the problem to a broader demographic or economic shift:** What may seem like a niche issue becomes a compelling opportunity when it's positioned within a broader movement. Investors are more likely to engage when they see that your solution taps into where the market is already headed, not just where it's been. Anchor your problem in undeniable trends like shifting consumer behavior, rising purchasing power in specific populations, or evolving regulatory and policy environments. This helps reframe your insight as timely and scalable rather than fringe. For *The Rest of Us*, it also reduces the burden of "proving" your market by showing that larger forces are already validating its growth.

MAKE THE PROBLEM THEIR PROBLEM

Sometimes it's not enough to explain a problem. You have to make your audience *feel* it, especially if they've never personally experienced it, or if they assume it lives far outside their world.

Rajia Abdelaziz learned this the hard way. Early in her fundraising journey, she opened her pitch with her own story: A frightening experience in college that led her to uncover the devastating statistic that one in four women is sexually assaulted. It was human, honest, and deeply motivating. She realized, however, that when she framed it this way, some listeners heard it as *her* problem, not *theirs*.

> Sadly, people were looking at it as, 'Oh, this young girl had a scary situation. She's passionate about this problem, for her. This will never happen to me or someone I love.'

So, she re framed it.

> When you switch the same exact story to be slightly more aggressive, where you make the person uncomfortable, where you say, this isn't a me problem, this is a you problem, that's when it hits. You've got a daughter, a sister, a wife, a mom. You're in trouble. You need to do something about it.

With this shift, people in the audience stopped seeing Rajia as just a passionate founder with a personal story. They started seeing themselves in the story, and themselves as the solution. She reframed the problem not just as a statistic or experience, but as an urgent call to action.

This is the power of reframing. When you anchor your problem in lived experience, don't stop at the personal. Extend the lens so your audience understands what's at stake for *them*. Ask yourself:

- What blind spots might the audience have?
- How can I make the problem tangible to someone who has never lived it?
- What framing makes this feel urgent, not optional?
- How do I move them from observers to advocates?

As Rajia put it:

Even if I'm a white male in my 60s who's never worried about my safety, it is my problem. Because someone I care about will be affected.

By the end of your Problem section, the investor should fully believe that the problem is real, big, painful, and solvable. Then they'll be ready for the next part: your solution.

The problem is the foundation.
If investors don't believe the problem is real, urgent, and solvable, nothing else in your pitch will land. This is the moment where they decide whether your idea is worth following.

Specific beats sweeping.
Broad claims like "everyone struggles with this" signal a lack of focus. Narrowing a big mission into a precise, concrete pain point shows you understand who hurts and why it matters.

Data makes the problem undeniable.
One or two sharp, sourced pieces of evidence do more than a dozen statistics. Use numbers to validate your insight, not overwhelm your audience, and always cite your sources.

Make it human and felt.
Data convinces, but stories connect. Pair your stat with a lived example that helps investors *feel* the problem, not just understand it intellectually.

For *The Rest of Us*, the burden of proof is often higher.
When the problem affects communities investors aren't part of, they may question its scale or importance. Counter this by translating lived experience into data and framing underserved markets as undervalued opportunities, not special cases. You're passionate and positioned.

YOUR SOLUTION

· **CLEAR**—Is the solution understandable based on its description?

· **WORKABLE**—Can the solution realistically be executed?

· **COMPLETE**—Is the solution comprehensive and does it fully address the problem?

Now that you've made a clear case for the problem, it's time to show how you solve it. This section should tie directly, and I mean *directly*, to the problem you just laid out. Don't make investors do the work of stitching your story together; they won't. You showed them the pain, now show them the painkiller.

This section is usually two to three slides, and it needs to communicate:

- What you're building
- Who it's for
- How it directly solves the specific pain points you described

STAY FOCUSED ON THE PROBLEM YOU JUST DESCRIBED

This is not the time to introduce something brand new. Stay consistent. If you've just convinced an investor there's an acute problem affecting a specific customer group, your solution should map cleanly onto that same group and that same pain. If it doesn't, your story starts to fall apart, and the investor will lose confidence.

Keep yourself honest by doing a quick gut check: *Does this clearly solve the problem I just described?*

Use header statements to keep your narrative tight and logical. When in doubt, reread your last Problem slide and ask whether this Solution slide answers the question: *So what do we do about it?*

SIMPLICITY AND CLARITY ABOVE ALL

Your solution should be easy to understand, even for someone far outside your industry. Most investors won't know your jargon or acronyms, and many won't ask what something means if they feel like they *should* already know. That's how you lose them. A lot of investor drop-off happens in the Solution section not because the solution is weak, but because they don't understand it quickly. Your job is to make it so straightforward they could pitch it back to you.

So, spell things out:

+ Write out any acronym the first time you use it (and put the acronym in parentheses).
+ Don't assume shared knowledge. Even *MD* could mean "managing director" *or* "medical doctor" depending on context.
+ Default to the version a fifth grader could understand. Simple doesn't mean simplistic, it means you've mastered your story.

And please, I'm begging you, don't show complicated, technical diagrams. I know it's tempting, especially if your product is technically impressive, but this isn't the moment to prove how smart the engineering is. Instead, do the work to pull out the key insight you want them to remember. Ask yourself: *What's the one thing they must understand about how this solves the problem?*

If you absolutely need to show an architecture sketch or workflow diagram, put it in the appendix. Then when an investor asks for it, you look prepared, thoughtful, and in control without overwhelming the main presentation.

SHOW *AND* TELL

Even when founders explain their solution clearly, many still skip the crucial step of showing it. I've seen countless decks where the solution is described only in text or represented by generic icons. That forces investors to imagine what the product might look like, which is never a good idea.

The visuals of your solution should make it more understandable, not more complex. You're not adding more content, you're reducing cognitive load by giving the investor something concrete to anchor to. Don't worry about polish. Investors don't expect finished design at pre-seed or seed.

Screenshots, mockups, or even rough photos of prototypes all work. Your goal is simply to help them picture what you're building.

A simple structure that keeps your solution crisp and comprehensible:

+ Picks one key use case, and
+ Shows a single, clear path through how a customer solves their problem using your solution.

This avoids feature overload while reinforcing the tight mapping between the problem you just described and the product that addresses it. You're still keeping the main explanation simple and now you're making it visual.

Let's look at a couple of example slides:

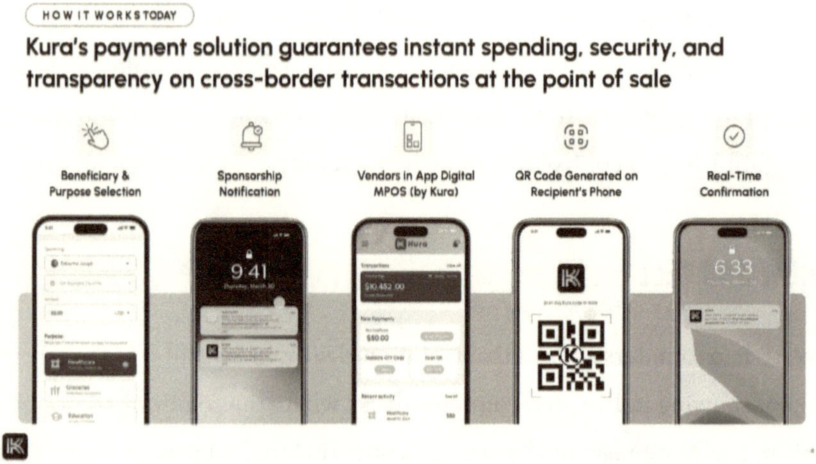

Figure 15.1

Kura uses a straightforward visual walk-through of a single cross-border transaction (see figure 15.1). Each screen shows one step in the user journey, so an investor can instantly grasp how the product works without reading paragraphs of explanation.

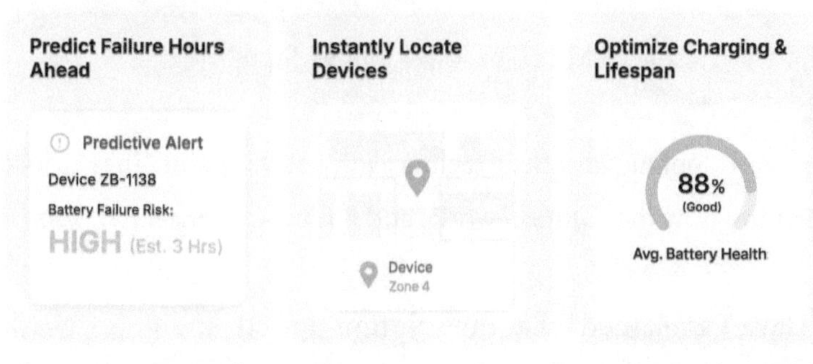

Figure 15.2

DeepCharge demonstrates three core problem-solution moments with clear, minimal visuals—predictive alert, device location, and battery health optimization (see figure 15.2). The slides avoid technical diagrams and instead highlight simple, investor-friendly outcomes.

This type of slide shows the investors how your solution works in the real world without needing a full demo or multiple feature breakdowns. You don't need to include every capability or feature. Focus on one meaningful path that reinforces your problem-solution fit.

IS IT REALISTIC AND COMPLETE?

Once you've shown what your solution is and walked through how it works, the next step is to make sure it feels credible and complete in the eyes of an investor. Even if they don't ask these questions out loud, they're wondering:

+ Could this actually exist based on what I'm seeing?
+ Does this truly solve the problem they just described, or only a sliver of it?

You don't need technical schematics or a full road map here. What matters now is that the investor can believe in the solution and connect the dots.

REALISTIC (IT FEELS FEASIBLE FROM WHAT YOU'VE SHOWN)

Investors aren't looking for a deep technical dive at this point. They're looking to understand how the solution works and if it makes sense. Ask yourself:

+ Have I explained what the solution does in straightforward, human language?
+ Does the use case I walked through make the solution feel achievable, not hypothetical?
+ Did I stay away from vague or inflated claims that create doubt instead of confidence?

The goal is to present your solution so cleanly that an investor can imagine it operating in the real world. A simple use case + clear visuals does more to build feasibility than any architecture diagram ever could.

COMPLETE (SOLVES THE ACTUAL PROBLEM FULLY ENOUGH TO MATTER)

Your solution doesn't need to tackle the entire ecosystem on day one. But it does need to address the core pain point you just spent time proving exists. To sanity-check yourself:

+ If a customer used the solution as shown, would the problem get meaningfully better?
+ Am I solving the central piece of the problem, or something adjacent?

+ Does my before/after (explicit or implied) show the relief the customer feels?

If you're intentionally starting with a narrower wedge, say so. Investors respect focus, especially at pre-seed and seed stages. What they need to understand is that your wedge actually hits the pain point, not something tangential. Tight alignment between the problem and solution is what makes your narrative feel inevitable rather than theoretical. That alignment alone removes an enormous amount of perceived risk.

JARGON AND GENERIC GRAPHICS: A QUICK NOTE

Skip anything that looks impressive but communicates nothing. Technical jargon that only insiders understand and generic graphics that don't convey real information both create unnecessary cognitive load. Stock illustrations, abstract 3D renderings, and placeholder icons (like two stick figures shaking hands in front of a globe) might look "designed," but they don't move your story forward.

Your job is to make the investor understand your solution quickly, not decode your terminology or guess at your visuals. Use simple, direct language and show visuals that reinforce your explanation. Don't assume understanding (we all know what happens when we assume); earn it through clarity and relevance.

TESTING, ONE, TWO, THREE

Once you've got your simple explanation and your language down, test it! (Actually, test everything in your pitch, but especially this.) Try it out with someone who knows nothing about your company or industry.

Say what your company does, then ask: *Can you tell me what you think we do?*

+ If they nail it—amazing.
+ If they get close—tighten your language.
+ If they miss the mark—simplify.

I've tested pitch descriptions with my grandma. I've asked my 15-year-old son if he can understand them. We've supported founders across deep tech, biotech, manufacturing, and everything in between. You can always explain your work simply, and you need to, because investors don't fund what they don't understand.

HOW IT'S DIFFERENT FOR *THE REST OF US*

This is often the moment when *The Rest of Us* get doubted because the people listening may not personally understand the problem you're solving. When investors don't share the lived experience behind the problem, your solution won't always feel "obvious," even if it's deeply intuitive to the communities you serve. If your product is culturally grounded, addresses a systemic gap, or rethinks a legacy model, it may fall outside their mental blueprint for what a "startup" looks like. That's not a flaw in your story; it's a limitation in their exposure.

Here's how to take control of that gap:

+ **Make the problem → solution link unmistakable:** If investors don't live the problem, they need a crystal-clear bridge showing how your solution directly relieves the pain you just described. No leaps or assumptions of existing knowledge.

- **Use concrete visuals rooted in real users:** Show what your solution looks like in the hands or lives of the people it's built for, especially those investors rarely see represented in pitch rooms. This builds both clarity and credibility.
- **Translate social relevance into business relevance:** If you're solving an equity-driven or community-specific problem, don't assume investors will intuit the market opportunity. Draw the line from unmet need → paying customer → financial upside.

When your solution touches a systemic issue, some investors might expect you to solve *all* of it. Resist the pull to overpromise if you're met with someone like that. Solving a meaningful, clearly defined pain point is enough, more than enough, to build a business. Be explicit about what you're solving now, why you're starting there, and how it becomes the foundation for future layers of impact and revenue. That grounded confidence is what earns investor conviction.

YOUR SOLUTION CHECKLIST

Before you move on, pause and run your solution through a quick gut check:

- ☐ Is it crystal clear what we're building?
- ☐ Can a nonexpert understand how it works?
- ☐ Does it directly solve the pain we defined in the problem section?
- ☐ Can someone visualize how a customer uses it?

If any answer is "not really," simplify before you move forward. You want your solution to feel obvious and inevitable, not aspirational or abstract. With this, you've now covered the three most important sections of your pitch, the emotional and logical backbone everything else rests on:

- **Mission:** why you're doing this
- **Problem:** what pain you're addressing
- **Solution:** how you remove that pain

These three pieces are what make an investor lean in long enough to care about the rest. Now that you've grounded your story in purpose, need, and fit, we can shift into the more mechanical (but equally important) part of your deck: how this becomes a business. Next up: your business model.

 TAKEAWAYS

The solution must map directly to the problem.

If your solution doesn't clearly solve the pain you just described, your narrative breaks and investors lose confidence.

Clarity beats complexity every time.

Jargon, technical language, and dense explanations are the fastest way to lose investors. Drop-off happens here because founders overestimate what the audience can follow in real time.

Show, don't just tell.

Screenshots, photos, mockups, or simple walk-throughs communicate more in five seconds than a paragraph of text ever will. The goal is comprehension, not polish.

Realistic and complete enough to believe.

Your solution doesn't need to be finished or feature-rich, but it does need to look feasible and capable of delivering meaningful relief to the customer you defined.

For *The Rest of Us*, simplicity is strategic.

Bias shows up fast in the solution section. Overexplaining or overengineering can unintentionally reinforce doubts about execution. A clear, grounded, user-centered solution signals competence and control and strengthens your credibility.

16

YOUR BUSINESS MODEL

- What are the company's **PRIMARY SOURCES OF REVENUE?**
- Are all **RELEVANT CUSTOMER SEGMENTS** addressed?
- Is the business model **LOGICAL?**
- **FINANCIAL VIABILITY**—Can this business model make enough money to return an investment?

Now that an investor understands why you're building your company and what you've built to solve the problem, they need to understand how this becomes a business. Your business model is simply the explanation of:

+ Who is paying you
+ What they're paying you for
+ How that revenue could grow over time

This is typically a single slide, but it carries real weight. Investors are evaluating not only *if* your business can make money, but whether it can make *enough* money for them to see a return on their investment. For *The Rest of Us*, this is one of the places where bias shows up fast. If you're underestimated, you're often over-scrutinized. That's why presenting your business model with confidence, even at an early stage, is critical. Clarity here reinforces the fact that you're not just mission-driven; you're building a real company.

IF YOU'RE PRE-REVENUE, THAT'S OKAY, BUT BE CLEAR

Even if you haven't started monetizing yet, you still need to communicate your planned business model and show that you know who your paying customer is. Be especially careful to distinguish between your end user and your paying customer as they are not always the same. If you're early, say so, but show that you've done the work to validate your assumptions. You can even break this into a "now" and "later" approach:

> *Right now, we're testing freemium onboarding, but longer-term we plan to monetize through tiered subscriptions based on user volume.*

That's honest, it's grounded, and it shows you're thinking ahead. Investors might assume that if you don't proactively bring up how you'll generate revenue, it's because you haven't thought it through. If you're from a group that isn't typically seen as a "business type," this kind of omission may get interpreted unfairly. Even a single sentence can flip that perception.

WHAT YOUR BUSINESS MODEL SHOULD COVER

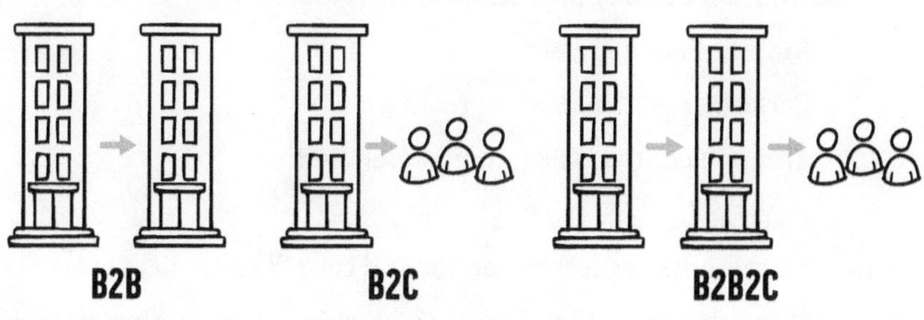

Figure 16.1

When we talk about business model, we're talking about a few related pieces. You don't need to put all of this on the slide, but you do need to be ready to talk through it with confidence (see figure 16.1).

+ **Who's paying you?** Are your customers:
  * Individuals (B2C)
  * Businesses (B2B)
  * A combination (B2B2C, channel-driven, marketplaces)

+ **What are they paying you for?** What is the unit of value?
  * Access (subscription or license)
  * Transactions (you take a percentage)
  * Per-user or per-seat pricing

- Packages, tiers, or flat fees
- Services or consulting hours

+ **How often do they pay?** Are you charging:
  - Monthly, annually, etc.
  - Per-use or on demand
  - Through contracts or volume-based tiers

There's no right answer, just be specific and clear. You can have more than one customer segment, both products and services, and multiple payment frequencies. The more predictable your revenue is, the more attractive it usually is to investors.

For *The Rest of Us*: if your customer base includes underserved groups, take extra care to show the economic opportunity there. Investors may unconsciously devalue markets they don't personally identify with. Back up your segment with data and clear logic around ability and willingness to pay.

ADD CONTEXT: UNIT ECONOMICS AND MARGINS

You don't need detailed financials on this slide, but a simple signal that you understand your cost to deliver goes a long way. For example:

We charge $50 per seat per month, and our cost to serve is $10, leaving a healthy margin that improves with scale.

That shows unit economics in plain terms: what you make per "unit" (seat, transaction, device, license) after direct costs. This shows you're building a business that can become profitable over time. Strong margins are compelling if you're in a nontraditional industry or not following a typical Silicon Valley playbook. A sustainable, profitable business is a strong signal—don't undersell it!

TALK ABOUT SCALABILITY

Even early on, investors want to know if this can grow. This is where you show that your model can scale. In simple terms, *scalability* means:

* Can revenue grow faster than costs?
* Can you serve more customers without hiring one person per customer?
* Do things get easier, cheaper, or more efficient as you grow?

For example, a digital tool with self-onboarding is more scalable than a service that requires a custom 1:1 setup every time.

You can signal this with a line like: *As we onboard more partners, fulfillment costs decrease, and margins improve.* That tells the investors you're already thinking about growth levers and operational efficiency.

ACKNOWLEDGE MODEL EVOLUTION (IF NEEDED)

Business models evolve, which is reality, not failure. You don't have to pretend you have everything perfectly nailed down, especially at the pre-seed or seed stage. Be clear about where you are now and how you're thinking ahead. For example:

We're currently charging through pilot partnerships, but we anticipate shifting to a SaaS-based model post-MVP.

or

Right now, we're focused on building and testing. Our early revenue plan is [X], and we've identified [Y and Z] as likely scale models. We're validating which path has the strongest signal.

That kind of transparency builds trust as long as you can explain the why behind your assumptions and direction. For *The Rest of Us*, this is particularly important. If your early model looks "scrappy" (services, manual onboarding, custom work), investors might assume that's the whole plan unless you explicitly articulate how it evolves. Spell out the arc.

AVOID COMMON RED FLAGS

Some phrases make investors instantly nervous because they sound like you haven't thought through monetization. Steer clear of:

+ *We'll figure out how to make money later.*
+ *We'll make money through ads* (unless you already have a large, engaged user base).
+ *It's free now, but we'll charge eventually* (with no plan for how or why).

Even if you're still exploring, you can frame it thoughtfully:

We've identified three potential monetization strategies and are currently testing conversion rates across two of them.

SHOW THE WORK BEHIND YOUR MODEL

You don't have to include all the research on your slide, but you do want to be ready to talk about how you arrived at your pricing and model:

+ Did you talk to potential customers about what they'd pay?
+ Did you look at comparable or similar products or services?
+ Are you anchoring to something they already spend money on?

In conversation or Q&A, it helps to say something like:

We talked to 50 potential customers, and 80% said they'd be willing to pay between $25–$50 per month for a solution like this.

If you've done this kind of customer discovery, say so proudly! *The Rest of Us* often over-validate but underreport. You probably have spreadsheets, surveys, or long email threads that could double as a dissertation—don't let that legwork stay invisible!

WHAT ABOUT FINANCIAL PROJECTIONS?

This question comes up in nearly every workshop and pitch review: Should financial projections be in the deck?

My honest answer is that you don't need to include financial projections in your core deck. You *do* need them in your appendix, ready for Q&A or later-stage conversations. The goal of your pitch deck is to convince someone you're worth spending more time with. That's it. You are not closing the deal with your deck. If someone is interested, they'll go deeper. That's when your projections matter.

HOW IT'S DIFFERENT FOR *THE REST OF US*

This guidance is especially important for founders who are underestimated because data shows a clear pattern where we're more often evaluated on precision, while others are funded on potential. According to DocSend's 2024 Funding Divide report,[63] business model slides from all-female teams received 41% more scrutiny than those of all-male teams. That gap shows up in how projections are judged too.

---

63   DocSend. The 2024 Funding Divide: The State of Startup Fundraising Across Gender and Race. DocSend, 2024. https://www.docsend.com/the-funding-divide-2024.

If you include projections too early, they can be used as a reason to pass. Even if your projections are more realistic than the next founder's hockey stick,[64] they may be judged more harshly. That's the double standard, and that's why I advise against leading with them. So, yes, build your model, absolutely, but use it strategically and don't let it become a premature filter. Your narrative should carry the meeting, not your spreadsheet. Especially if you're someone who doesn't look like what the investor expects a "CEO" to be.

IF YOU DO INCLUDE PROJECTIONS

If you choose to include a projections slide, or you're specifically asked for one, anchor it in credibility and restraint:

- **Keep it believable:** You don't need perfect accuracy, and no one expects that. But don't manufacture a hockey-stick chart just to look like you're going to "crush it."
- **Avoid unrealistic jumps:** If you're projecting $100,000 in revenue this year, and then suddenly $10 million next year with no team or infrastructure changes, that's a red flag.
- **Show your work:** The assumptions behind your projections are far more important than the numbers themselves.

Investors know you're making educated guesses. What they care about is: *How did you get to this number, and what would need to happen for that to be true?* That might mean things like:

---

64   A hockey stick chart shows revenue or growth that stays flat for a while and then suddenly shoots up, forming a shape that looks like a hockey stick. It's often used (and overused) in startup decks to suggest rapid, exponential growth, sometimes without realistic justification.

+ *We assume 5% conversion of free to paid users.*
+ *We expect to close three new enterprise contracts per quarter based on our pipeline.*
+ *Our average revenue per customer is $500 annually, based on early pilots.*

If you can show how the numbers are built from real-world inputs or early indicators, you give your projections credibility and show you're running your business with intention. You don't need to have all the answers, and you don't need a CFO, you just need to show you've asked the right questions and you're thinking like a business leader. Figure 16.2 shows an example of a projections slide that communicates growth clearly while grounding the numbers in believable assumptions.

EXAMPLE FINANCIAL PROJECTIONS SLIDE

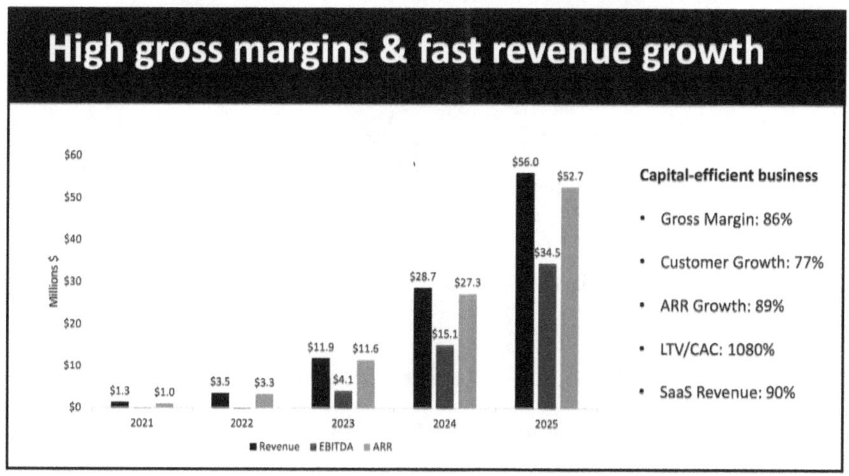

Figure 16.2

Now that your business model is clear, the investor's next question is about the size of the opportunity. How big is the market, and how much can you capture? Let's talk market size.

The Business Model slide answers: "How does this become a business?"
You've shown your mission, problem, and solution—this is where you prove it can make money.

Pre-revenue is fine; clarity isn't optional.
Even if you're early, you need to show you've thought about who pays you, what they pay for, and how revenue grows. A simple "now vs. later" framing builds credibility.

Differentiate between end user and paying customer.
They aren't always the same. Showing you understand the distinction avoids red flags.

Keep it focused and believable.
Overly complicated or vague business models signal weakness. Investors want to see logic, viability, and scalability, not financial fantasies.

For *The Rest of Us*, this section is over-scrutinized.
We are often unfairly doubted on our ability to make money. A clear, confident, grounded business model combats bias by showing you've thought it through.

17

MARKET SIZE

· **SIZE/DEPTH**—Is the market large enough for the company to achieve venture-scale (10x or more) growth and returns?

· **VALIDITY**—Are the assumptions you've made about your revenue opportunity evidence-based and believable?

Welcome to the section that strikes fear into the hearts of many early-stage founders: market size. This chapter is on the longer side, and that's intentional, so get comfy!

Let's come right out and say it: This part of the pitch can feel like a guessing game, even when you're doing your homework. One of my own investors, who's both deeply experienced and very successful, put it bluntly: "Fuck market size. It's all made up and doesn't mean anything."

In some ways, he's right. The exact number matters less than your ability to make a believable, compelling case for why there's meaningful money to be made, but don't let that fool you into thinking this slide doesn't matter because it absolutely does. Once you've shown how your business makes money, the next logical question from an investor is, "How big could this get?" That's why I recommend placing your market size slide right after your business model. You've just explained who's paying you and what they're paying you for, so now it's time to show how many of those customers are out there and how much revenue potential that creates.

WHY THIS SLIDE MATTERS

This section isn't about proving your precision with economic forecasts. It's about using real-world data and sound logic to quantify a big enough opportunity to make your business worth betting on. Investors need to believe that:

+ There are enough potential customers.
+ They will spend real money.
+ Your business can scale to generate enough revenue that they can earn a profit on their investment.

This slide shows that you're thinking in financial terms, not just mission terms.

THE CONFLICTING ADVICE TRAP

Ask ten investors how to calculate market size, and you'll get eleven opinions. One will tell you TAM, SAM, SOM. Another will say just show revenue potential over five years. Someone else will demand third-party analyst reports. Then your accelerator advisor will tell you to just show the size of your "beachhead."

They're all right. And all wrong.

There's no one-size-fits-all method here. What matters is that your logic is clear, your numbers come from credible sources, and your framing reflects how your market actually works. If you feel like you're going in circles with this slide, you're probably on the right track. Market size is part data, part storytelling, and part theater. Your job is not to be perfectly "correct" (that's impossible anyway). Your job is to be consistent, thoughtful, and believable in the way you size your opportunity.

This is key: Don't get defensive.

This slide can trigger a lot of pushback, even when you've done the research. This is especially true for *The Rest of Us*. Investors will challenge your assumptions, ask for different cuts of the data, or simply say the market feels small because they don't intuitively understand it. That doesn't mean your market is small, it means you need to calmly walk them through your reasoning. Defensive energy can read as uncertainty. Clear, grounded confidence reads as credibility.

For founders who are underestimated or building for communities investors aren't part of, "We don't think the market is big enough" is a common rejection. It often translates to "We don't understand the people you're building for." Your job isn't to justify the existence of your market, it's to make it legible to someone who can't see it without your lens.

For Derek Ali, Grammy-winning audio engineer and founder of EngineEars, understanding how to frame the opportunity in a venture-backable way was a key turning point. His deep expertise in a niche segment of the music industry gave him credibility and clarity, but early on, his pitch focused too narrowly on the initial product, which was a platform for audio engineers to manage and monetize their work.

Building in such a niche field of the music industry didn't look venture backable. I didn't realize that going out to funds and positioning only our beachhead market as the opportunity was going to result in no's. They would say, 'I don't see the value in investing in just a mixing platform for audio engineers. What's the broader scale?'

Investors weren't seeing the bigger picture because Derek wasn't yet painting it for them. His lived experience and intuition had led him to a clear and focused starting point, but the *vision* for where it could grow needed to be just as clear. Once he reframed the pitch to include the longer-term market opportunity of leveraging the platform as a launchpad for much larger infrastructure plays in music tech, the investment interest shifted.

Once I understood that I needed to communicate the investment opportunity of what was to come later versus what we were building now, we refined our pitch and secured a $1.5 million pre-seed extension.

His experience is a common one. Many underestimated founders, especially those operating in overlooked markets, are laser-focused on their immediate customer's needs (which is good!) but don't frame the full arc of the opportunity when fundraising. Derek added:

I probably took 500 calls during the time that I wasn't communicating the larger, visionary market size. People wanted to talk just because of who I am, but then during the calls, I realized these investors weren't listening. I could tell by their tone; it almost felt robotic. I knew something wasn't connecting, but they weren't giving me direct feedback. Once we figured out how to talk about the larger opportunity of what we were aiming to build, investors started paying more attention.

An effective market size slide tells the investor a few key things:

+ You understand how to define your Total Addressable Market (TAM) in a way that's relevant to what you are doing, not a vague Google search.
+ You've done the math to show that this is a big enough opportunity to support a successful, scalable business and give investors a potential return.
+ You've thought through your rollout strategy, starting with a focused segment or target market to prove traction early on.
+ You're not trying to be everything to everyone. You know your near-term opportunity and are focused on executing within it for the next 12–18 months.

Too often, market sizing slides present irrelevant top-down stats ("The wellness industry is a $4 trillion market … "), try to be overly clever or complicated, or skip over segmentation and real math. We're not doing any of that here. We're going to walk through it step-by-step in a way anyone can calculate, no MBA required.

WHY INVESTORS CARE SO MUCH ABOUT MARKET SIZE

Market size isn't about how much revenue you will generate; it's about how much is possible in the space you're operating in. It's one of the quickest ways an investor can assess if your business has the potential to meet their return expectations. And the expectations are very different between venture capitalists and angel investors.

HOW VCS THINK ABOUT MARKET SIZE

As we covered previously, venture capital has its own business model. VCs raise money from outside parties, limited partners (LPs), and they are expected to generate strong returns on that money. To attract future LPs, funds are expected to deliver outsized performance, often aiming to return 2–3 times the size of the fund over a 10-year period.

That's why VCs aren't just evaluating your company; they're evaluating whether your *potential exit* could materially move the needle on their fund.

Let's say a VC manages a $100 million fund. If they invest in 20 companies, and most won't return much or may fail, they need at least one or two companies to return $100 million or more just to break even, let alone generate a profit for their LPs. This is what's meant when you hear phrases like:

+ "We need companies that can return the fund."
+ "It's not venture scale."
+ "It's not investable for us."

It's not a judgment of you as a founder or the quality of your business. It's a function of how their fund is structured. They're looking for businesses with the potential to grow 10x, 20x, or even 100x because that's what the math of their model requires.

You'll often hear that investors want to see a $1 billion total addressable market (TAM). That doesn't mean they expect you to capture all of it; it means they need to believe there's enough market potential that, with strong execution, your company could deliver a massive return.

Here's what's important to remember: **This is their opinion.** It's based on how they've interpreted your pitch, what they understood (or missed) during diligence, their existing portfolio, their fund size, their personal biases, and their experience. It is not a definitive statement on whether your company is "good enough" nor is their view of the market necessarily more accurate than yours.

Venture math isn't intuitive, and it's rarely explained to founders. Many brilliant entrepreneurs hear "not venture scale" and internalize it as a verdict. But it's not. It's a reflection of one investor's perspective, filtered through their unique lens of incentives, constraints, and assumptions. Those can be wrong, especially when you're building for a customer or community they don't understand.

Your job is to communicate the scale and urgency of your opportunity clearly. Their job is to decide whether it fits their model. Whether they say yes or no, *neither answer defines your worth or your company's potential.*

WHY ANGEL INVESTORS ARE DIFFERENT

Angels are typically investing their own money, not managing capital for others, and they don't have the same return pressure as VCs. This gives them more flexibility in what they fund and why. Angel investors might define success as simply helping a business grow, achieving a small exit, or even just getting their money back. They're often driven by impact, passion for a space, or belief in the founder just as much as financial return.

As a result, you don't always need a billion-dollar TAM to raise angel capital. But you do still need to show that you've done the work to understand your market and opportunity.

A QUICK NOTE: MARKET SIZE ≠ FINANCIAL PROJECTIONS

Before we get into the details, let's clear something up that causes a lot of confusion—market size is not the same thing as financial projections. They answer different questions and belong in different places in your pitch (see figure 17.1).

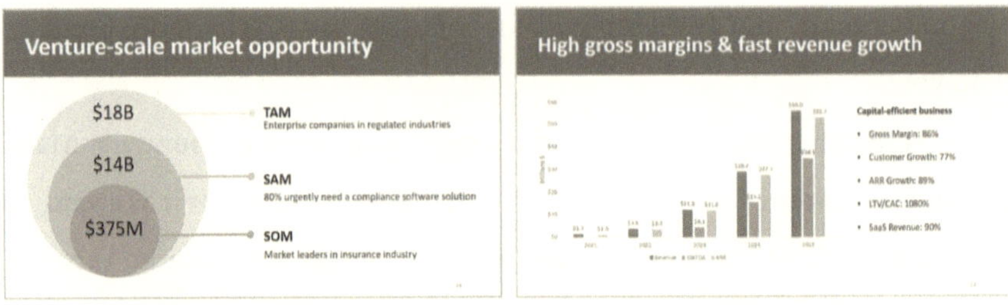

Market Size

Forward-looking
opportunity.

Projections

Near-term sales and
cost assumptions.

Figure 17.1

Your market size is a forward-looking estimate of the total revenue opportunity for your business. It tells investors how much money could be made if your company successfully served your target customers. It doesn't include costs, margins, or how many people you can reach today.

Your financial projections, on the other hand, are near-term forecasts tied to your current strategy and cost structure. They reflect how your revenue (and expenses) might grow over the next one to three years based on what you know now.

Think of it like this:

+ Market size = total pie
+ Projections = your first few slices

You need both but they serve very different purposes. Market size helps investors understand the potential for scale, return, and long-term upside. Projections help them assess your execution strategy and milestones. As we covered in the business model chapter, don't lead with projections in your core deck. Keep them in your appendix so you're ready when asked, without letting premature scrutiny derail the conversation.

That's why market size gets its own section in the main deck, while projections stay behind the scenes until they're relevant. One sets the stage for potential; the other supports diligence once an investor is already interested.

Now let's talk about how to define that pie in a way that's specific, believable, and investor ready.

MARKET SIZE CALCULATION METHODS

Calculating a credible market size is one of the harder parts of building a pitch deck. It's easy to feel overwhelmed because the advice is inconsistent, the math feels abstract, and it's rarely explained in a way that founders can immediately apply.

There are two general approaches to market sizing: top-down and bottom-up.

TOP-DOWN MARKET SIZING: LOOKS IMPRESSIVE, PROVES VERY LITTLE

A top-down market size usually comes from secondary research or industry reports. You start with a big number from a firm like McKinsey, Statista, or IBISWorld and work your way down. For example:

The luxury apparel market is worth $93 billion globally. If we can capture just 1% of that, that's a $930 million opportunity.

The problem with this method is that it's not specific to your business. That 1% number is arbitrary. It doesn't tell an investor who your real customers are, what they'd pay, or how likely it is that you'd win that piece of the pie. Top-down sizing also tends to overinflate your addressable market. You're counting all of something, not the specific portion you're building for. The information might be directionally helpful, but it's not credible when it comes to your actual business opportunity.

BOTTOM-UP MARKET SIZING: HARDER TO FAKE, EASIER TO TRUST

A bottom-up market size starts with your own customer segments and pricing strategy. It's built from the ground up, using real-world assumptions about who will buy from you and what they'll pay. This is how investors calculate market size during due diligence. You're better off doing it now before they do it for you.

The number may sound smaller than a top-down method, but it's specific, it's actionable, and it shows you know your audience. *The Rest of Us* are more likely to be challenged on our market size, even when it's rational. Investors might have limited exposure to the communities or industries you're serving, so your market may be underestimated. That's not your fault. Present your market clearly and confidently, backed by real assumptions. A strong bottom-up size helps close that credibility gap.

From here on out, this chapter will walk you through how to calculate a bottom-up market size and define the components that make it work.

MARKET SIZE TERMINOLOGY: TAM, SAM, AND SOM

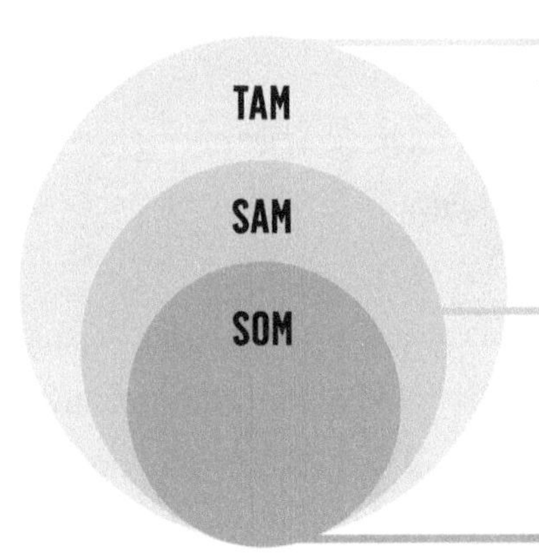

TOTAL ADDRESSABLE MARKET

All your potential customers if you had 100% market share.

 # POTENTIAL CUSTOMERS × $ AVG. ANNUAL REVENUE/CUSTOMER

SERVICEABLE ADDRESSABLE MARKET

Realistic % of customers you can actually reach or who can actually buy your offering.

$ TAM × % CUSTOMERS YOU CAN REASONABLY SELL TO

SERVICEABLE **OBTAINABLE** MARKET

Realistic % of customers you think you can convert or who will actually buy your offering.

$ SAM × % CUSTOMERS YOU COULD REASONABLY CAPTURE

Figure 17.2

You've probably heard the acronyms TAM, SAM, and SOM but you might still feel unsure about what they really mean or how to calculate them for your business. Let's break it down in simple terms, with clear math and logic behind each layer (see figure 17.2).

TOTAL ADDRESSABLE MARKET (TAM)

TAM is your total revenue opportunity if you had 100% market share and indicates the potential of your company at scale. It's the full size of the pie.

To calculate it: Number of potential customers × Average annual revenue per customer.

The math is simple in concept. If everyone who *could* buy what you're selling *did* buy what you're selling at the price you're selling it, it would be this many dollars.

This is about scale. Investors, especially venture capitalists, are typically looking for TAMs in the $1B+ range because they need the opportunity to support big exits. But that doesn't mean you should stretch the truth to hit that number.

Example: If you sell a $100/month subscription to therapists and estimate 200,000 potential US customers, your TAM would be: 200,000 × $1,200/year = $240M

SERVICEABLE ADDRESSABLE MARKET (SAM)

SAM is the portion of your TAM that you can reach. Not all potential customers are realistically within your target or accessible via your sales model.

To calculate it: TAM × % of reachable or relevant customers.

Think about distribution, access, and market constraints. For example, if you're targeting older adults and know that only 30% use smartphones regularly, your SAM will be smaller than your TAM. Or, if you are selling to doctors, you'll likely want a conservative estimate of the percent you can reasonably reach given they are notoriously hard to sell to.

SAM doesn't mean you will win these customers or that the revenue amount is in your financial projections; it's that you could potentially sell to them with the right strategy and resources.

SERVICEABLE OBTAINABLE MARKET (SOM)

SOM is your realistic near-term sales opportunity, usually for the next 12–18 months, which aligns with how long your current fundraise is expected to last.

To calculate it: SAM × % of customers you can realistically convert soon.

This is your proof-of-concept, or beachhead market. It's where you'll focus post-funding to prove traction, refine your go-to-market strategy, and set up for growth. Your success in capturing this slice of your market is indicative of how you'll do when you expand to the larger market.

Think about things like where you and your customers are located and if geography will help or hinder reach and sales, how strong your competition is and if you can reasonably expect to take market share from them right away, and how you will reach those customers based on your marketing plan and distribution channels. Once you accept money from investors, they will use your SOM as a reference point, as it relies heavily upon your research and assumptions.

A word of caution: If your SOM is in the billions, it signals a red flag. Investors may think your assumptions are unrealistic or that you haven't thought through your early adopter market for the next 1–2 years.

A NOTE ON GEOGRAPHY

Unless you're launching globally from day one, it's typical to present US numbers only. If global expansion is part of your plan, you can add a note or include a global TAM/SAM later in your appendix.

A commonly accepted VC shortcut is the Global TAM = US TAM × 3.

If you are focused on a country outside the US but pitching to US-based investors, it presents a different level of risk for them because they might not be familiar with that market. They understand the US market because they live in it, and they often subconsciously assume every other market must be smaller, riskier, or harder to scale. Joel Mutua encountered this issue:

> 95% of our investors were US-based and none had ever invested in Africa before. I had to explain the market from scratch, over and over again. It wasn't a lack of belief in me; it was a lack of understanding.

For founders like Joel, fundraising often means doing double the work: pitching the business *and* educating investors on an entire geography, regulatory system, and consumer behavior landscape. That's an exhausting layer of labor that many founders never have to think about. BUT, it also means you get to shape the narrative and turn the unknown into an opportunity.

A few strategies that help:

+ **Show scale through analogy:** Help investors see the parallels. *Nigeria's fintech ecosystem is one of the fastest-growing in the world, with adoption and innovation patterns echoing what the US experienced a decade ago, but at a larger, mobile-first scale* is more compelling than *The Nigerian market is large.*[65]

+ **Ground your credibility in local traction:** Highlight partners, pilots, or regulatory wins that demonstrate you're operating in that market and understand how to thrive in it.

---

65   Nigeria is home to more than 220 million people, 70% of whom are under age 30, and mobile penetration exceeds 90%. Its fintech sector now attracts more than one-third of all venture funding in Africa, according to McKinsey & Company, "Fintech in Africa: The End of the Beginning," 2022.

- **Use third-party validation:** Reports, global publications, or government data help close the knowledge gap. Don't assume investors will seek this out on their own.
- **Connect investors to local voices:** Introduce them to advisors, customers, or other respected founders who can vouch for the market dynamics.

Investor education shouldn't be your full-time job, but it's often part of the path for global founders. The more you can anticipate what they don't know, and bridge that gap with clarity and confidence, the more control you'll have over how your opportunity is perceived. Remember, a lack of familiarity is *their* blind spot, not *your* flaw.

EXAMPLE 1: B2B SAAS

Let's walk through how to calculate TAM, SAM, and SOM using a fictional B2B SaaS company (see table 17.1). Here, we're using a company that sells corporate licorice subscriptions (because licorice is obviously universally adored and boosts morale. If you disagree, let's pretend you didn't say anything).

COLUMN 1: SEGMENT YOUR MARKET

Start by identifying your customer segments, which are the distinct groups you plan to sell to. These segments should be mutually exclusive, so you don't accidentally double-count customers. In this example, the company breaks out their market by company size: large, medium, and small companies. You could segment by industry, location, buyer type (e.g., HR vs. Operations), or any other criteria that make sense for your business.

EXAMPLE: B2B SAAS

SEGMENTS	# CUSTOMERS	$ AVG ANNUAL REVENUE/ CUSTOMER	US TAM	% SERVICEABLE	US SAM	% OBTAINABLE	US SOM
Large Companies	40,000	$20K	$800M	90%	$720M	15%	$108M
Medium Companies	80,000	$12K	$960M	90%	$864M	8%	$69.1M
Small Companies	200,000	$8K	$1.6B	75%	$1.2B	4%	$48M
TOTAL	320,000		$3.4B		$2.8B		$225.1M

Table 17.1

COLUMN 2: ESTIMATE MARKET SIZE PER SEGMENT

Next, you'll fill in the number of potential customers for each segment. Use credible sources wherever possible (census data, industry reports, LinkedIn Sales Navigator, etc.). It doesn't need to be perfect, just make a clear, good-faith estimate. See the end of this chapter for some recommended credible sources to find sizing data.

COLUMN 3: ANNUAL REVENUE

In the third column you're going to put how much one of those customers would pay you, on average, in a year (ARR). This can be different amounts, or even entirely different revenue models, for different segments. Multiply the number of customers by the ARR to calculate your TAM for that segment. Finally, estimate what percentage of customers in each segment you can realistically serve (SAM) and convert soon (SOM). These percentages are assumptions, but they should be grounded in your understanding of how reachable or likely to convert these customers are.

WHY TABLES HELP

Using a table like the one shown in table 17.1 makes your thinking, and math, transparent. It also makes it easier to play with assumptions to see how they affect your market size. You'll notice the total TAM here is $3.4B, with a SAM of $2.8B, and a SOM of $225M. That last number, the SOM, is what the company is focused on for the next 12–18 months as its proof-of-concept market. Investors love this format. It shows you're strategic and realistic, not just tossing around big numbers.

SLIDE DESIGN BEST PRACTICE

Once you've worked through the math, build a slide that clearly communicates your TAM, SAM, and SOM with a graphic and a brief summary. Include:

+ A visual of your segments and calculations. Put the table you made in an appendix slide once you get to deeper conversations.
+ Short descriptions of each customer group
+ Dollar values for each market tier
+ A clear citation of your sources
+ A note about your pricing assumptions, if helpful

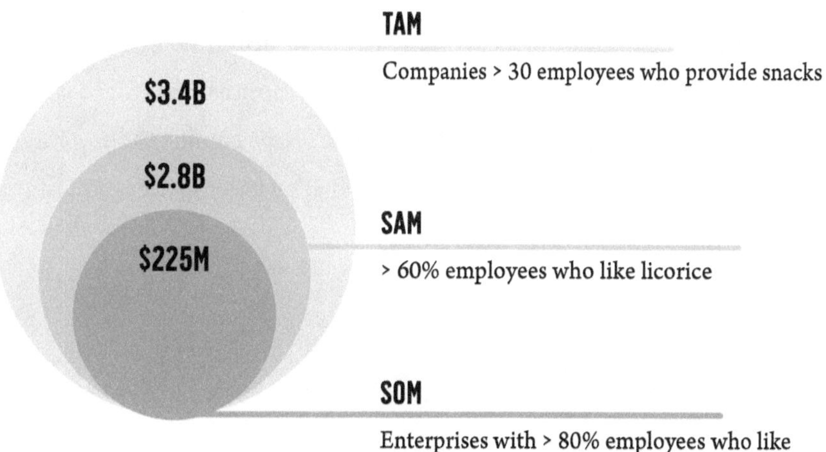

Figure 17.3

EXAMPLE 2: B2C CLOTHING

Let's look at a second example, this time, for a fictional B2C clothing company that sells direct-to-consumer. In this case, segmenting by company size (like we did in the B2B example) wouldn't make any sense. So, we've segmented by age groups of women, which is more relevant for this market. This kind of demographic segmentation is common in consumer businesses.

You'll immediately notice that the number of customers is much higher, but the revenue per customer is much lower. That's typical in B2C models, especially for lower-priced goods like clothing. Unlike high-dollar SaaS licenses, consumer businesses rely on large volumes of customers spending smaller amounts.

You'll also see in table 17.2 that the SAM and SOM percentages are lower, which is completely reasonable. Saying you can reach or convert 90% of women aged 20–39 would be unrealistic. Instead, we're using modest and believable percentages for how many of these potential customers are reachable and likely to buy within the next 12–18 months. That SOM is what they're targeting with their current fundraise. It's large enough to show there's potential but narrow enough to show focus. That's what investors want to see.

EXAMPLE #2: B2C CLOTHING

SEGMENTS	# CUSTOMERS	$ AVG ANNUAL REVENUE/ CUSTOMER	US TAM	% SERVICEABLE	US SAM	% OBTAINABLE	US SOM
Women 20–29	22,023,000	$100	$2.2B	60%	$1.3B	3%	$39.6M
Women 30–39	21,811,000	$70	$1.5B	50%	$763.4M	2%	$15.3M
Women 40–49	20,307,000	$55	$1.1B	40%	$446.8M	1%	$4.5M
TOTAL	64,141,000		$4.8B		$2.5B		$59.4M

Table 17.2

SOURCES FOR SIZING DATA

A big part of making your market size credible is showing that you used solid sources to back up your assumptions. Even if your numbers aren't exact, the logic behind them and where they come from should be clear. Here are some go-to source you can use to gather credible sizing data:[66]

+ **BLS.gov:** The US Bureau of Labor Statistics offers detailed information about industries, businesses, and workforce size.

+ **Census.gov:** A rich source for population data, household income, age demographics, geographic segments, and more.

+ **Industry or trade associations:** Most industries have associations or consortia that publish publicly available reports or summary stats.

+ **Specialty analysts:** Many analyst firms release press briefings, infographics, or summary data from expensive reports. You can often find these by searching news sites or browsing through PRNewswire and other syndication services.

+ **Investor presentations from large incumbents:** Public companies often share slide decks or earnings presentations with excellent market research. These are goldmines and totally fair game to use.

Include your sources in a small-sized font at the bottom of your slide. That builds trust and saves time when you hit diligence later.

---

66   At the time of writing, it is reasonable to wonder whether US government data can still be trusted given the current administration's actions. Federal datasets from agencies like BLS and Census are still among the most rigorous and reliable sources available. They're produced by nonpartisan experts who follow strict statistical standards that don't change administration-to-administration. If you're uneasy, cross-check figures with independent research firms or multiyear historical data.

CROSS-CHECK YOUR ASSUMPTIONS

As you build your bottom-up market size, keep coming back to these questions:

* Are your customer segments mutually exclusive and specific?
* Are the average annual revenue values realistic per segment?
* Are your sources cited and credible?
* Does your SOM reflect what's possible in the next 12–18 months?

When in doubt, share your market size worksheet with your team, advisors, or mentors. Ask for feedback on your logic and numbers. If something feels off to them, take the time to rework it. *The Rest of Us* may be asked to defend our numbers more aggressively, especially if we're targeting a customer base that investors don't intuitively understand. Having clear logic, segmentation, and sources is the best way to own that conversation with confidence.

HOW IT'S DIFFERENT FOR *THE REST OF US*

This is the part of the pitch where we're either dismissed or discredited because the legitimacy and size of the market isn't immediately recognizable to investors. "We don't think the market is big enough" is often code for: "We've never looked at this community or segment as buyers before." This is not your fault, but it is your challenge. Your job is to make the market undeniable. Here are some tips:

* **Use bottom-up math, not top-down headlines:** If you read this chapter, then you already know to do this. It's so important that I'm going to state it again. When your audience isn't familiar

to investors, generic stats (e.g., "Black women spend $x billion annually … ") won't cut it. Start with segmentation and pricing, and build credibility based on your actual business model and go-to-market plan.

+ **Explain why your audience is powerful:** If you're building for plus-size shoppers, neurodivergent professionals, Black teens, single parents, immigrants, or any other particular segment, spell out the spending power, loyalty, and trendsetting influence they hold. Always assume your investor does not know. If you've used the lessons from Part I to find your ideal investor personas and you think they do know, you can always ask them first! I do this all the time with the phrasing, *I never want to assume that someone knows all the information I do; are you familiar with the stats about where venture funding goes?* You'll be surprised how many people want you to say them even if they come from the space.

+ **Ground your TAM/SAM/SOM in your near-term plan:** Especially in consumer or culturally specific businesses, your SOM might look smaller, but smaller is fine if it's focused and realistic. It shows execution readiness and combats the potential interpretation that you lack ambition.

+ **Anticipate scrutiny:** Yes, you'll likely have to defend your assumptions more than others. That's why every segment, source, and revenue model must hold up under pressure. When your market is unfamiliar, clarity becomes your equalizer.

Jenny Rudd, founder of Dispute Buddy, was raising her pre-seed round when a VC fund told her the only thing standing in her way was her market size.

We'd been talking for a while and I said to them one day, 'What's in between now and you making an investment?' And they said, 'We just need to do some calculations of your market size.' I said, 'Okay.'

A few weeks later, they passed on the deal.

They said, 'I'm really sorry. We're not going to invest because your market size is too small.' And I thought, that's so weird.

Dispute Buddy, a platform that extracts evidentiary content from mobile devices for use in legal settings, addresses a global problem. Jenny couldn't believe the fund truly thought the opportunity was small. A year later, her CFO asked to see the VC's market size calculation.

My CFO looked through the spreadsheet they sent through with their workings and said, 'Jenny, they've made a huge error. They added up all of what they think is the potential units you could sell, and then instead of multiplying it by the dollar value, they just entered that number of units as the total market size and put a dollar sign next to it.'

In other words, the investor had miscalculated the total addressable market by orders of magnitude, turning a many billions-of-dollar opportunity into a false few-million one.

I thought, oh my gosh, this is amazing. They'll now invest in me because that was the only thing really in the way.

Jenny approached them with care, giving them time to process the error. She hoped they would acknowledge the mistake and be excited that they could now invest. Particularly as they'd said previously, "If anything changes with your market size, let us know, as we really believe in you as a founder." But they responded with:

> The first thing they said was, 'Well done for finding that error. That's really impressive.' And then they said, 'Yeah, it's not just the number. It was more the feel we had about the market.'

She realized immediately it was all a lie.

> What is the point of doing all this work to calculate market size if you just didn't really feel it?

Market size is often used as a proxy for perceived opportunity, but in early-stage investing, it can also be a stand-in for subjective bias. Investors ask for spreadsheets but make gut decisions. Jenny's story reminds us that:

+ You must calculate your TAM clearly and explain your logic in simple terms.
+ Don't assume investors will do the math correctly, or at all.
+ If your market is misunderstood, ask for their assumptions.
+ Sometimes the "market size" reason is just a polite way to say no.

> They made a mistake, and they never apologized. They wasted my time. I wish they'd just told me up front, 'We aren't feeling it.'

The Rest of Us aren't just proving our businesses are viable; we're expanding the definition of what's considered "investable."

MARKET SIZE SUMMARY

- Your TAM should be aspirational and demonstrate the full future opportunity.
- Your SAM shows you understand the real-world limits on reach.
- Your SOM reflects your realistic short-term sales focus and go-to-market priorities.

This is one of the trickiest slides to get right, but it's also one of the most impressive when done well. You don't need to get every number perfect; you just need to show that you've done the work to understand your market and build a case for its potential.

Up next, it's time to look at where your company fits into the competitive landscape and how to tell that story clearly on a slide.

Market size matters, but it's fuzzy math.

Even experienced investors admit it's "all made up." What matters is showing you can define and frame a credible opportunity that's big enough for growth.

Investors use this slide as a filter.

After seeing how you make money, their next question is, *How big can this get?* This slide is where you prove scale potential.

Bottom-up beats top-down.

Top-down (industry reports, giant numbers) is vague. Bottom-up (your actual customers × realistic pricing × conversion) is specific, actionable, and credible.

Use TAM, SAM, SOM with clarity.

TAM (total potential pie), SAM (your reachable portion), SOM (what you can realistically capture in 12–18 months). This shows you understand both scale and focus.

For *The Rest of Us*, this section is a common excuse for bias.

"We don't think the market is big enough," often really means, "We don't understand your audience." Your job is to close that gap by grounding the math in lived reality and presenting it confidently.

COMPETITION

· **STRENGTH OF DIFFERENTIATION**—Is the solution significantly unique relative to competitors?
· **DEFENSIBILITY**—Are the solution's competitive advantages likely to persist? Are they proprietary or secured?

Your competition slide isn't about proving there's *no* competition, it's about proving that you deeply understand the landscape and where your company fits. It's tempting to say "we have no competition" to show how unique your solution is, but to investors, that's a red flag. It usually signals one of three things:

+ There's no real market.
+ You haven't done your research.
+ Customers aren't paying to solve this problem yet.

Competition means the problem is real and people are paying to solve it; it validates the market. That's a good thing! Your job is to show how you're different, and better. If you are truly defining a new category, consider framing it in this way: *Here's how people try to solve this today, and why it's not working.* Remember, even sliced bread had competition. It was called "bread."

FRAME THE NARRATIVE

Before diving into visuals, start by answering these questions in your own words:

+ What alternatives do customers use today?
+ How do people currently solve this problem?
+ Where do those solutions fall short?
+ Why is now the right time for your solution to win?

Answering these will help you decide what competitors to show, and which benefits to highlight. You're not just comparing features; you're positioning your company.

USE A COMPETITOR TABLE TO SHOW DIFFERENTIATION

There are two common ways to map the competitive landscape: a competitor table (see figure 18.1) and a 2×2 matrix. Both can work, but the table is usually stronger at the early stage because it's clearer, more concrete, and grounded in real customer decision-making.

USE A CUSTOMER-CENTRIC TABLE

	YOUR LOGO	COMPETITOR LOGO	COMPETITOR LOGO	COMPETITOR LOGO	COMPETITOR LOGO
CUSTOMER BENEFIT #1	✓	✗	✗	✓	✗
CUSTOMER BENEFIT #2	✓	✗	✗	✗	✓
CUSTOMER BENEFIT #3	✓	✗	✗	✓	✗
CUSTOMER BENEFIT #4	✓	✓	✗	✓	✓
CUSTOMER BENEFIT #5	✓	✗	✗	✗	✗
CUSTOMER BENEFIT #6	✓	✗	✓	✗	✗

Figure 18.1

When making a table, put your company in the first column. Add 3–5 of your most relevant competitors in the remaining columns. Picture yourself as one of your paying customers:

+ You have a problem and you're evaluating solutions to solve it. What is in your consideration set? These can be other companies or status quo ways of doing things and workarounds that require a behavior change. You can also include indirect competition, like tools or habits that solve the problem in part, even if they weren't designed to. Your competition isn't always obvious or intentional, and it isn't always another company. Sometimes it's spreadsheets, avoidance, manual labor, or one overworked staff member duct-taping a process together. If it's part of how the customer solves their problem today, it belongs in the table.

+ Along the rows, list the customer-facing features, benefits, or outcomes you're weighing to make your decision about which solution to choose. Each row should describe something specific and valuable from a user perspective, not just industry buzzwords. They should represent things a customer would evaluate when choosing a solution. Think in terms of value: provides real-time insight, supports cultural dietary needs, automates administrative tasks, reduces downtime, etc.

+ Then, fill in the chart with checkmarks and *X*'s to show which solutions provide each benefit.

Your column should logically show all checkmarks; that's the point. You've identified what matters most to the customer and built a solution that meets those needs. But no competitor column should be all *X*'s. If nothing in that column solves anything meaningful, it's not really competition, and it signals you haven't researched the landscape. Try to cluster competitors' *X*'s in ways that reveal clear "white space." This helps the investor instantly see where others fall short and where you uniquely deliver value.

Be sure to use the header to make a statement about your differentiation. An example might be: *The only digital platform that combines flexible meal planning and culturally relevant nutrition* or *The first payments solution designed for cross-border micromerchants.* Your table would then show how your competitors miss those key features. Maybe they only offer generic meal plans, don't support cultural dietary needs, or require expensive subscriptions. You define the rows, so make them count.

You can see how nice and glanceable this format is; it's easy to look at this and immediately grasp which companies are in close competition and how they stack up. Another great aspect of the table is that you define the customer features and deliverables that you believe are the greatest value adds. This gives investors a view into how you have defined your offering in a customer-centric way.

WHY TO AVOID THE MATRIX (USUALLY)

The 2×2 matrix (that beloved X/Y grid where somehow everyone ends up "up and to the right," see figure 18.2) is sometimes requested by investors who want to see a broader view of the landscape. It's not wrong to use it, but it's highly subjective and can come off as vague or even performative if not done well.

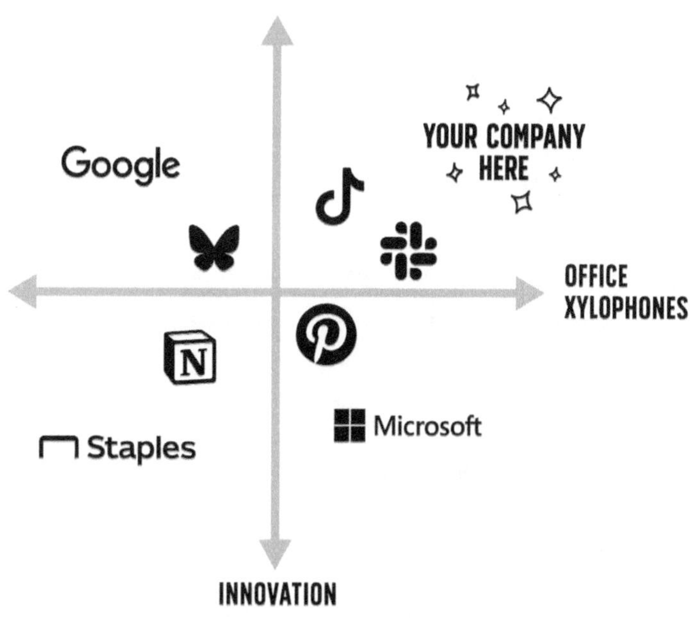

Figure 18.2

If you decide to include one, make sure your axes are clearly labeled and meaningful (e.g., "Affordability" vs. "Specialization," not "Innovation" vs. "Awesomeness"). For example, don't use "AI Sophistication" as an axis unless your users care about that. Be honest about where your competitors land in the quadrants. No one believes you're in a magical quadrant all by yourself unless there's real logic behind it.

If you're thinking, *Wait, how is it that every founder is in the top right?* It's because, spoiler alert: They put themselves there. I hope the message of controlling your narrative is coming through in this book loud and clear, but that doesn't work if the story is easy to pick apart or is based on flights of fancy. This matrix requires the investor to first agree with your framing of the axes, then your selection of competitors, and then your placement of each company. That's a lot of steps—and a lot of room for doubt.

So, if you do use a matrix:

+ Keep it in your appendix unless a specific investor asks for it.
+ Make the axes make sense in the context of your market.
+ Be real about the trade-offs and where companies sit.
+ Don't try to out-clever the slide—just use it to clarify your positioning.

If you're not sure your matrix will hold up under a quick glance and a skeptical eyebrow raise, go with the competitor table instead. It's clearer, more customer-centric, and harder to fudge.

WHAT INVESTORS MEAN BY A *MOAT*

You might have heard the term *moat* tossed around in fundraising. It's investor speak for how your business protects itself from competitors over time. The idea is borrowed from the literal moat around a castle, something that keeps others from easily getting in. In pitch language, it answers: *What's stopping someone else from copying you and winning?*

Some moats are straightforward, like patents or exclusive licenses. Many others are less obvious, especially for founders building in overlooked markets or with novel business models. You may already have a moat, but investors might not recognize it unless you name it clearly. Here are some common types of moats investors look for:

+ **Proprietary technology:** A unique algorithm, product architecture, or system that others can't replicate.

+ **Network effects:** Your solution becomes more valuable as more people use it (think marketplaces or platforms).

+ **Brand loyalty:** Deep trust with a specific user base that's hard to earn.

+ **Switching costs:** It's painful or costly for customers to move away from you.

+ **Distribution advantage:** A sales channel or partnership competitors can't easily access.

+ **Data advantage:** Unique data that compounds in value over time.

+ **Community:** A loyal, engaged community that becomes part of your moat through advocacy and retention.

A moat can absolutely be built on trust with a historically underserved audience, or your lived experience that gives you access others don't have. Those are real barriers to entry. They simply need to be articulated in a way investors intuitively understand. If your advantage isn't a patent or proprietary tech, you might need to translate it into investor language. Here are examples of how to do that explicitly:

- **Community-led moat:** *We've built a 25,000-person community of Black caregivers over five years. Competitors have tried to reach this audience and failed because they don't have the cultural trust or leadership presence we've established.*
- **Data moat:** *Our first 4,000 users generated dataset X that no competitor has access to. This data improves our model accuracy with each use, creating increasing differentiation over time.*
- **Distribution moat:** *We're the only platform with a signed distribution agreement with the three largest clinics in this region. That gives us access to 80% of the market at launch.*
- **Founder-experience moat:** *Most competitors approach this market from the outside. Our lived experience gives us insight into access barriers and customer behavior that others routinely miss. That's why our retention is 3x industry norms.*

When you're talking about defensibility on your competition slide or in conversation:

- Be honest about what gives you staying power.
- Show why your advantage strengthens over time.
- Tie it directly to customer behavior. Why do they choose you, and stay with you, over alternatives?

Now that we've grounded what *defensibility* means in practical terms, let's look at how to communicate differentiation when you're building something outside the standard B2B SaaS template.

HOW IT'S DIFFERENT FOR *THE REST OF US*

If you've ever gotten a blank stare after explaining your product to someone unfamiliar with your customer base, you're not alone. That disconnect is often a reflection of their limited exposure, where investors may not even realize your customers exist or that they spend money in the category you're building for. Bridge that gap without apologizing for it. ***Helping an investor understand a market they aren't familiar with isn't pandering; it's leadership.***

If you're building a solution for a population that's been historically underserved or overlooked, you may need to:

+ Educate investors about your segment's behaviors, spending power, or unmet needs.
+ Include nonobvious competitors, like outdated tools, piecemeal workarounds, or human processes.
+ Emphasize what incumbents don't offer that your target audience really needs, especially if it's about cultural nuance, affordability, accessibility, or trust.

Example: *Our target customer doesn't use the mainstream solution because it doesn't account for X, or it's cost prohibitive. We're the only one solving that pain in a way that is inclusive and accessible.* This helps investors understand not just how you fit in the existing landscape, but why your company is a necessary addition to it.

FINAL TIPS FOR YOUR SLIDE

- Add a header statement that summarizes your differentiation clearly.
- Keep your design glanceable and don't crowd it with too many rows or competitors.
- Always cite your sources if you're using competitor data.
- Think about positioning more than just "better features." You're building a brand, not a checklist.

Ready to move on? After you've shown investors why your company stands out, it's time to talk about why now. Timing is everything, so let's dig into why the market is ready for your company to succeed.

 TAKEAWAYS

Competition is validation.

Saying *we have no competition* is a red flag. It tells investors there's no market, you haven't researched, or customers aren't paying to solve the problem. Competition proves the problem is real and valuable.

Frame the narrative before the visuals.

Start by identifying what alternatives customers use today, how they solve the problem now, where those solutions fall short, and why now is the right time for your solution.

Customer lens > founder lens.

Build your competitor set from the customer's perspective, not your pride in uniqueness. Even the "status quo" (DIY, hacks, habits) is competition.

Competitor tables win.

Tables with customer-facing benefits or features are easier for investors to process than 2×2 matrices. Keep rows specific and tied to real customer value, not jargon.

Moats = future differentiation.

Investors look for how your edge will hold up: IP, network effects, unique partnerships, or cultural insight they can't copy.

19

WHY NOW

· **MARKET READINESS**—Is it an optimal time for this solution to come to market? Is there demonstrated traction?

· **FUNDRAISING RATIONALE**—Is it an appropriate time for the company to be raising capital? Does the valuation reflect current performance and KPI achievement? Is an appropriate amount being raised?

"Why Now" doesn't show up in every pitch framework, but investors are evaluating it constantly. They want to know why *this moment* is the right time for your solution to exist, and why *this stage* is the right time to fund your company. This section often includes two slides.

TWO TYPES OF "WHY NOW"

There are two distinct lenses investors use when assessing timing:

1. **Macro timing: Why is the world ready now?**
   What external forces, like technological advances, shifting consumer behavior, social movements, regulatory changes, or economic trends, are aligning to make this the moment for your solution?

2. **Micro timing: Why are YOU ready now?**
   What traction or progress have you made that makes this the right time to infuse capital and take the business to the next level?

Your "Why Now" section should speak to both. You want investors to feel confident that you're not too early for the market, and not too early in your own journey to put their money to work.

MACRO TIMING: THE WORLD IS READY

Some ideas are objectively great, but they've failed because the timing was wrong, and the market wasn't ready to adopt them. Maybe infrastructure didn't exist yet, or customers weren't ready to change their behavior. Maybe the economy or policy landscape created friction. You want to demonstrate that your solution is riding a tailwind, not pushing uphill into a gust of skepticism.

Ask yourself:

+ What's changed recently that makes your company viable today?
+ Is there a shift in customer behavior that benefits you?

- Has a new policy, platform, or partnership opened the door?
- Is there a cultural or economic "zeitgeist" around your problem?

If you're solving a problem that's been historically overlooked, draw a clear line connecting broader shifts like demand for inclusive tech, ESG momentum, DEI commitments, etc., to your business. ***Show why the market is finally paying attention to something you've known all along.*** This is where you can show a validating quote from an investor, expert, or customer. Sometimes someone else's words make your timing that much more undeniable.

MICRO TIMING: YOU ARE READY

Now it's time to show that you're ready to put capital to good use. You don't need to have everything figured out; you need to show that the progress you've already made gives you a strong foundation to build on.

One of the most effective tools here is a traction timeline. Use a simple chronological format (by month, quarter, or year) to show:

- Major product or service milestones (launches, MVPs, etc.)
- Customer acquisitions or pilots
- Revenue growth (if applicable)
- Partnerships, awards, or press
- Team expansion
- Fundraising activity (grants, accelerators, notable angels, etc.)

So many founders think they're not ready to raise because they don't have revenue, but traction comes in many forms. Investors want to see signs of momentum, clarity of thought, and conviction. Joel Mutua reframes traction as something accessible:

> If I could do it again, I'd focus on traction, but not just revenue. Real traction: knowing your customer, building defensibility, showing proof you can grow. Traction is more than numbers.

Don't cram in every single event in your company's history. Highlight moments that reflect meaningful momentum or significantly increased company value (see figure 19.1). Then show what this round of funding will unlock next. That's what helps investors connect the dots between where you've been and where you're going.

This can be especially powerful if you've done a lot with very little (which, let's face it, is the story for *The Rest of Us*). If you've bootstrapped, crowdfunded, or "seed-strapped" your way to traction, say it proudly! When explained with confidence, it's resourceful and credible and speaks to how far you'll make future money go.

Figure 19.1: Slide from Amanda Drobnis,
Founder & CEO, Hilltop Bio

COMMON MISTAKES TO AVOID

- **Over-indexing on trends?** Pair the trend with a long-term behavior shift.
- **No traction yet?** Use pre-traction proof points like sign-ups, letters of intent, and pilot feedback.
- **No urgency?** Paint a picture of what success looks like in six months, with or without that investor.

This section is what creates fear of missing out (FOMO). It's where you show that your company is inevitable. The customers are ready. The traction is building. With capital, you're about to hit the gas. You aren't begging anyone to get on board because the train is leaving the station, and you're already in the conductor's seat. It's now or never, investor.

This is the part of your pitch that makes investors feel like they'll miss out if they don't act now.

HOW IT'S DIFFERENT FOR *THE REST OF US*

You might be riding a wave investors haven't noticed yet, or one they haven't learned how to value. Timing rooted in social change, access, cultural insight, or community need is real, but it isn't always visible to people outside the ecosystem you serve. This is your moment to make that momentum legible.

Use this section of your pitch to build a sense of urgency around *why you, why this,* and *why now,* even if it's not immediately clear to those outside your community or market. Make the urgency explicit. If investors aren't living your customer's reality, they won't instinctively understand what's unfolding and why this is the moment to act.

Here's how to do that without overexplaining or falling into justification mode:

- **Connect social or cultural shifts to business momentum:** If your audience or market segment is experiencing rising attention, spending, or policy support, show that trajectory and then position your company within it.
- **Highlight your efficiency and traction-to-resource ratio:** If you've built meaningful progress with constrained resources, frame it as a competitive advantage. It demonstrates operational leverage and makes a strong case for what additional capital can accelerate.
- **Turn urgency into opportunity:** Timing isn't a plea, it's a window. Make the case that this is an inflection point for your category and that early investors have a rare chance to participate before the curve steepens.

PUTTING IT TOGETHER

Think of this section as your urgency engine. You're showing investors that the world is ready, and so are you. If they don't move now, they'll miss it.

Timing isn't always meticulously orchestrated. Sometimes you go out to raise because the business is accelerating. Other times, it's because you're being pushed by a board member, a shift in strategy, or a feeling that if you don't move now, the window might close.

That's what happened to Suelin Chen. After bringing on a new investor who joined her board, the focus shifted to speed. She felt pressure to grow the team, increase revenue, and raise again quickly. But Suelin, ever thoughtful and measured, wanted to get the business fundamentals right first. Still, she decided to test the waters by raising a small bridge round of $500,000 to buy time and extend runway.

She didn't expect what happened next.

> It kind of happened accidentally, but worked out like a hack. I got a cold inbound email from a high-net-worth individual who loved what we were doing and offered to invest. That had happened a few times before, and it gave me confidence our platform was resonating with people. So, I said, let's take that check and also try to raise a little more.

That first check of about $150,000 was a spark. Then came another. And another. Before she knew it, she was 80% of the way to her $500,000 target. The round picked up so much momentum they kept raising. And raising. In total, they pulled in $3.6 million through what became a rolling, oversubscribed party round with a mix of funds and angel investors who had some knowledge of the aging space.

> We were overwhelmed with interest, so we just kept bumping up the amount. We were closing more than 50% of investors we pitched. It was wild.

Momentum is contagious, which you can reflect in both your demeanor and your deck. The more people who say yes, the easier it becomes for others to follow, not because the fundamentals have changed, but because the timing and perception have.

No matter how you get there, the "Why Now" story is yours to tell, and you get to define the urgency in terms that are true to your vision.

Timing is everything.

Even brilliant ideas fail if they arrive before the world is ready. Investors want to know why your company needs to exist now and why now is the right moment to put capital into it.

Macro & micro timing.

Macro timing shows external trends (tech shifts, cultural zeitgeist, policy changes, economic momentum) that make this moment ripe for your business. Micro timing shows your traction and progress: what you've accomplished that makes you ready to scale with new funding.

Proof matters more than predictions.

A traction timeline with milestones like product launches, customers, partnerships, and revenue makes your readiness tangible.

For *The Rest of Us*, this section is fuel against bias.

We often hear "we're not sure the market is ready" when really investors are unfamiliar with our communities. Framing timing around real shifts and scrappy proof flips that script. Doing a lot with very little is a credibility signal.

20

GO-TO-MARKET (GTM)

· **CUSTOMER IDENTIFICATION**—Are you familiar with your target customer(s)?

· **PATH TO PURCHASE**—Do you have a clear sense of how to acquire new customers across segments?

· **VALUE CREATION**—How will you retain your customers over time?

This might be one of the most misunderstood sections in a pitch deck, and one of the least clearly explained in the advice founders get. "Go-to-market" (GTM) can mean ten different things depending on who you ask, but what investors are really looking for is the answer to one question:

How will you find your customers, convert them, and keep them?

Your GTM section reduces the investor's fear that you'll struggle to get traction. This is not about proving you'll go viral. It's about showing that you have a thoughtful, realistic plan for identifying, acquiring, and retaining the people or businesses who will pay you. This is typically one slide.

THINK IN PHASES: NOW/NEXT/LATER

I recommend using a Now/Next/Later framework. It helps you stay grounded in the early-stage tactics without losing sight of your long-term ambition.

- **Now:** Your early adopters and your current tactics
  Who are you reaching today, and how are you reaching them? What are you testing? What's working? Early GTM is about validation:
  - Are you finding the right people?
  - Is the messaging landing?
  - Are you doing this quickly and cheaply?

- **Next:** How you scale what's working
  Once you validate something, what will you double down on? Which partnerships, channels, or tools unlock more predictable growth?

- **Later:** Your path to broader reach and exponential scale
  What future channels become viable once you've proven product-market fit? Will you layer in new channels, add sales teams, explore affiliate models, or seek distribution deals?

Investors don't expect you to know every detail now, but they do want to see that your growth ladder is logical.

DON'T JUST LIST CHANNELS—STRATEGIZE THEM

A lot of GTM slides look like this: "social media, paid ads, PR, word of mouth." That's a marketing bingo card. Investors want to know why those channels specifically make sense for your business.

Go a level deeper. Show you've thought about where your audience is and how they make decisions. Instead of "content marketing," say:

> *Our customers are actively searching for solutions on YouTube and Reddit. We're producing short-form educational videos based on keywords from user-generated content, driving low-cost customer discovery.*

That's concrete and shows you understand where your people are and how they behave. A great GTM strategy is about thinking through what you want to happen as a result of what you're doing. For Rajia Abdelaziz, her early channel strategy focused on product-led virality. Her GTM wasn't "press"; it was product-led storytelling amplified by genuine customer advocacy. One of her very first customers turned into a national media moment that put invisaWear on the map, with nearly no marketing spend.

> We develop the technology and bring it to market with an Indiegogo campaign, which brought in $50,000 in revenue.
>
> A couple months later, a young woman went missing in the Boston area and reporters called me asking to do a local story. After seeing the segment, a woman buys one of our necklaces for her niece. A week later, her niece is in a serious car accident; she's trapped in the vehicle and can't reach her phone because it got tossed. But she remembered she had an invisaWear necklace on. She uses our product, and it ends up saving her life by calling for the police and an ambulance.

That was one of our first big success stories. The family called every news station in Boston. They told them, 'This product you aired a story about last week? It saved our daughter's life.'

ABC picked it up nationally. We hadn't even been on the market for a year, and we brought in hundreds of thousands of dollars in sales just from that ABC story about a piece of jewelry saving a young woman's life.

The follow-up coverage broadened our market reach by saying our product was perfect for realtors, college students, and seniors who don't want to wear a big clunky device. I proudly wrote an investor update about it and was able to say we were on track to do a million dollars in our first year, with barely any marketing spend.

Rajia's story highlights what a smart channel strategy can look like when you understand your product's emotional impact and how your customers spread the word. Investors don't expect you to have millions in revenue already, but they do want to see traction that aligns with your GTM approach, and a clear line between your strategy and your outcomes.

ALIGN STRATEGY TO CUSTOMER VALUE

One thing investors will assess is whether your GTM matches your customer lifetime value (CLV).

+ If your customers pay you $5,000/year, a high-touch outbound sales process like reps or industry events might make sense.
+ If your customers pay $50/year, you'll need a low-cost acquisition model, likely product-led growth, SEO, or virality.

Even if you don't have precise customer acquisition cost (CAC) or CLV numbers yet, show that you understand the logic. For example:

Because our average contract value is $18,000/year, we plan to use a targeted outbound strategy with sales development reps (SDRs), supported by LinkedIn Ads and warm intros from early partners.

This shows you understand the math behind the channels you're choosing.

RETENTION IS PART OF ACQUISITION

Customer acquisition doesn't end with the sale. Keeping people engaged and delivering consistent value is a core part of GTM, especially for investors thinking about long-term growth. If you've built anything around onboarding, community, or support, highlight it in this section. For example:

We have a 3-step onboarding process that gets users set up in under 10 minutes, followed by weekly tips and a private Slack community. That's helped us retain 78% of customers over 6 months.

This type of statement tells investors:

+ Your product delivers value quickly.
+ You know how to keep customers engaged.
+ You're thinking beyond the top of the funnel.

HOW IT'S DIFFERENT FOR *THE REST OF US*

You may be using channels or approaches that traditional investors don't immediately recognize as valuable. That doesn't mean your GTM is weak, it means the investors aren't familiar with the ecosystems you operate in. This is where you take control of the narrative.

You might be reaching customers through WhatsApp groups, cultural community networks, diaspora organizations, parent groups, affinity clubs, barbershops, churches, or other deeply trusted, yet often invisible, channels. These are real distribution systems. They're just not the ones that show up in VC blog posts.

Investors won't automatically see the power of those channels unless you spell it out. Not defensively—intentionally.

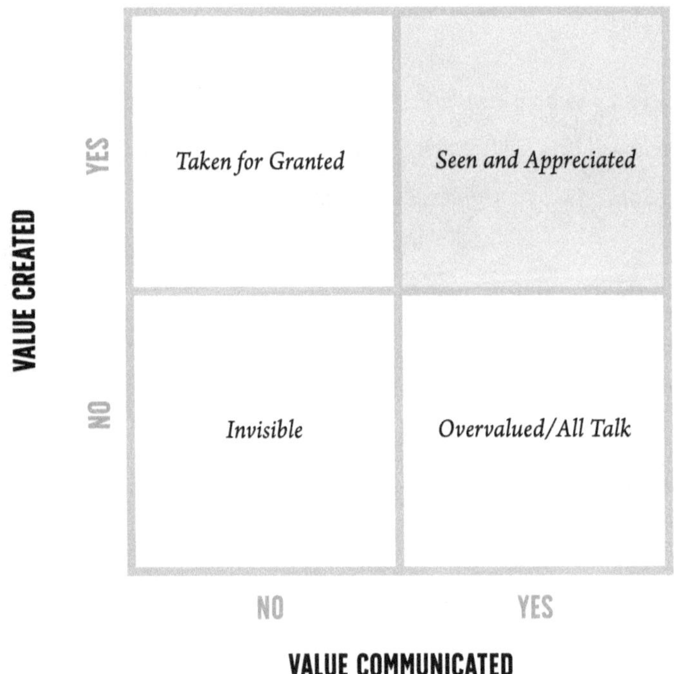

Figure 20.1

To anchor this, let me introduce a lesson I learned early in my career that shaped how I think about GTM and, honestly, how I think about communicating value in general:

Value created remains hidden unless you show it.

My first job out of college was at a boutique management consulting firm. Whenever I overdelivered for a client, I'd proudly march into my boss's office and tell him about the results. He'd look at me, pause, and ask: "Did you tell the client that?"

Then he'd stand up, walk to the whiteboard, and draw a 2×2 matrix (because we were consultants, of course he did). (See figure 20.1.) He'd label one axis "Value Created" and the other "Value Communicated." Then he'd point to the quadrant labeled "Value Created/Not Communicated" and say, "That's where most people accidentally live."

It stuck with me. Value created but not communicated isn't recognized or appreciated, and quickly becomes taken for granted. The same dynamic shows up in your GTM. If your early growth came from WhatsApp referrals in immigrant parent groups, or from church bulletins, student ambassadors, neighborhood leaders, culturally trusted influencers, or a product moment that traveled through your community long before it hit traditional channels, that's not "cute" or "scrappy." It's signal, it's distribution, and it's proof, but investors won't automatically understand what that traction means unless you connect the dots for them.

This is especially true when your audience's buying patterns differ from the ones investors are familiar with. If they've never seen a company grow through barbershops or online groups or community-based onboarding, it's not that your strategy isn't scalable; it's that their own frame of reference is limited.

Sometimes, the gatekeeper isn't the customer at all, but the distribution channel itself. That's the world Elijah Davis had to navigate.

One of the hardest parts was not creating the product; it was getting people to recognize that I was the one who created it. In the cannabis, consumer packaged goods (CPG), and beverage industry, the gatekeepers decide who gets shelf space, who gets distribution, and who gets taken seriously. As a Black man, I learned very quickly that they do not treat everyone the same, even if you have an MBA, emotional intelligence, and creativity.

At trade shows, our booth would be packed with people lining up, grabbing samples, and telling us our products were the best thing on the floor. But when the conversation shifted to business and capital, the energy changed. Instead of asking how they could carry or purchase our brand of products, they would ask, 'Would you white label this for us?' as if I were the manufacturer instead of the founder. As if my innovation somehow belonged under someone else's name.

He had taken all the risks by finding a manufacturer, developing an innovative product, and investing in a brand presence. Still, many potential partners didn't see him as the brand owner. They saw him as a potential supplier for their own ideas. Elijah continued:

That was the pattern. I was early. We created something original. In 2023, we launched Platinum915 CannaShots, the first ready-to-drink, alcohol-free, hemp-derived Delta-9 THC shot on the market. Instead of support, I was intentionally overlooked. Meanwhile, founders from other demographics were given the benefit of the doubt, capital, shelf space, and PR for less innovative products. They were scaling while we could not even get a meeting or a single dollar of support.

Today, two years later, hemp and hemp-derived products generate more than $28 billion dollars. The beverage category I helped pioneer is thriving, while I am still bootstrapping. Platinum915 is starting to receive support, and I am grateful for it. But the truth is, we should have received it then. The products deserved it then. I kept going anyway, and I will keep going. Systemic barriers are real. That is the world we are in, but it does not have to be the world we stay in.

His story illustrates something crucial: your GTM isn't just "marketing." It's how you enter real-world power structures, and sometimes those structures weren't built with you in mind. That's why when you're building your GTM strategy, it's important to:

- Call out any channel friction or gatekeeping that affects access.
- Explain the realities of how your customers find and adopt solutions.
- Highlight how you've already succeeded despite those constraints.
- Frame these challenges as opportunities you know how to navigate, not barriers you're stuck behind.

A resourceful GTM is not a compromise. It's proof that you know how to create demand without privilege, pattern matching, or inherited distribution.

FINAL GTM THOUGHTS

Your GTM strategy doesn't need to be perfect or permanent, but it does need to be intentional. Think like a customer. Speak their language. Show that you know how to find them, earn their trust, and keep them engaged. A brilliant solution doesn't matter if the right people never encounter it or if the person who controls access never lets you through the door.

Your GTM is both a plan for acquiring customers and a window into how you navigate real-world dynamics, including the ones that aren't always designed with you in mind. It shows how you turn insight, resourcefulness, and persistence into momentum.

TAKEAWAYS

GTM is about traction risk.

Investors worry: *Can this founder actually get customers?* Your GTM shows you have a thoughtful approach to identifying, acquiring, and retaining paying users, not just hoping something will go viral.

Think in phases: Now/Next/Later.

+ **Now:** Who are your early adopters, and how are you reaching them today with scrappy, low-cost tactics?
+ **Next:** What channels, partnerships, or tactics will you scale once validated?
+ **Later:** What long-term growth levers unlock exponential reach?

Strategy beats channel lists.

A long list of marketing channels like social, PR, ads, etc. is not a strategy. Show why those channels fit your audience and how you'll use them.

Retention is part of GTM.

Acquisition is only half the job. Keeping customers engaged proves long-term value. Highlight onboarding, community, support, or any stickiness mechanisms you've built.

For *The Rest of Us*, GTM is credibility.

Founders from underestimated groups are often asked, *But how will you find customers?* Your GTM is where you demonstrate that you already know where your people are because you are them or you deeply understand them. Scrappy traction becomes a differentiator, not a weakness.

21

TEAM

REMEMBER

*Don't underestimate your team's value! Early-stage investors typically **bet on people** over initial products.*

*Removing the **risk** that...*

- There isn't founder-market fit
- The solution can't be executed by the people working to build it

- **QUALIFICATION**—Why is the team well positioned to solve the given pain point?
- **EXECUTION CAPABILITY**—Does the team have the skills, knowledge, and/or talent to successfully build the business?
- **BALANCE**—Do team members possess complementary capabilities?

At the early stage, investors aren't betting on your fully baked product. They're betting on you and your ability to execute, adapt, and attract others to the mission. That makes your Team slide a lot more important than many founders realize. Your product will change. Your market might shift. Your go-to-market could pivot. What investors really want to understand is: Why are YOU the right person to lead this company, and who's building alongside you? This is typically one slide.

BOOKEND THE PITCH WITH PEOPLE

In the Core 10 Pitch Framework, you open with your origin story and mission. After walking through the business itself, you close with you again, this time as the CEO who is building the company day by day. It's an intentional narrative to start with purpose and end with proof. Investors meet the human behind the idea and leave with confidence in your ability to turn that idea into a company.

WHAT TO INCLUDE

If you're a first-time founder or someone who doesn't "look like" the archetype investors are used to backing, your lived experience becomes part of your edge. You are often closer to the customer's reality than anyone else in the room. Make that explicit:

As a parent of a child with food allergies, I've lived this problem for five years. That personal experience, combined with my background in supply chain operations, gives me a unique edge in building a better distribution solution.

A strong Team slide helps you demonstrate:

+ **Founder-market fit:** Why you are uniquely suited to this market through your lived experience, background, skills, or motivation. Founder-market fit is the alignment between who you are and the problem you're solving, and it signals to investors that you have the insight and commitment to navigate this space better than anyone else.

+ **Execution capability:** Your team has the operational, technical, or leadership skills needed at this stage. Tie roles to the actual work ahead. Keep it specific and tightly aligned to what your business needs now.

+ **Complementary skills:** You don't need a full team or co-founders, but you should show that you're thinking holistically. Highlight the functions that matter and how you're covering them, even if through fractional support, contractors, or advisors. If you're a solo founder, clarity here is extra important.

If you're worried because you don't have co-founders, please know that you don't need them. Many successful companies start with a solo founder, and investors don't take issue with that. You *do* need to show that you're not building in isolation. Even if your team is your cousin building your site at night and a part-time intern learning as they go—own it.

Investors know that one person can't do everything, so a slide with only your headshot raises questions about capacity and risk. Even if you're pre-revenue or pre-product, show that others are involved. You want to demonstrate that you're building with support, not trying to do it all alone. For mission-driven or social-good companies, the people who show up early signal the strength of your vision. Passion-fueled teams often join early for equity or below-market salaries, and they tend to stay when things get hard because they're building a product with purpose behind it.

One person doing all the things is an execution risk. Showing everyone building with you, in whatever capacity they operate, decreases that risk.

ADVISORS MATTER

If your network doesn't include advisors with startup exits or tech experience, don't be discouraged. What matters is whether the people supporting you bring relevant knowledge and help. An academic, a clinician, a former manager who helps you vet hires—they all count.

You don't need to give bios for every advisor, but you can absolutely include:

+ Logos of relevant employers or institutions.
+ One-liners like "Marketing strategy," "Healthcare policy," or "Technical development."
+ A brief note on how they help, like "Recruits and screens engineers," or "Leads our sales efforts on commission," or "Advises on accessibility testing."

Melissa Wood built her team of advisors from the very beginning, long before fundraising. They're in her pitch deck because they all have industry expertise, recognition, and are tangibly moving the business forward.

> A few of them are mentors of mine along with advisors to the company. They're out there advocating for me, helping me with strategy, and making key introductions.

This is the definition of *builder capital*. People contributing time, energy, and expertise before the company has the resources to hire full-time. It reduces execution risk because it shows you're not building in isolation and you're not waiting for capital to get started. You define what an *advisor* means for you and your company. Maybe your former manager, with whom you maintained a strong relationship, is helping you set up org charts and training processes. Or an engineering lead from a previous job is writing your product requirements documents (PRDs). Those are valid advisors. They show you're not just collecting names, but you're putting people to work.

Don't wait for formal titles or LinkedIn clout—if someone's helping you move faster or smarter, they count.

STRUCTURING THE SLIDE

Keep it scannable (see figure 21.1). You want investors to grasp who's building the company in under ten seconds. A few formats that consistently work:

+ **Name + Role + Logo strip**
  Simple, effective, and space-efficient. In your verbal pitch, layer in the context:
  I spent eight years running clinical ops at a major hospital system …
  Before starting this company, I led sustainability programs for a national CPG brand …

+ **Name + One-line credential + Area of responsibility**
  This keeps everything clean while showing exactly why each person matters.
  Jasmine Chen, 10+ years in edtech curriculum design, leading user research & GTM.
  Luis Ramirez, former head brewer at award-winning craft brewery, overseeing production & supply chain.

- **Advisors section**
  Use smaller headshots or logos plus functional labels.
  Regulatory strategy, Retail distribution, Clinical validation, Food safety, Manufacturing, etc. This works especially well in sectors like healthcare, climate, consumer goods, or regulated services, where domain-specific expertise matters.

Make it clear who is full-time, part-time, fractional, or advisory. Investors want to know who is responsible for execution versus who is lending guidance. The goal isn't to impress them with headcount; it's to show you have the right people in the right seats for this stage.

HOW IT'S DIFFERENT FOR *THE REST OF US*

The Team slide can feel especially fraught when you don't have a co-founder with a big exit or a roster of ex-Google advisors. Your early team might not look like what investors expect to see in "venture-backed" startups. That isn't a weakness; it's context, and it's your opportunity to own the narrative of what credibility looks like.

There's also a real double standard at play. Solo founders from underestimated backgrounds, especially women and founders of color, are often judged through a harsher lens. Building solo can get misread as a lack of momentum rather than a deliberate, strategic, resilient choice. That's why your narrative matters. Show how you're gathering support and assembling people who are skilled and care about the work.

Here are a few ways to take control of the narrative:

- **Reframe proximity as power:** You're closer to the problem, the community, the customer, and the insights. That's founder-market fit, and it's one of the strongest unfair advantages a founder can have.

Header statement calls out specialized expertise

Clear titles

Relevant logos

Friendly pictures

Advisors by function

Short description of fit for the role

Figure 21.1

+ **Show what you've built with what you've had:** Resourcefulness, execution, and traction without big budgets or a stacked team signal grit and capability. Investors take those cues seriously when you frame them clearly.

+ **Redefine advisor value:** The person who deeply understands your customers or your regulatory landscape may be far more valuable than someone with a résumé full of logos. Explain why your advisors matter and how they actively contribute.

+ **Be up front about gaps and how you're addressing them:** Naming gaps is not a liability if you immediately show your plan. *I'm leading product and customer research. I've brought on an advisor with 20 years in healthcare UX to guide accessibility testing. Our next hire will be a part-time dev with HIPAA-compliant systems experience.*

Rajia Abdelaziz modeled this approach brilliantly. She launched her company while still in college, and instead of saying, "I just graduated," she reframed her experience to highlight credibility and commitment:

> Rather than saying I graduated college, I said: 'I just turned down a six-figure offer from Google. I had been a software engineer at Amazon, programming wearable devices and educating C-level executives on Apple Watch technology.'

That framing did three things:

1. Established technical credibility.
2. Positioned a major career sacrifice as skin in the game.
3. Neutralized age bias without hiding anything.

Rajia didn't stop there. She knew that investors would still wonder if a 21-year-old could lead a company. So, she answered the question before they could ask it:

> I have two brothers. One of them was 14 when I first started the company. He's now 22 and he's now invisaWear's COO. He actually 3D printed the first invisaWear when he was 14, and he's the reason we raised our first half a million dollars. My second brother is a year younger than me, and he's the reason we have 3 million followers on social media and bring in 30% of the company's monthly revenue. I literally started joking about it with investors. I'd say, 'Now, you're probably wondering, why would I give a 21-year-old hundreds of thousands of dollars?' Thankfully, I've got an incredible team of advisors and mentors who have all been there, done that.

It worked because she centered competence, conviction, and support without a whisper of deference or an apology.

A great Team slide and story address risk directly. Rajia didn't wait for investors to surface their concerns; she answered them with facts and confidence. As she put it, "It's not just a slide. It really matters what you put on there."

One more truth: Investors often carry unconscious images of what a "strong leader" looks or sounds like. If your leadership style, background, or communication doesn't match that image, you may get read as less capable. You don't need to perform someone else's version of leadership. Instead, articulate how your leadership works, including how you build trust, drive outcomes, and grow your team.

Also, don't undervalue nontraditional advisors. Many of us come from networks without VCs or repeat founders, but we do have clinicians, community leaders, operators, educators, policy experts, or industry veterans who roll up their sleeves for us. Time, sweat, and judgment are real capital and absolutely count.

Finally, if you've ever felt impostor syndrome while building your Team slide because it doesn't look like a startup org chart, you're not alone. Investors don't need pedigree; they need clarity. Show the people and partners who make you effective today. That transparency builds far more confidence than pretending you have a fully built-out team before you're funded.

FINAL THOUGHTS ON YOUR TEAM

Even if you don't have a "dream team" just yet, you can show that you understand what capabilities are needed, are clear about your strengths and gaps, and are actively bringing in the right people to help you grow. That kind of self-awareness and direction builds trust, and at the early stage, trust is everything.

TAKEAWAYS

Investors bet on people, not just products.
At the early stage, your solution may pivot, your GTM may change, but you—your skills, and your ability to attract others—are what investors evaluate.

Your Team slide bookends the story.
The Core 10 Pitch Framework starts with you (mission + origin story) and ends with you again as CEO and builder. It's an intentional arc that begins with purpose and closes with proof.

Founder-market fit is your superpower.
If you don't match the "traditional founder," your lived experience becomes an advantage. It often means you're closer to the customer than anyone else in the room.

A team isn't just co-founders.
Advisors, fractional hires, contractors, and community partners all count. Investors want to know you're not building in isolation.

For *The Rest of Us*, this is where bias cuts both ways.
Investors may expect more proof and polish, but your scrappy support systems like cousins coding at night, part-time interns, and trusted advisors signal resilience, creativity, and the ability to move mountains with limited resources. Reframe them as strengths because they are.

22

WRAPPING IT UP

Ending your pitch with a Thank You slide isn't just a formality; it's your final impression. Whether you're presenting live and this slide sits on the screen during discussion, or an investor is scrolling through your deck at 11:00 p.m. in bed (yes, that really happens), this is what lingers. Make it count.

Your Thank You slide should include:

+ A sincere, human thank-you.
+ Every way someone can contact you: website, email, and social links. Hyperlink them and also spell them out in case the deck is viewed in a non-clickable format.
+ The social platforms where you're active or reachable.
+ Optional asks beyond fundraising—join a newsletter, test the product, or request a specific introduction.

Even if you're sending the deck with no idea who's opening it, keep your sign-off gracious and confident. "Thank you" or "Thanks for your consideration" works, but you can go a little warmer with something like, *Thank you for spending time with our story* or *We appreciate your time.* The best closings sound like you and reinforce your personality or brand. If you can spark a smile, even better; people remember that, and it nudges them toward booking a call.

Here are a few examples for inspiration:

- *We appreciate you spending time with our story. We know your inbox isn't empty.*
- *Thanks for spending time with our deck. We hope it was more compelling than your last Zoom meeting.*
- *If you made it here, thank you. We don't have a surprise prize for the last slide, but we should.*
- *Thanks for meeting us here. We're building something that matters, and your time means a lot.*

Be sincere in your thank-you. That can feel strange when you're not in the room or when someone is watching a recording or scanning slides without you there, but they're still choosing to spend time learning about you and your company. That deserves appreciation.

Remember, you never know what's happening behind the scenes. Just because you don't hear from an investor, it doesn't mean they aren't sharing your pitch with others in their network or keeping tabs on your progress. The importance of your passion and authenticity can't be overstated and a genuine, gracious close can have a lasting impact.

AFTER THE PITCH: FINANCIALS, FUNDRAISING ASK, AND EXIT STRATEGY

Some important topics don't belong in your Core 10 because including them too early can distract from the story your pitch needs to tell.

What *doesn't* go in your Core 10 deck:

+ Detailed financial projections
+ Your fundraising ask (amount, instrument, terms)
+ Your exit strategy

All three matter, and investors will eventually want to see them. They work better in your appendix or as part of a follow-up conversation. Your Core 10 is about earning the next meeting, not answering every question investors might someday ask.

Now let's break down how to handle each of these pieces strategically, especially in the early stage.

1. FINANCIAL PROJECTIONS

Do you need them? Yes.

Do they need to be in your core deck? Usually not.

Do they need to be accurate? Also no (but kind of yes).

Everyone knows early projections are guesses. What matters is the logic behind them. What do you believe will happen? Why? What would need to go right to hit those numbers?

If your projections are in the core presentation, be prepared for investors to zero in and potentially spend too much time there. At the early stage they often raise more questions than they answer. A deep dive into financials can derail the conversation and force you to pull the discussion back to the real goal of earning a second meeting. That's why projections belong in your appendix. They're available if needed, but they don't distract from the narrative.

Financials also include sensitive information you might not want freely circulating. The practical reality is that investors typically won't sign nondisclosure agreements (NDAs) before a first pitch. They see hundreds (if not thousands) of pitches a year across overlapping markets and simply can't keep track of what they're obligated to keep confidential. Signing NDAs for every intro meeting would create legal liability for them and bottleneck their entire pipeline.

If an investor asks about your projections, you can bring up the appendix slide if you like, or say something like: *We have a full model built and are happy to walk you through it during a follow-up conversation.*

The goal of your first pitch is to spark curiosity and schedule another conversation, not to get a check.

If you do include projections, make them believable. I'm not saying your projections should be accurate and represent what's really going to happen because that would mean you can predict the future, in which case, please contact me ASAP, I have some questions for you. Unrealistic or fanciful assumptions that create a chart that looks like a hockey stick just to have one can damage your credibility. If an investor is interested and goes into due diligence, they will likely want to see the full model. If you get to that point and your model is based on ridiculous assumptions or it isn't believable that you can achieve exponential growth in that timeframe, you're just shooting yourself in the foot and wasting your own time.

Highlight things like:

+ 3–5 years of grounded growth scenarios.
+ Revenue, cost of goods sold (COGS), headcount, and major spend categories.
+ Metrics that matter for your business model or go-to-market plan like profit margin, customer acquisition cost (CAC), retention rate, etc.

What's important is the logic behind your numbers. What needs to happen to achieve that growth? What are the assumptions powering your projections? Everyone knows you're making things up with your projections, but *why* do you think this is what might happen? The assumptions behind them are what's more important to explain. Your projections show *how you think*, not what will happen.

2. EXIT STRATEGY

Should you talk about an exit strategy? Like so many things in fundraising: It depends. Shocker, I know.

In most cases, early-stage investors don't expect a detailed exit plan. They want to know you're building something valuable that could be acquired or go public someday, not that you've already picked your acquirer.

There are a few exceptions:

+ Angel groups that explicitly ask for it
+ Verticals where exits are tied to product strategy (e.g., biotech)
+ Corporate VCs that may be eyeing acquisition at the time of early investment

If it's relevant, include it. Otherwise, you can say:

*We're focused on building long-term value and will evaluate strategic paths
as the business matures.*

Translation: I'm not ignoring this, but I'm also not forcing a story just to check a box.

3. THE ASK

This one gets a bit technical, so buckle up (see figure 22.1).

You **cannot** publicly include your fundraising ask in every version of your deck due to general solicitation regulations. If you upload a deck with lines like "We're raising $500K on a SAFE with a $6M cap," and anyone who is not a verified accredited investor can access it, you could unintentionally violate securities rules by soliciting the general public. This means no posting your deck on social platforms like LinkedIn.

This is one of those legal "gotchas" that disproportionately affects under-networked founders who don't have exposure or access to quality fundraising guidance.

So, what do you do?

Put the ask slide in your appendix. When you're sending your deck to a known investor or pitching it live, move it into the core deck, PDF it, send it, then move it back into the appendix. Keeping it out of the core lets you use the pitch for broader purposes without having to worry that you're violating a regulation.

Your ask slide should include:

+ How much you're raising
+ Instrument (SAFE, convertible note, priced round)
+ Key terms (cap, discount, valuation)
+ How you'll use the funds (major buckets and rough percentages)
+ **Most importantly:** the milestones this round unlocks

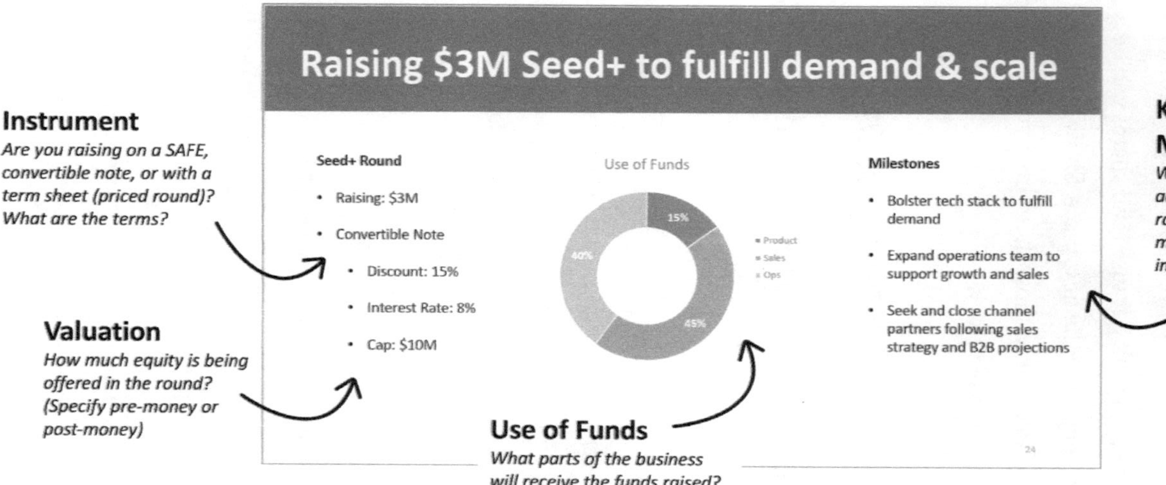
Round Size
How much money are you raising?

Raising $3M Seed+ to fulfill demand & scale

Instrument
Are you raising on a SAFE,
convertible note, or with a
term sheet (priced round)?
What are the terms?

Seed+ Round
• Raising: $3M
• Convertible Note
    • Discount: 15%
    • Interest Rate: 8%
    • Cap: $10M

Valuation
How much equity is being
offered in the round?
(Specify pre-money or
post-money)

Use of Funds
15%
40%
45%
Product
Sales
Ops

Milestones
• Bolster tech stack to fulfill
  demand
• Expand operations team to
  support growth and sales
• Seek and close channel
  partners following sales
  strategy and B2B projections

KPIs / Target
Milestones
What will you be able to
achieve with the capital
raised? How are you
measuring the results of the
investment over time?

Use of Funds
What parts of the business
will receive the funds raised?

Figure 22.1

Investors want to know what their money enables, not just how you'll spend it. That's what turns your raise into an investment opportunity. The purpose of raising is to build more value into the company by achieving milestones you otherwise couldn't or would take too long, so that when you go to raise your next round, you have a higher valuation and everyone who invested early will benefit because their shares will be worth more. Money is the vehicle to get you to the next place. Show investors how spending it will get you there. If you only show them how you're going to spend it, you're not telling the complete story.

HOW IT'S DIFFERENT FOR *THE REST OF US*

This is the final stretch of the pitch, and even though it feels procedural, this is often where bias hits the hardest and founders start to overthink. You may be familiar with the quiet panic of:

+ *I've never made a financial model before. What if they tear it apart, or I did it wrong?*
+ *Exit strategy? I'm just trying to get customers!*
+ *What if I'm asking for too little or too much? I don't want to look like I don't know what I'm doing.*

You are not behind, and you're not alone. You've simply been outside the rooms where these conversations are casually demystified for others. Here's the mindset shift:

+ **Financial projections don't need perfection, just logic:** If you can explain the assumptions behind your numbers, you're doing it right.

+ **Exit strategy isn't required unless it's relevant:** You're allowed to be focused on building, not selling.
+ **Being careful with your Ask slide isn't insecurity, it's legal compliance:** Many investors don't understand solicitation rules; you protecting yourself is professionalism, not tentativeness.

And yes, bias shows up here too. *The Rest of Us* are often grilled harder, questioned more, and expected to have every detail polished. That dynamic isn't fair, but it's precisely why your calm, grounded finish matters. A human thank-you can be the thing that lingers. It can be the moment an investor decides they want to get to know you better.

YOU DID IT!

You made it through all ten sections of your pitch deck! That's no small thing. Many people never even get started.

Pause for a moment.

Take a slow breath in through your nose until your lungs fill with air and then slowly exhale through your mouth until your lungs empty.

Now imagine this: You're about to hit "send" on an email with your pitch deck attached. It's going to someone you deeply admire. An investor whose experience, network, and values feel aligned with what you're building. Maybe they're a dream check, or maybe they're the one who could open a door that's been locked for too long.

You've worked hard on this deck. You've thought intentionally about every slide, every message, every moment of the story you're telling. It's no longer just a collection of stats and opinions; it's a guided journey. A story with a heartbeat.

As the investor opens the deck, they lean in. Your header statements pull them through, each one like a step on a trail, guiding them through your vision. They see the problem and nod, yes, this matters. They reach your solution and raise an eyebrow—interesting. By the time they get to your Why Now slide, they're sitting up straighter.

A question pops into their head, maybe a concern about risk or market fit, but before they even have time to dwell, they see you've addressed it. Not defensively, but thoughtfully. Strategically. They smile. They're starting to believe in your ability to navigate what's ahead.

Slide by slide, you build trust. You connect the dots between opportunity and execution. You turn uncertainty into curiosity, and then into excitement.

When they reach the final Thank You slide, they don't just see a founder. They see a leader and a person with conviction and a personality. They don't just see a pitch. They see a possibility and an urgency to learn more so they don't miss the bus.

Take one more breath.

That's the power of a strong pitch deck.

Your final impression lingers.

The Thank You slide isn't filler, it's your last chance to leave them with warmth, humanity, and professionalism.

Gratitude builds connection.

A sincere, personal closing makes you more memorable. Investors are humans too, and acknowledging their time with warmth signals confidence.

Don't stop at "thanks."

Use the final slide to make it easy for people to act: contact you, follow your work, or support you in ways beyond money like introductions or newsletter sign-ups.

After the pitch comes the real conversation.

Investors will often ask about financials, exit strategy, and the fundraising ask after the Core 10. These may not go in the main deck but should be ready in your appendix.

For *The Rest of Us*, closing strong is a credibility signal.

We sometimes undersell ourselves at the end out of humility or nerves. Ending on a gracious, confident note while making clear, specific asks flips the script from grateful for attention to worth investing in.

23

PITCHING WITH PURPOSE: ADJUSTING YOUR DELIVERY

PRESENTING YOUR PITCH

Your pitch deck is more than a static document. It's a living, breathing tool that can adapt to different settings and audiences. It's designed to introduce your company to investors, but it becomes more powerful when you deliver it. Whether you're pitching on a demo day stage, applying for an accelerator, sitting one-on-one with a potential investor, or recording a video to share, the way you *present* your deck matters as much as what's in it.

Before every pitch, ask yourself this question: **What is my goal for this conversation?**

Goals vary widely. It could be to spark initial interest, get selected, book a second meeting, clarify fit, test a hypothesis, or build a relationship. Once you know what outcome you're aiming for, you can choose the mode of delivery that moves you toward it.

Goals are the outcomes you want. Modes are the way you deliver the message. To make this tangible, I'm anchoring the chapter around three delivery modes you can shift between:

+ **Perform:** Capture attention.
+ **Inform:** Build understanding.
+ **Dive Deep:** Explore nuance and strengthen conviction.

Having names for them helps you prepare deliberately instead of defaulting to one-speed-fits-all pitching.

It's also really helpful to have a general timing rule of thumb. Your presentation should take about one-third of the meeting. The other two-thirds should be dialogue, questions, and connection, which is where trust is established and relationship-building happens. If you present for 15 minutes in a 20-minute meeting, you've left almost no space to build a relationship or understand what the investor cares about. That alone can cost you the follow-up.

PERFORMANCE MODE (1–3 MINUTES PRESENTING)

This is your stage-ready, spotlight-on, make-them-remember-you version of the pitch. Think demo day, competitions, or any highly selective application process where you're one of many voices trying to stand out. If you've ever attended a demo day, pitch competition, or even watched *Shark Tank*, this pitch style will be familiar to you.

Performance-style pitch delivery is typically high-energy and designed to be memorable. Founders are trying to capture the attention of an audience and stand out among other presenters in a live or recorded setting. This style of pitching is also relevant to application processes for accelerators, fellowships, or grants, where a founder is looking to be selected from a pool of other candidates.

Your goal in this delivery mode is to inspire people to find you during networking time, learn more, and exchange contact information.

Performance mode benefits from:

- Vivid imagery (paint a picture in their minds)
- Personal anecdotes
- Memorable turns of phrase
- Confident delivery (even if your heart is pounding and your hands are sweaty)

Unless you love public speaking, you will likely feel awkward and uncomfortable, if not downright terrified. Glossophobia, the fear of public speaking, affects roughly 75% of people and is considered the most common phobia.[67] That's okay. Think of it like stretching a muscle you haven't used before. You're learning to show up in a way that commands space, and that's part of building founder presence.

Now, go ahead and roll your eyes and say, *I don't believe you,* but I was terrified of public speaking most of my life.

My first memory of truly being afraid of presenting was freshman year of high school. Public speaking was a required course, and we had to give a 10-minute instructional presentation on anything we chose. I picked how to bake chocolate chip cookies because I thought it would be easy, and people would be inclined to like it since they'd be thinking about cookies.

I. Bombed. So. Hard.

When I walked to the front of the class my heart was pounding, my face felt hot, which meant it had definitely flushed (ohmywordhowembarrassing), and I had a ringing in my ears. I instantly forgot everything I was going to say and just read the words off the poster I had made, forcing myself to talk and nervously stammer until the 10-minute timer was up.

---

67 Ambitions ABA. "49 Fear of Public Speaking Statistics," February 24, 2025, https://www. ambitionsaba.com/resources/fear-of-public-speaking-statistics.

I had a similar experience in college when it came time to defend my honors thesis, and again when I joined a management consulting firm and was invited to present my work to a client. Heart pounding, hot face, ringing ears.

Then I discovered the secret. Magically, my fear went away and now I even *look forward to and enjoy* being on the professional stage.

I'm going to share this secret with you.

Are you ready?

It's the silver bullet.

The answer to all your fears.

Okay, I'm gonna share it now.

The answer is … **practice**.

Whoa, slow down—don't get mad. This isn't a joke. I *guarantee* that the more you practice, the faster your anxiety will turn into excitement. Presenting is a skill, and as with any skill, you need to put in the work to learn it and get better at it.

Practicing doesn't mean standing alone in your office reading your slides out loud, although that's certainly part of it. It's important to put yourself in uncomfortable situations and pitch in front of a crowd even if you don't "need" to for the business.

Any founder you see pitching from a stage who you find impressive—whose presentation skills you envy—know that they practiced the shit out of it to get that way. You can be like that too.

SAME PITCH, DIFFERENT ROOM

You can deliver a pitch flawlessly. You can rehearse it, refine it, and feel the energy of the audience when it lands just right. But sometimes the problem isn't your performance, it's who's watching it.

Rajia Abdelaziz was invited to give what she thought was a friendly, low-stakes demo pitch. The goal of the event was to educate other entrepreneurs by watching an established founder pitch to a panel of judges.

> We got on stage in front of 200 people. Myself, my co-founder, and a panel of five judges. I thought I was doing something good, giving back to entrepreneurs by showing what a real investor pitch looked like. I opened with the same stats I always use: One in four women are sexually assaulted. I shared that we were on track to hit $1 million in our first year.

Then a male panelist announced, into a microphone, that he'd never heard of women worrying about their safety.

> Before I could even respond, the women in the audience started arguing with him. I said, 'With all due respect, sir, it sounds like the women in the audience disagree.'

Then another judge interrupted the pitch to ask if she and her co-founder were in a romantic relationship.

> He literally said, 'Are you together?' in front of 200 people. When I said no, he announced he would never invest in a company where the co-founders were dating. It was humiliating. I felt like crying.

Despite handling the situation with professionalism and grace, Rajia left the stage feeling demoralized. But the story didn't end there. A few days later, a man who had been in the audience reached out. He'd told his female colleague, a successful founder and investor, what had happened. She had also experienced gender bias while fundraising and was furious about the recounted story, but also curious about invisaWear.

She invited Rajia to pitch again, this time to her all-woman executive team.

> Every single woman in the room shared a personal story about safety. The woman told me she had originally planned to invest up to $500,000. After hearing from her team, she doubled it to $1 million.

Same pitch. Same founder. Entirely different room. Sometimes the difference between rejection and a $1 million check isn't your pitch, but who's listening.

INFORMATION MODE (5-10 MINUTES PRESENTING IN A 30-MINUTE MEETING)

If Performance Mode is about capturing attention, Information Mode is about earning a second conversation. This is the version of your pitch most founders will deliver again and again over Zoom, in conference rooms, across café tables, or in coworking spaces. It's the one where the audience is small, curious, and giving you real time. It can feel calmer and more intimate, but because you're closer to the goal line, it also feels higher stakes.

In this mode, you're not performing, you're teaching. You're walking someone through the architecture of your business with enough clarity and confidence that they leave both informed and intrigued. This is where the Core 10 really works. Each section becomes a stepping stone, building understanding in a deliberate arc.

Your goal here isn't applause. It's continuity. You want the person across from you to say, "I'd like to dig deeper, let's schedule another call." It's important to bear in mind, however, that information isn't received equally.

Some investors want you to walk them through slide by slide without interruption. Others wave off slides entirely and say, "Just talk me through the business." Some flip through the deck faster than you can narrate. You can ask, "What's most helpful for you?" but how you carry the room still matters as much as the facts you're explaining.

For *The Rest of Us*, these meetings can be emotionally exhausting. There's often a layer of silent translation happening underneath the pitch where you're interpreting tone, redirecting subtle dismissals, managing micro-bias, and navigating energy in the room that isn't quite neutral.

Derek Ali remembers this feeling vividly:

> I honestly felt like the process was … they might have looked at me like, 'He's a music guy. He doesn't know what he's doing in tech.' I didn't have the lingo yet. I didn't have all the data they wanted. So sometimes, it felt like they were pivoting the conversation toward my co-founder, who they assumed must be the one who really understood the business.

For someone like Derek, who had reached the top of his field with multiple Grammy wins and albums that defined a generation, this shift into tech came with a harsh psychological reality of not being taken seriously.

> There was a lot of insult, honestly. It was like, 'This guy's not ready yet.' And to a certain extent, I understood. I didn't have experience in tech. But it was discouraging. I'd built a legacy in music and now I was getting dismissed by people who hadn't accomplished anything close to what I had in my field.

That feeling of being talked over, underestimated, or ignored, isn't uncommon in information-mode meetings. It's a form of micro-dismissal: the polite nod, the lack of follow-up questions, the attention given to someone else in the room.

> I started asking myself, am I just shooting myself in the foot every time I take a call? Should I just stay in music and 'stay in my lane'?

But what Derek did next is what separates a founder from everyone else:

> I could either just take these lashings and learn from them, or I could give up. And I decided to get beat down over and over until the timing was right. Every time I got knocked down, I reminded myself, 'You're uncomfortable because you have room to grow.' That's what being a founder is.

This is why modes matter and why your delivery needs to shift with the audience, the moment, and the goal. This is also why the same meeting that once drained you can eventually become the one that funds you because growth happens in the rooms that misunderstand you before it happens in the rooms that back you.

DEEP-DIVE MODE (10+ MINUTES PRESENTING IN A 45+ MINUTE MEETING)

Deep-dive mode is where the real conversations happen. By the time you're here, you're no longer proving you're worth meeting, you're showing you're worth backing. The power dynamic shifts. They're leaning in. They want to understand the inner workings of your business well enough to justify a yes.

These meetings often sit inside the due diligence phase, which means the tone changes too. The curiosity is sharper, the questions more detailed, and the stakes feel heavier.

A deep dive can feel like an interrogation if you aren't prepared for the texture of it. But remember that investors don't ask detailed questions to poke holes. They ask because they're looking for reasons to move forward. This is where you help them cross the bridge from interest to conviction. In deep-dive mode, expect the conversation to stretch across the full anatomy of your business. You're not delivering a linear pitch anymore; you're navigating a live, multidirectional discussion.

You'll likely find yourself:

+ Moving fluidly between your Core 10 and your appendix materials.
+ Talking through technical or domain-specific details, sometimes with specialists the investor brings in specifically to evaluate you.
+ Changing your flow in real time as questions surface, reteaching parts of the story, reframing assumptions, or expanding on choices.
+ Diving deep into the areas that anchor your company's potential like market size, go-to-market machinery, user insight patterns, financial logic, retention dynamics, or product defensibility.

Early in the meeting ask, *What would be most helpful for us to spend time on today?* This does two important things. It sets a collaborative tone instead of a defensive one and it ensures the meeting centers on *their* decision-making path, not your slide order.

You can also set expectations beforehand by sending a short email proposing an agenda or highlighting two or three areas you're ready to explore in depth. Deep-dive meetings work best when both sides know what success looks like. The goal isn't to lecture. It's to co-create understanding.

Think of this mode as moving from "pitching" to "partnering." You're no longer trying to impress someone from across a table. You're working shoulder-to-shoulder with them to determine whether this is a good fit for both of you.

UNDERSTANDING LENGTHS

Pitch length isn't just about time management but intentionally choosing how you'll guide your listener. Different lengths naturally lend themselves to different delivery modes, and each mode opens up different types of goals. The length of the pitch doesn't dictate what you're trying to achieve; it simply shapes the container you're working within.

Here's how pitch length tends to map to the modes you'll draw from:

MATCHING PITCH LENGTH TO MODE AND GOAL

LENGTH	MODE	GOAL
1 minute	Perform	Spark curiosity quickly; create an emotional hook.
3 minutes	Perform	Be memorable, clear, and dynamic; set the tone for deeper dialogue.
5 minutes	Inform	Deliver the full narrative (Core 10) with clarity and flow.
10 minutes	Inform/ Deep Dive	Add details, address early questions, and build conviction.
20+ minutes	Deep Dive	Customize heavily for an investment decision; co-pilot the discussion.

Table 23.1

The key is not to memorize these as fixed rules, but to recognize how each length shapes what you can reasonably accomplish and how to choose the mode that supports your intent.

THE ONE-MINUTE PITCH (AKA THE ELEVATOR PITCH)

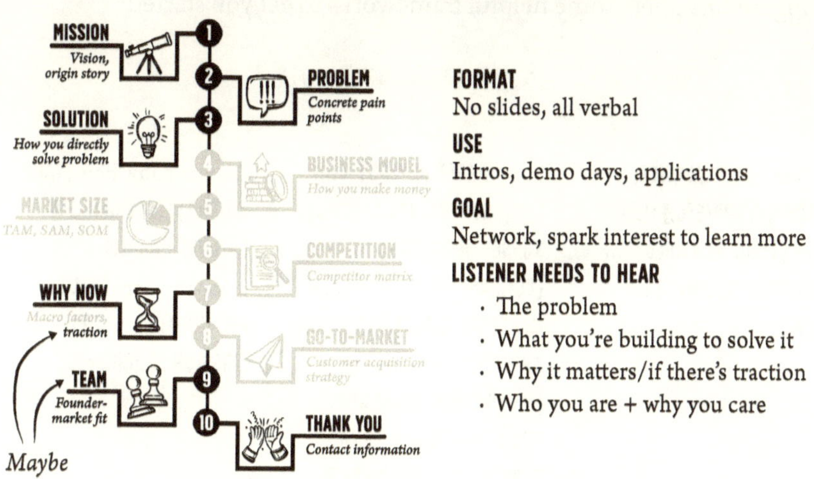

Figure 23.1

Despite being the shortest pitch you'll ever give, the one-minute version is often the hardest to get right. You're distilling your entire company into a handful of sentences (see figure 23.1). But the goal here is simple: spark enough excitement that someone wants to keep talking with you.

A strong one-minute pitch communicates:

+ A one-line summary of what your company does
+ Why it matters

+ One or two compelling facts (traction, impact, or market size)
+ Your "why," the emotional or personal anchor for your work

You rarely have visuals in this format (maybe one slide if you're lucky). That means your words have to paint the picture. Lean into moments of pain, transformation, or analogy. You're not trying to give someone the whole story; you're trying to give them a reason to *want* the whole story.

Figure 23.2 offers some helpful frameworks to get you started:

COMMON STARTING POINTS

We are a **[TOOL/DEVICE/PLATFORM/APP/ETC.]** that does **[VALUE PROVIDED]** for **[CUSTOMER SEGMENT]** by **[HOW]**.

For **[TARGET BUYERS]** who are **[SEGMENT/KEY ATTRIBUTE SUBSET OF BUYERS]**, **[COMPANY NAME]** provides the **[TOOL/DEVICE/PLATFORM/APP/ETC.]** with/that **[DISTINCTION/WHAT SETS YOU APART]** because of **[PROOF YOUR DISTINCTION IS LEGIT]**.

Do you know how **[TARGET BUYERS]** **[EXPERIENCE A SPECIFIC PROBLEM]**? Our company does **[VALUE PROVIDED]** by **[HOW]** so that **[MISSION IS ACHIEVED]**.

Figure 23.2

Across all the frameworks and templates people teach, one theme stays consistent: the "why this matters" moment arrives early. You don't have enough time to cover everything, so lead with what differentiates you or what emotionally hooks your listener.

THE THREE-MINUTE PITCH

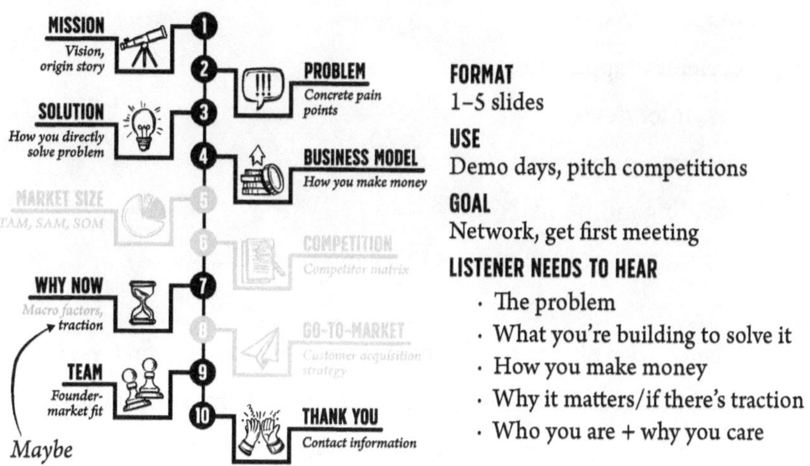

Figure 23.3

A three-minute pitch follows the same structure as the one-minute pitch, but with just enough breathing room to expand on a few critical elements (see figure 23.3). It's still in the performance family with high energy, but you have more space to add nuance.

You can typically include:

+ A quick overview of your business model.
+ A brief introduction to your team (beyond just yourself).
+ Slides that support your narrative rather than complicate it.

Even with this "extra" time, three minutes flies by. It's shockingly easy to overstuff this format. Choose visuals that make your point faster and avoid visuals that invite new questions you won't have time to answer. Even if you don't think you'll ever need a three-minute pitch, having one in your back pocket is a gift to your company because it becomes a Swiss Army knife for:

+ competitions
+ accelerator applications
+ press interviews
+ partnership conversations
+ recruiting moments
+ anytime you need to make a sharp impression fast

Performance-style pitching will almost always feel strange at first, especially if you're used to more conversational interactions with investors. Discomfort is totally normal here. Performance skills and conversational skills are different muscles, and founders grow both over time.

THE FIVE-MINUTE PITCH (AKA THE CORE PITCH)

5 MINUTE PITCH: YOUR CORE PITCH

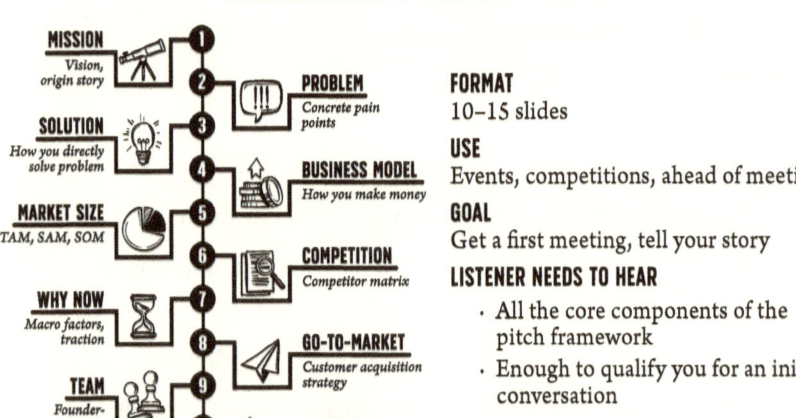

Figure 23.4

This is the pitch you'll use the most. Five minutes is enough time to walk through the full Core 10 and still leave space for questions. It lives in the inform mode, but you can layer in performance energy depending on the setting.

The biggest mistake founders make here is rushing to cram in every detail. Five minutes forces discipline. Remember: clarity over completeness.

10-MINUTE AND 20-MINUTE PITCHES

20-MINUTE PITCH: MAKE THE MOST OUT OF MORE TIME

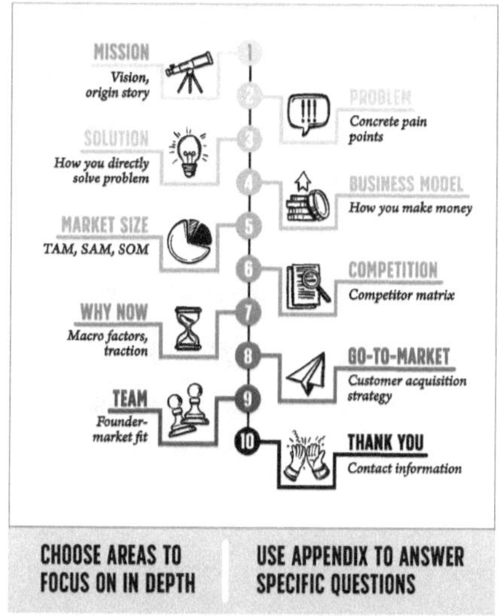

FORMAT
~30 slides, including financials + ask

USE
Meeting 2+ w/ prospective investor

GOAL
Consideration for investment

LISTENER NEEDS TO HEAR
- A review of the core pitch (unless they indicate otherwise)
- More detail to help answer their questions—remember, to uncover their needs and interests, you'll want to ask questions, too!

Figure 23.5

Once you're in deeper conversations, your pitch becomes a dialogue tool rather than a scripted performance.

A 10-minute pitch gives you space to:

+ Explain technical or operational mechanics.

+ Illuminate customer personas.

+ Articulate deeper GTM logic.

+ Proactively address questions you know always come up.

It's also where you begin tailoring your pitch to the specific listener's curiosities or concerns. The follow-up questions you've been getting serve as clues: What consistently needs more context? What consistently excites people? Use your extra time there.

Twenty minutes or more? You're no longer presenting a pitch; you're co-piloting an investment decision. A pitch that is delivered over twenty minutes or more will typically be a highly bespoke session aimed at helping a potential investor learn what they need to make an investment decision. Though you may briefly touch on each of the aspects of your core pitch, it's also entirely possible that the listener will indicate that they want to spend time diving deeper into specific sections. Longer pitches are also where leveraging your appendix may come into play. Often, more granular questions can be addressed by specific appendix slides, which also showcases your preparation and expertise.

Since these longer calls or meetings are typically aimed at addressing the individual investor's particular questions, it's important to understand what they care about. Put your listener first by inviting them to share what's most interesting to them or where they'd like to spend the most time during the discussion. By tailoring the pitch to the potential investor's needs, you'll make it easier for them to reach a final investment decision on your company and show that you respect their time. While it may seem counterintuitive to begin a pitch by asking questions, getting into the habit of tuning in to your listener will help you focus the discussion on the points that matter most.

CONFIDENT FUNDRAISING LANGUAGE (SAY THIS, NOT THAT)

Investors are always listening for subtext. They're not just hearing your words, they're interpreting what those words imply about your confidence, your readiness, and whether you see yourself as someone building a venture-scale company. That means the language you use matters. A lot.

We can slip into certain phrases out of humility, politeness, or self-protection and unintentionally frame our pitch as a request for help, rather than as an investment opportunity. Words like *hope, need*, or *try* drift into a charity narrative, as if you're seeking support for a cause instead of offering someone a chance to buy equity in a company designed to grow in value.

Fundraising is not philanthropy. I mean, unless you're running a non-profit, then it is, but that's not what we're talking about here. You are selling ownership in an asset that you expect will be worth more in the future. Your language should reflect that.

COMMON PHRASES TO REFRAME

INSTEAD OF...	TRY...
We hope to raise …	We are raising …
We need funding to …	With this funding, we will …
We think this could be big.	We know this is a $X billion market and we are positioned to capture it.
We want to …	Our next milestone is …
We believe this will work.	Here's the traction proving it's working.
We're trying to …	We are …

Table 23.2

These shifts aren't about posturing or bravado, but speaking in the language of the environment you're in.

HOW IT'S DIFFERENT FOR *THE REST OF US*

How you show up in the room (or Zoom) is judged before you even say a word. If you're an underestimated founder, whether that's based on your race, gender, age, location, accent, education, disability, industry background, or simply not being a carbon copy of every other founder they've funded, your delivery becomes more than communication. It becomes perception management. An unfair but familiar reality.

While some founders can show up in a hoodie and "wing it," many of us don't get that grace, nor would it represent our character or identity. Still, we can find ourselves in a no-win situation:

+ Our polish is misread as lacking grit.
+ Our passion gets labeled "emotional."
+ Our confidence reads as arrogance, or worse, as "trying too hard."

So yeah, how you pitch matters. It matters in ways that feel like they shouldn't … but do.

Adjusting your delivery doesn't mean becoming someone else, but rather learning to dial parts of yourself up or down strategically, depending on the room, while staying true to your voice. This is precisely where many underestimated founders shine! We've been navigating this kind of audience awareness our whole lives. We've had to be excellent storytellers, compelling communicators, and sharp observers just to be taken seriously. As with many things I point out in this book, that isn't a weakness; it's a skill set. You're already more practiced than you think.

What makes this particularly tricky is that the most visible pitch environments like demo days and competitions, weren't designed to accommodate nuance. High-energy performance-style pitching rewards flash over depth. Short-form pitches are often hostile to complex business models, underserved markets, or products grounded in cultural insight, trauma, or community care. You often have to fight twice as hard to be heard. What's new, amiright? But we're here to win anyway.

PERCEPTION TRAPS TO WATCH FOR

These traps have nothing to do with your actual capability and everything to do with investor bias. Being aware of them helps you stay grounded in your delivery rather than internalizing someone else's projections. Here's what to watch for and how to reclaim the narrative when it happens.

PERCEPTION TRAP	WHAT THEY MIGHT THINK	HOW TO REFRAME OR RESPOND
Calm Delivery	"Lacks passion"	Tie in *why* it matters to you with personal motivation (your origin story).
Confident Delivery	"Too aggressive"	Anchor confidence in *data* or *mission-driven* language.
Detailed Explanations	"Too complex"	Use analogies or metaphors to simplify without dumbing it down.

PERCEPTION TRAP	WHAT THEY MIGHT THINK	HOW TO REFRAME OR RESPOND
Less Polished Visuals	"Not investable"	Highlight traction, progress, and resourcefulness. Leverage sites like Canva.
Formal Tone or Attire	"Too corporate"	Wear clothes you find comfortable and representative and speak in your natural language and tone.

Table 23.3

DELIVERY MYTHS BUSTED

A quick debunking of the advice that doesn't apply equally to all founders.

MYTH	REALITY FOR US
"Just be yourself"	You can be yourself, and also strategic. They're not mutually exclusive.
"They care more about the idea"	They care about *you*, and they will read you differently based on bias.
"You don't need to rehearse"	If you're underestimated, you're scrutinized more. Preparation is power.
"It's just a casual chat"	Informal settings still carry judgment. Show up like it matters, because it does.
"The best pitch always wins"	Nope. The most *relatable* pitch often wins. You have to build the bridge.

Table 23.4

You are not here to contort yourself to fit someone else's template of what a "founder" should sound like. You're here to reshape that template by honoring your voice, your story, and your strategy. Mastering delivery isn't about performing a character; it's about amplifying your clarity and presence so that, whether you're on stage, in a boardroom, or across a tiny coffee shop table, you walk in knowing you can own the moment. When you pitch from that place, you're not performing at all, you're connecting, and connection is what gets people to say yes.

The deck isn't the pitch, you are.
Your slides are a guide; your delivery determines whether investors feel your conviction.

Every pitch has a purpose.
Before any meeting, ask: What's my goal for this conversation? Tailor your delivery, not just your slides, to that goal.

Three delivery modes matter.
+ **Perform:** Short, high-energy, designed to be memorable (demo days, competitions).
+ **Inform:** Balanced and clear, focused on building understanding (1:1 meetings, investor intros).
+ **Dive Deep:** Collaborative, detail-oriented, showing conviction and expertise (follow-ups, diligence).

Leave room for dialogue.
Presenting should only take ~1/3 of the meeting time. The other ~2/3 is where trust is built through conversation.

For *The Rest of Us*, performance anxiety is real, but not fatal.
Public speaking fears are normal. What matters is practicing delivery until you show confidence, even if you don't feel it. Presence is a muscle you build.

Bias shows up in the room, not the slides.

We are often judged more on tone, confidence, and delivery than privileged peers. Knowing this isn't fair, but preparing for it, helps level the playing field.

24

RUNNING THE MEETING: ADAPTING TO INVESTOR PREFERENCES

You've practiced your pitch. You've tailored your delivery for the setting. Now comes the part you can't fully script: the meeting itself.

Even if you've delivered the same pitch a hundred times, every investor meeting has its own rhythm. People bring different personalities, preferences, experience levels, and expectations into the room. Some investors love structure. Some thrive on open conversation. Some want you to drive; others want to grab the wheel immediately.

If you're newer to fundraising or simply used to settings where expectations are explicit, this unpredictability can feel intimidating. But you don't have to guess! You can show up as yourself and steer with empathy. Investors are often just as nervous—especially angels, part-time investors, or people who are "angel curious" but early in their journey. They're trying to look competent too.

I recently spoke with someone who wanted to start angel investing. She had watched the founder's pitch video, reviewed the deck, and already taken a first meeting. Still, she said:

> I don't know what else to ask … and I don't want to look like an idiot.

I talk to a lot of people who are interested in angel investing but hesitate to act. They're smart, accomplished, and financially ready, but unsure how to engage in a meaningful way. They're afraid of asking the wrong question. Or sounding inexperienced. Or wasting a founder's time. Founders often assume these investors know how to evaluate their opportunity, and when a check doesn't come through, they take it as a sign of misalignment or lack of conviction.

The reality is often that they just don't know how to talk to each other. Founders aren't taught how to build relationships with first-time or nontraditional investors. Investors aren't taught how to build trust with early-stage founders.

This chapter is about how to navigate that dynamic. We'll look at common meeting formats, how to prepare for each, and how to gently guide the conversation in a way that works for you. You'll also learn how to handle one of the most hotly debated questions in fundraising: should you send your deck ahead of time?

The more meetings you take, the more you'll notice a pattern: investors aren't just evaluating your business, they're evaluating what it's like to work with you. The ability to adapt while staying grounded in your own communication style is one of the most powerful signals you can send.

Let's get into how to do that.

COMMON MEETING FORMATS (AND HOW TO PREPARE)

Investor meetings tend to fall into a few recognizable patterns, especially when you have 5–10 minutes to present. The format may shift mid-conversation, but knowing the common modes will help you adapt without scrambling.

Before we break them down, here are a few universal truths:

TIPS FOR ANY FORMAT

+ Have your deck open and ready even if they say, "No slides." Investors often change their mind once they realize visuals help them anchor your story.

+ Know your traction and key numbers. Investors often jump straight to them, even if it's not where you planned to start.

+ Be ready to share your screen or send the deck quickly, which means closing tabs and silencing notifications so you don't reveal more than you intend.

+ Have short summaries of each Core 10 section prepared. Some meetings end up time-compressed, and you want to be able to land your message even if the format shifts.

1. "SHOW ME YOUR PITCH"—FULL PRESENTATION FIRST

This is the classic. The investor wants you to walk them through your deck from start to finish with minimal interruption. They'll hold their questions until the end.

This is your cleanest path to delivering your Core 10 exactly as intended. Your narrative arc stays intact, and you get to build conviction slide by slide. Prepare by:

+ **Knowing your transitions cold:** You should be able to move from Problem → Solution → Market with smooth, intentional pivots.
+ **Keeping slides anchored in one main point (your header statement):** This ensures the investor isn't reading ahead or getting lost in details while you're speaking.
+ **Practicing more than you think you need:** When you're nervous, you talk faster, skip key lines, or wander into tangents. Repetition guards against that.
+ **Having appendix slides ready:** Anything technical, nuanced, or math-heavy should live there so you can pull it up on demand without cluttering the main story.

This format works in your favor when you want a clean, uninterrupted narrative, especially if your story benefits from strong pacing and emotional or logical buildup.

2. "LET'S JUST CHAT"—NO DECK AT ALL

Sometimes an investor opens with, "We don't need the deck, just tell me what you're working on." If you weren't expecting it, it can feel destabilizing. But it's honestly often the best format. It's personal, conversational, and gives the investor a sense of you separate from the visuals.

Prepare by:

+ **Having your one-minute and three-minute versions ready:** These become your narrative spine.

+ **Creating a "deckless outline":** Use your sentence headers from the Core 10 as talking points:
  - *Mission/Origin → Problem → Solution → Business Model → Market Size → Why Now → Competition → GTM → Team → Thank You.* These anchor you even when you're not clicking through slides.

+ **Being ready to say, "Happy to send the deck afterward"** so they don't feel like they're missing anything.

This format also lets you learn about them. Pay attention to their reactions, their questions, what they latch onto, and how they communicate. And yes, this is absolutely a moment where founders should ask questions, too. You don't need a full investor diligence questionnaire here, but you can gently probe:

+ "What drew you to take the meeting?"
+ "How do you typically support founders post-investment?"
+ "What kinds of companies or markets do you feel you understand best?"

Think of it as a mutual vibe check, not an interview.

3. "LET'S GO THROUGH THE DECK TOGETHER"—INTERACTIVE REVIEW

This format has become increasingly common, especially on Zoom. The investor either opens the deck on their end or asks you to share your screen so you can walk through it together. They'll pause to ask questions as they go. Prepare by:

+ **Knowing which slides tend to trigger questions.**
+ **Practicing your narrative with interruptions built in:** You should be able to resume cleanly after a detour.

- **Feeling comfortable jumping ahead or circling back based on where their curiosity leads:** This flexibility signals confidence and mastery.
- **Having your bank of appendix slides ready to pull up** if they help in the flow of conversation.

Interactive reviews can feel chaotic, but they're almost always a positive sign. Curiosity is engagement and engagement is interest. Just keep the tone conversational, focused, and positive, even if the questions start piling up.

GUIDING THE FORMAT WITH CONFIDENCE AND KINDNESS

You don't always have to wait for the investor to dictate the flow. If you've practiced a particular structure or want to keep the meeting clean, it's completely appropriate to suggest a format.

You might say:

- *I have a short version of my deck I'd love to walk you through. It's about 6 minutes and gives the full picture. Then we can spend the rest of the time on discussion and questions. Does that sound good to you?*
- *I'm happy to talk through this conversationally or walk you through my slides, whatever you prefer. Is there a format that works best for you?*
- *I've found it helpful to start with a quick walk-through of the deck to set context, then dive into the parts that are most interesting to you. Does that work for you?*

The key here is offering rather than insisting. Investors will appreciate your proactive approach, and it shows you're thoughtful and organized.

SHOULD YOU SEND YOUR DECK AHEAD OF TIME?

Ah, the age-old question founders love to debate: *Do I send my deck before the meeting or hold it until we're face-to-face?* There's no "right" answer, but there's a thoughtful, strategic way to approach the decision.

Founders often worry that sending the deck early means losing control of the narrative. Someone could skim it in under three minutes (which is the industry average), make a snap judgment, and silently pass. Yes, that happens. But withholding the deck doesn't guarantee a better outcome either. Some investors interpret it as friction, or worse, as a sign you're unprepared. If your goal is to build trust, making access difficult can send the wrong signal.

So the real question isn't *if* you should send it. It's *why* they're asking and what version you send.

KNOW YOUR WHY

When an investor asks for your deck, pause and consider the intent behind the request. Are they:

+ Trying to prep for the meeting? Great. They want to show up informed.
+ Screening for whether to take the meeting? Still fair—they're busy and need context.
+ Passing the deck to an associate? Very normal, and common at funds. Just remember the associate becomes your first audience.
+ Avoiding a meeting entirely? Here, think twice. Not every request earns your materials.

Understanding why they want the deck lets you respond collaboratively but also protect your story.

A BALANCED APPROACH: SEND THE DECK, KEEP THE STORY

If an investor asks for your deck ahead of a meeting, I recommend sending it, but a version that keeps you in control of your narrative.

+ **Send a streamlined version:** Strip out anything that relies heavily on your voice to make sense like deep product architecture, financials, or dense appendix materials. Send the Core 10 only and leave the nuance for the conversation.

+ **Pair it with a short video:** This is where you can really shine. A simple, authentic video of your origin story, a minute of context, or you walking through the high-level narrative carries your energy, credibility, and clarity in a way a deck never will. (We'll get into how to create a strong video pitch in Chapter 26, but for now, know that it's a powerful complement to your slides.)

+ **Frame expectations in the email:** A gentle guide helps them read the deck the way you want them to: *Here's a high-level version of our deck and a short video for context. I'd love to walk you through the full narrative and answer questions live.* This positions you as thoughtful, prepared, and in control.

This approach keeps you in control of your narrative while respecting the investor's time and preferences. It also shows that you're thoughtful, prepared, and confident.

WHEN YOU SHOULDN'T SEND IT

You're not obligated to send your deck just because someone asked. You can, and should, hold back when:

- You're concerned the deck will be misinterpreted without your voice.
- The investor feels transactional or dismissive.
- The request feels like a filter rather than the start of a relationship.
- You simply don't trust the context or intent.

Here's a warm, confident way to decline:

I find the narrative is much clearer when I can walk you through it. Happy to send the deck afterward for reference.

If someone refuses to meet without seeing the deck first, especially early in the relationship, ask yourself whether that's a partner you want. As underestimated founders, we are too often forced into proving ourselves before anyone even shows up. You deserve an investor who values engaging with you, not just scanning your slides.

HOW IT'S DIFFERENT FOR *THE REST OF US*

Investor meetings often come with an added layer of performance, whether anyone acknowledges it or not. You're pitching through a filter of bias and unfamiliarity, and you may not be given the benefit of the doubt that others receive automatically.

Here's what that means in practice:

You might feel pressure to overprepare, but also not come off too polished. To be confident, but not *too confident*. To be personable, but not overly casual. This balancing act isn't in your head; it's a very real survival skill for founders navigating rooms not built with them in mind.

When I was fundraising $10 million for my last company, I had to make a snap decision at the start of every pitch meeting: *Do I talk about my kids, or not?*

When you're a woman, you're judged at every age, so you often need to decide what's the lesser risk based on who's in the room. I look younger than I am, so when I didn't bring up my kids, I was usually called "young lady" and perceived as determined but inexperienced. When I did mention my kids, I was no longer too young, but now I was a mom, and therefore risky because my family obligations would supposedly be prioritized. I have yet to meet a dad who has to weigh that calculus while fundraising.

Julie Moir Messervy shared how age bias shows up differently, but just as persistently:

> I'm exactly of the generation when women started working outside the home. I am 74, and, long ago, I had to fight my parents to even attend graduate school. When I became a mom, daycare barely existed; we had to create it. I had to learn to step outside of my comfort zone and my family system to promote myself and bring my ideas into the world.
>
> How I approach my age depends on who I'm talking to. I know it can introduce perceived risk, so I've built a team that offsets that for investors. My VC partner and COO are both in their 40s. One is a Black man; one is a white man. I'm a woman, and the rest of my team are all women, including our head of marketing and design. I feel like I have a dream team. We just have to keep going, and keeping going is the hard part.

Suelin Chen shared how bias showed up while she fundraised through two pregnancies:

When I was pregnant, besides the very first angel who wrote a check, nobody wanted to invest. But as soon as the baby was out and I was back on email, people felt comfortable that I was okay and back to work. My experience of being pregnant was that I was basically invisible to the business world. They only see your belly, and they don't see you as a competent business person.

I remember once being at a CEO event put on by one of my institutional investors, and I was *really* pregnant. I was chatting about my business with this very experienced executive coach who said, 'Just remember the most important thing …' and in my head I was thinking, *Oh, is it about the team? Prioritization? Leadership?*

Then he patted my belly and said, ' … take care of this baby.'

This was at a business event! It was so weird and invasive. It felt like a microaggression because all of a sudden, you realize you're not being perceived as a CEO the way everyone else is. You're just a walking incubator.

Bias also doesn't always look like aggression or exclusion. Sometimes it shows up in the form of surprise, and that can be just as revealing.

These stories reveal how deeply ingrained stereotypes, even among professional investors who work closely with you, can shape perception without people realizing it. It also shows how praise can carry a double edge when it's rooted in assumptions that don't represent your identity or character.

When someone tells you, *I didn't expect you to be so confident,* or *You're actually really strategic,* underneath is an assumption that you wouldn't be. The moment you defy that expectation, you expose it.

Earlier in the book, we heard Jenny Rudd's story about a venture fund walking away from her deal, citing a market size that was "too small." After months of conversations, multiple meetings, and even an investment commit-tee review, she thought she was close to closing. Instead, she was dismissed.

Later, her CFO discovered that the VC had made a basic error in their calculations. They had entered the number of units Dispute Buddy could sell as if that number was the dollar value of the market. They had reduced a billion-dollar opportunity to a few million.

When Jenny explained the error, there was no apology or accountability. The investors didn't own their mistake. Perhaps worst of all, they didn't acknowledge the time she'd spent or the reputational damage of having a VC out in the ecosystem calling her market small.

So, Jenny made a decision.

> I went back to them about a week later and said, 'Hey, look, I've had a think about it, and I just don't think that we're the right fit for investment, so thanks very much. If you'd like some feedback on my decision, let me know.'

The VC replied with a vague, friendly brush-off.

> 'We love you. We love what you're about. We love how you operate. Thanks.' And that was it.

Jenny took back control of the narrative. She exited on her terms with grace, clarity, and strength.

> I've lost so much respect for them. They can't own their own mistakes. They're not telling the truth about how they make decisions. They wasted my time. I wish they'd just told me right at the beginning: We don't feel this is for us.

REFRAMING QUESTIONS TO CONTROL THE NARRATIVE

Even as more women and diverse investors become angels, bias still shows up, especially in the questions founders get asked.

Research shows a clear pattern:

* Men are asked *promotion-based* questions: "How will you become a billion-dollar company?"
* Women are asked *prevention-based* questions: "How will you stop competitors from overtaking you?"

Prevention-based questions often push founders into defensive, risk-minimizing answers, which leads investors to perceive the business as less ambitious, even when it's equally strong. The best way to counter this is to reframe the question.

A simple response framework is:

* "That's a great question. I think what you're asking is [restate the question in a promotive way]."

For example:

* Investor: *How will you keep competitors from stealing your customers?*
* You: *That's a great question. I think what you're asking is how we're building defensible assets that give us a long-term advantage. Here's how we're doing that . . . .*

You're not dodging the question, you're actually elevating it. You shift the frame from *fear* to *potential*, which is exactly where your narrative belongs.

Although the original research centered on gender, every founder can use this technique.

MAINTAINING YOUR AGENCY

Bias shows up differently for all of us. You can't control how someone shows up in a meeting, but you can control your structure, tone, and the energy you bring into the room.

When bias is revealed, whether in words, tone, or behavior, how you respond is also within your control. Not every moment is "us versus them," and not every comment comes from malice. I've been in plenty of situations where I've turned an uncomfortable interaction into a teachable moment, offering a nonjudgmental but informative response, and seen that person experience a genuine shift in perspective.

You may feel hesitant to suggest a meeting format or to proactively guide the flow of conversation but let me be clear: You are allowed to lead. You don't need permission or to defer to the investor. It's not pushy to say, *Here's what I've found helpful,* or *I'm going to walk you through a few slides first to give context.* Framing your pitch delivery with thoughtfulness signals professionalism, not presumptuousness.

Also remember that investors may subconsciously expect you to prove more and assume less. While another founder might get a casual, *Cool, I get it,* you may need to lay more groundwork. That's not fair, but it is something you can plan for.

Structure creates safety for both you and your audience.

Here are a few tactics I recommend:

+ **Structure creates safety:** The clearer your plan, the more confidently you'll pitch, and the easier it will be for investors to follow your story.

+ **Format can be a tool of inclusion:** Don't be afraid to adapt the format to highlight your strengths. A walk-through with your deck open might show your visual storytelling skills. A casual chat might highlight your passion, grit, and personality.
+ **Silence is where bias often hides:** If someone seems distracted or disengaged, don't automatically assume it's your fault. Check in with curiosity: *Would it help to focus on a specific part of the business?* That gently puts the ball back in their court without defensiveness.

Above all, don't shrink or shape-shift into what you think someone else wants. You have every right to be in the room, and your unique background, voice, and lens are valuable. The more you own your delivery style and practice it with intention, the more control you'll gain in how others receive it.

BUILDING MENTAL MUSCLE

Of all the founders I've interviewed, and the thousands I've interacted with over the past six years, Rajia Abdelaziz has faced some of the most direct and repeated bias during fundraising. She's encountered many of the worst tropes women and founders of color face, including dismissal, ageism, gendered questions, and blatant ignorance around the problem she was solving.

So I asked her: *How do you stay optimistic? How do you not fall into a defeated stance?*

It was very, very difficult, to be honest with you. It was not easy. I had a lot of childhood trauma growing up. I was raised in a very strict Middle Eastern household. I would come home with an A-minus and my mom would say, 'You're a disappointment.' I have spent my life in situations where I work my hardest but it's never good enough.

Rajia doesn't bypass the hardship; she's honest about the toll it takes, but she's also trained herself to process it differently. She takes a scientific approach to mindset, building reflection and reframing into her daily routine.

> I gratitude journal every single day and write down three things I'm happy about. Even if I can't think of anything, I write observations like, I'm alive and breathing. 150,000 people went to bed last night and didn't get up. Any one of them would trade places with me right now. I'm grateful I talked to a customer who's having problems and at the end she was happy with her device and her purchase. It trains your brain to look for the good and keeps you positive.
>
> Every no was like a punch in the face, and you have to get up and say, 'That no could be leading me closer to one yes. What feedback in that no is actually valid? Even if I'm being discriminated against, is there anything in here I can use to my advantage?'

You do not have to earn your worth by surviving pain, but if it ever feels overwhelming, know that building your mental muscle is part of the founder journey, too. Rajia's story is one of survival, reflection, and self-preservation. It's a reminder that resilience isn't just a trait some people are born with. It's a skill that can be learned and strengthened.

Elijah Davis spoke about pain through a metaphor of growth and transformation:

> I was a seed buried in dark soil, needing nutrients and water, capital and support, to take root and grow. Without them, survival was difficult. The darkness was heavy, especially as a Black man navigating a world that did not always create space for people who look like me. Yet even in that shadow, roots were forming. I was learning and growing, becoming stronger even if it went unseen, much like faith.

The early pain—the moments of being unseen, unsupported, and isolated—was not wasted. It shaped me, strengthened me, and brought me to a place where, with faith, I could flourish, pursue my passions, and stand fully in the light, unafraid and unbothered. Entrepreneurial pain was part of my evolution. Pain is not a setback but a catalyst. It transforms, sharpens, and propels you into arenas aligned with your purpose and passion. The struggle does not define you. How you rise from it does!

Elijah draws a distinction between pain in his life and pain in entrepreneurship. Life pain is raw, personal, and unavoidable. It taught him how to survive. He refers to it as "my relationship with pain in life," something deeply familiar and woven into his identity. Entrepreneurial pain is different, but it's not unfamiliar. It's frustrating, yes, but it's also fuel. He uses it to motivate and push forward.

This is one of our superpowers as members of *The Rest of Us*: We are not new to struggle. We've often faced worse. The startup world may be unjust, but it isn't our first encounter with injustice. We endure not because we want to prove ourselves to the system, but because we already know our worth. As Elijah said:

I'm not trying to prove anything to anybody. I already know I can do it.

Julie shared a similar reflection on how her mindset evolved as she stepped into her role as CEO:

Four years ago, I felt very *un*confident. I had a fear of fundraising, of doing it right and of knowing how to talk to my investors. I had to learn that they're a collaborator, and not an enemy. I had to learn how to work with them.

When my investor repeated that they were in this because of *me*, that gave me a greater sense of confidence and responsibility. I knew I couldn't pass the responsibility off to anyone else. I had to step right into it.

Mindset work isn't a one-time effort. It's a practice. Confidence doesn't always come first, either. Sometimes action has to lead, and confidence catches up later.

Meetings are unpredictable by design.

Investors vary wildly. Some want structure, others want a casual chat; some want you to lead, others want to take the wheel. Your ability to adapt without losing your voice signals collaboration, resilience, and executive maturity.

Investors are often nervous too.

Many angels, especially first-timers or nontraditional ones, aren't sure what to ask and fear sounding inexperienced. That means you're sometimes guiding someone who's figuring it out right alongside you.

The real test isn't your slides, it's the relationship.

Meetings aren't simply business evaluations. Investors are assessing what it would be like to work with you. Empathy, adaptability, and clarity make you more memorable and trustworthy.

For *The Rest of Us*

Bias shows up just as much in meetings as it does in pitches through the questions you're asked, the assumptions made, or how your tone and presence are interpreted. By preparing multiple ways to tell your story and practicing how to guide the room, you maintain control of the frame instead of being defined by it.

FEEDBACK: WHAT TO TAKE AND WHAT TO TOSS

HOW TO HANDLE FEEDBACK

A tricky area for founders is learning how to handle feedback, especially when it comes from investors. You'll get comments about your pitch, your business, your model, your market, and even your customers. When someone critiques your deck, they're implicitly critiquing the strategy behind it. Because the pitch is simply the story of the business, feedback on one inevitably bleeds into the other.

There is no universal standard for how a pitch "should" look or how a business "should" grow. Investors don't operate from the same playbook. They each prioritize different things, shaped by their own background, portfolio, and worldview. Some obsess over financial mechanics. Others want a clear wedge into the market. Others want an emotional story. Their feedback reflects their preferences, not an objective assessment of what your company must change.

That's why qualifying the source of feedback is as important as the feedback itself. Ask yourself:

- Does this person understand my customer or my market?
- Do they have relevant experience that makes their advice grounded?

+ Are they giving feedback as someone who might invest, or as someone who will never write a check?
+ Will they be part of my long-term journey, or is this a drive-by opinion?

A partner at a VC fund who is actively considering your deal will give you feedback with a different lens than someone casually reviewing your deck at a coworking space. A potential customer may highlight gaps that matter; a random observer may project their biases. Not all feedback carries equal weight and pretending it does will drain you.

It's tempting, almost reflexive, to adjust your pitch every time someone with a big title or big checkbook offers an opinion. But doing that too frequently will erode your clarity and confidence and you'll end up with a pitch that shape-shifts to satisfy whoever you spoke to last, rather than one that represents your actual strategy. Worse, you may unintentionally contort your business around advice that isn't meant for your stage, your model, or your market.

Chasing every piece of feedback is a recipe for founder burnout.

BUILDING A FEEDBACK FILTER

What you want to avoid are knee-jerk reactions. Investors, operators, mentors, accelerators, pitch coaches—everyone has opinions. If you rewrite your deck every time someone says, *You should . . .* , you'll quickly lose the through line of your own strategy.

I've watched founders spiral into exactly this trap of getting feedback, immediately changing the deck, pitching someone new, getting different feedback, and changing the deck again. Soon they're saying things like, *Wait . . . that slide was in the last version. I wish you'd seen that one instead.* That's a sign your pitch is being crowdsourced rather than led.

Here's a better approach that applies to both your pitch narrative and the strategic decisions behind it:

+ **Pause:** Don't change anything in the first five minutes, or even the first day. Emotional reactions make terrible editors.
+ **Reflect:** Consider who gave you the feedback, in what context, and with what level of experience or alignment with your business.
+ **Pattern match (it's good this time):** When you hear the same feedback from multiple, diverse sources, especially investors who might fund you, that's usually a real signal.
+ **Decide intentionally:** Only incorporate feedback that makes your pitch stronger *and* still feels authentic to you.

The operative word here is *you*. *You* are the founder. *You* are building the business. *You* are inviting investors into your world—lucky them! If someone suggests reordering your deck, adding jargon, or "pitching like Company X," and your gut screams no, trust that too. If a line or slide feels off every time you say it out loud, trust that.

Ricquelle Jeffrey shared her strategy for "sifting out the nonsense and keeping the good stuff":

> I believe in intuition. I know people might think it's fluffy, but I do believe you know in the first minute or two if someone will be an advocate or ally of yours.

She says the first sign of a positive signal is simple but powerful:

> Is this person taking me seriously? Do I have to keep overexplaining myself, or are they looking at me like I'm their equal? That makes a

big difference, especially for long-term partnerships. If they treat you like an equal at the beginning, it's a sign they'll treat you like one after they invest, too.

On the flip side, Ricquelle looks for signs of overselling as a red flag:

Are they overselling themselves? Are they claiming things that sound too good to be true? You can always ask: 'Can you share some examples of what you've invested in or helped fundraise for?' If someone's exaggerating and you ignore your gut, it can be a costly mistake.

She learned this lesson the hard way:

I was working for a medtech company and we were pitching to this angel investor who claimed he had raised $20 million for an academy in Johannesburg. But something felt off. We couldn't verify much about him. I remember telling the founder, 'I don't think we should share any more information.'

She decided to move forward. We gave him access to the data room, financials, everything. Two weeks later, we found out he was a scammer. He had a history of scamming others, and when we tried to reach him, he was gone, but now he had all of our information.

She also emphasized evaluating the source of the feedback ahead of the advice itself:

The source matters because that includes any preexisting experience or biases that the person might have about your situation. You need to understand what their motivation is for the information they're giving you. Also assess the style in which they're giving you advice. How are they responding to you? Were they considerate in their delivery? Even in the initial email and conversations you can tell a lot. It's why when I'm pitching, I start by asking the investor to tell me more about their journey. I want to know their 'why' first.

Melissa Wood also spoke about the importance of intuition:

This is the number one reason why we have turned down investment so far. My partner and I have both said, if either of us has a gut feeling about somebody or something, the investment, team member, anything, we walk away. We've had discussions with two investors we were considering and in both cases we each had a gut feeling that it just wasn't a good fit. We don't have any regrets.

SEEKING OUT MEANINGFUL, FRIENDLY FEEDBACK

An underrated skill in fundraising is learning where to get feedback in addition to how to digest it. Your goal isn't to build an echo chamber or collect as many opinions as possible, but to curate a cross section of voices that reveal patterns without pulling you off your center.

Here's what that mix could look like:

+ **Mentors who've built before:** They understand the realities of scaling, not just the aesthetics of a deck. Their feedback tends to weigh both story and strategy.
+ **Coaches who specialize in communication:** They help you sharpen clarity, flow, and delivery, which are things founders underestimate until they feel the difference.
+ **Investors who've seen hundreds of pitches:** They know what catches attention and what triggers concern. But remember,

they're giving feedback through the lens of their own thesis, stage, and personal biases. Very helpful, but not mandatory.

+ **Friends and family with fresh eyes:** They'll show you where the story gets confusing. If someone outside your industry can follow your pitch, your message is strong.

+ **Peers in the trenches with you:** Fellow founders understand the micro-signals investors respond to. They also know when advice you received is nonsense because they've heard it too.

You want diversity of perspective, not volume of opinions. Five thoughtful reviewers beat twenty random ones every time. When people from very different vantage points note the same moment in your pitch ("this slide feels dense," "I didn't get your revenue logic," "your origin story needs one clearer line"), that's when you know it's worth tightening.

You'll hear different things from each feedback source and that's exactly the point. Look for consistencies, not outliers. That's how you sharpen your deck without letting it spiral out of control. Also, clarify whether you're asking for content feedback or delivery feedback. Are you looking for input on the actual slides and flow, or how you show up when you pitch? If you don't tell someone what you want, they'll give you whatever commentary pops into their head, which might not be what you were looking for.

WHAT INVESTORS MEAN BY *COACHABLE*

If you've talked to any investors, or read anything written by them, you've likely come across the word *coachability*. It's a trait that nearly all investors say they're looking for in founders, but what does that mean, exactly?

Coachability doesn't mean doing whatever someone tells you. It means you can take in new information, evaluate it, and make thoughtful decisions without becoming rattled or defensive. Investors look for coachability because they're assessing leadership risk. A founder who can synthesize feedback, adjust when needed, and stay steady under pressure is far more likely to build a resilient business, and therefore deliver a better return. When they say they want a "coachable founder," they're really trying to understand whether you:

+ Can absorb critical feedback without shutting down or getting combative.
+ Know how to evaluate advice rather than blindly follow it.
+ Demonstrate self-awareness, maturity, and growth capacity.

By the way, the fact that you're reading this book and intentionally leveling up your skills already tells me you are coachable. Don't overlook that. A few simple ways to demonstrate that skill in real time:

+ **Write down feedback:** Even if you disagree, it signals that you value the input and are taking the conversation seriously. Investors notice this.
+ **Ask clarifying questions:** Something like, *Can you tell me more about what felt unclear on that slide?* shows curiosity and openness.
+ **Follow up:** If you incorporate someone's suggestion, or even a tiny part of it, close the loop:
  Your point on positioning stuck with me. I tightened that section; appreciate the nudge.

Being coachable doesn't mean changing your pitch to please everyone. Demonstrate you heard them and you're thinking about what they said.

HANDLING FEEDBACK IN THE MOMENT

Getting feedback in real time can feel like trying to catch an arrow mid-flight. You're processing emotion, evaluating logic, maintaining tone, and deciding what to say next, all while being watched. Here are tools to help you stay clear and confident without committing to anything on the spot.

WHEN THE FEEDBACK IS CONFUSING OR OFF BASE

Use curiosity to slow the moment down with questions like:

- *Can you help me understand what led you to that conclusion?*
- *What part of the business model are you responding to?*
- *Are you imagining a different type of customer/problem?*

This forces the other person to articulate their assumptions, and it can reveal if they misunderstood something, which is fixable.

WHEN YOU NEED TO ACKNOWLEDGE WITHOUT AGREEING

You don't owe anyone instant compliance. Use "hold and evaluate" language:

- "That's helpful context; let me sit with that."
- "I appreciate you raising that. I'll take a deeper look."
- "Interesting point. I'll think about where that might fit."

This communicates openness without surrendering direction.

WHEN THE FEEDBACK CONTRADICTS YOUR STRATEGY

Do your best not to get defensive and use comments that reflect your confidence in your plan:

+ "That's one way to approach it. Here's why we're making a different bet … ."
+ "I hear you. Our focus right now is on X because it directly drives Y."

Strong founders don't pivot because someone with a title says something; they explain their reasoning.

WHEN FEEDBACK IS CLEARLY ROOTED IN BIAS

You don't have to call out bias directly every time. Personally, I do this whenever I can, but I don't in situations where it will drain my energy. If I feel someone does not have an open mind to hearing a different view from their own, or if they don't respect my identity and position, I don't think it's worth my time. If you do call it out, one strategy is to protect the framing:

+ "Our customers have a different lived reality than what you're describing. Here's what we're hearing from them … ."
+ "I want to make sure we're asking the right question. The real issue isn't X; it's actually Y … ."
+ "Let me reframe that in the context of the market we serve."

You can redirect the lens without escalating tension. If the bias is blatant or harmful, you can also draw a boundary:

+ "I want to keep the conversation focused on the business, not identity dynamics."
+ "That framing doesn't align with how we view our customers or our mission."

There are so many potential sources of capital and types of investors out there. If you are placed in a position where you're defending your integrity, it's nearly always best to end the conversation early and exit that meeting.

WHEN FEEDBACK HITS AN EMOTIONAL NERVE

This is universal. Even seasoned CEOs feel it. What matters is how you regulate:

+ Take one breath. Literally one.
+ Slow your speech by 10%.
+ Return to a clarifying question like, *What specifically makes you say that?*

Presence is power.

HOW IT'S DIFFERENT FOR *THE REST OF US*

Feedback often lands differently for us because it's rarely just about the pitch. When you're underestimated, feedback carries more weight because you've been conditioned to believe you have less margin for error. That chronic awareness changes how you hear things.

Not all feedback is actually about your business and advice is not always good. Sometimes it's about someone's discomfort with your identity, your story, your tone, your emotional register, or the fact that your solution centers people they don't intuitively value. Let me say this plainly: Some "feedback" is bias dressed up as expertise.

Here are some real examples founders, me included, have heard:

+ *You should bring on a male co-founder.*
+ *This feels like a nonprofit idea.*
+ *You might want to dial back the emotion in your story.*

None of that is helpful business advice. That's someone revealing their blind spots.

Here's how to protect your confidence and sift through feedback:

+ **Build a trusted inner circle:** Have a few people who know your company and values well enough to help you evaluate feedback before acting on it.
+ **Practice filtering without absorbing:** You can acknowledge feedback, write it down, and still choose not to carry it. Discernment is not defensiveness.
+ **Name the bias when you see it:** Sometimes you need to say to yourself: *This comment is rooted in someone else's narrow idea of who a founder should be. That's not my problem to solve.*

You aren't looking to shield yourself from feedback with these tactics. They are meant to help you recognize what strengthens your business and distinguishes it from what reflects someone else's limitations.

You're not being defensive. You're being discerning. There's a difference.

THE CASE FOR VIDEO PITCHES

One of the most powerful tools for managing feedback, especially when you want to maintain control of your narrative, is a pitch video. A video lets you:

+ **Standardize the story** across audiences so no one's first impression depends on what mood you were in or how chaotic the meeting was.
+ **Show, not just tell:** Your tone, presence, pacing, and facial expressions convey conviction in ways slides alone can't.
+ **Create space between feedback and reaction:** You're not being asked for on-the-spot responses, which means you can reflect before deciding what (if anything) to adjust.

Sometimes founders worry that a video will feel too formal or impersonal, but I've found the opposite to be true. A good pitch video humanizes you. It brings your mission, your "why," and your energy to life. It creates an emotional connection that a cold deck can't, and it ensures that everyone, whether it's the partner, the associate, or the angel who only skims emails at midnight, gets the same clear, compelling baseline.

For *The Rest of Us*, this can be a quiet equalizer. If you suspect someone might misinterpret your tone, underestimate your technical depth, or dismiss your delivery style in a live setting, a pitch video helps offset those dynamics. It gives you a way to be seen and heard in your strongest form.

We walk through how to create an effective pitch video in Chapter 26.

Feedback is subjective, not universal truth.

Each investor prioritizes different things (financials, team, story, market, vibe, etc.). Their feedback reflects their personal lens, not a definitive rule.

Chasing every suggestion erodes your voice.

If you change your pitch every time someone comments, you'll end up with a Franken-deck that's inconsistent, confusing, and exhausting to maintain.

You need a feedback filter.

Pause before making changes. Reflect on who gave the feedback, why, and whether it aligns with how you think about the business.

Pattern recognition matters.

If you hear the same note from multiple, diverse sources, that's usually a signal. Not a mandate, but a clue worth investigating.

You own the story.

Investors are not co-founders. They don't operate your business—you do. Your pitch must feel authentic, grounded in your voice, and natural to deliver.

Diverse perspectives sharpen clarity.

Yes, seek advice from mentors, peers, coaches, and investors, but weigh it intentionally against your own instincts and vision.

For *The Rest of Us*

When you don't come from legacy networks, feedback often feels higher stakes, as if every comment must be followed or you'll "blow it." You don't owe every opinion equal weight. Some feedback is insight, some is bias, and some is projection. Trust your gut, honor your voice, and resist shape-shifting to satisfy every investor preference.

26

BENEFITS OF A PITCH VIDEO

WHY YOU NEED A PITCH VIDEO

Let's start with a statistic that should make you feel slightly ragey: Investors spend an average of just **2–3 minutes** reviewing a pitch deck before deciding whether to meet with a founder.[68] That's barely enough time to skim a takeout menu, let alone digest a business opportunity. It's certainly not enough time for someone to understand *you*—your vision, your drive, your "why."

A static deck forces investors to evaluate you in the least human way possible. It strips out the things that make someone want to lean in, including your tone, energy, clarity, and conviction. If your only shot at getting in the door is a PDF, you're handing over control of your narrative to a medium that can't do your story justice.

The Rest of Us are often judged more harshly and given less benefit of the doubt. When you don't come through a warm intro or share a lived experience with the investors reviewing your materials, your deck is often read with more

---

68   Data from DocSend's 2024 Funding Divide Report, which includes analysis of investor behavior, June 5, 2024, https://www.docsend.com/blog/docsends-2024-funding-divide-report-the-gap-for-underrepresented-founders-widens/.

scrutiny and less benefit of the doubt. That means your first impression has to work harder, travel farther, and overcome more noise.

Your presence is often your greatest asset, and a pitch video puts the human back into the process. It lets investors "meet" you long before you're in the room together, and it gives you the ability to guide tone, pacing, emotion, and narrative from the very first second. In short, a pitch video lets you lead with your strongest differentiator: yourself!

TWO TYPES OF PITCH VIDEOS (AND WHY YOU WANT BOTH)

When I say, "pitch video," I'm actually talking about two different tools, each serving a different purpose, just like the different modes of pitching we talked about earlier (Perform, Inform, Deep Dive). Think of these videos as asynchronous extensions of those modes.

1. YOUR INTRODUCTION VIDEO (ORIGIN STORY CLIP)

Length: 1–2 minutes

Purpose: Spark curiosity and build connection

Pitch Mode Parallel: Perform (short, memorable)

This is your hook. It's the video you attach to cold outreach, applications, or LinkedIn posts. You're not explaining your whole business in this video, you're helping someone understand why they want to meet with you.

Focus on your *why*:

- Why you started the company.
- Why this problem matters to you.
- Why now is the moment to solve it.

Think of it as your movie trailer, not the full film. You want investors to say, "I want to learn more."

2. YOUR PITCH VIDEO (FULL DECK RUN-THROUGH)

Length: ~5 minutes

Purpose: Clearly communicate the business opportunity

Pitch Mode Parallel: Inform (walk through the Core 10)

Bonus Effect: Frees your live meetings to become Deep Dive mode (questions, strategy, relationship-building)

This version mirrors a live investor meeting. You present your Core 10 as if the investor is in the room, except now you control the pacing and the narrative. When investors watch this before meeting you, the live conversation becomes far more productive. Instead of explaining basics, you're answering thoughtful questions.

Use this video when you:

+ Reach out cold and want to send more than just a PDF.
+ Apply to accelerators, angel groups, or pitch competitions.
+ Respond to "Can you send the deck?" with something more compelling.
+ Want control over how your story lands, instead of hoping someone "gets it" in a 2-minute skim.

VIDEO TYPE COMPARISON

VIDEO TYPE	INTRO VIDEO	PITCH VIDEO
LENGTH	1–2 minutes	~5 minutes
PURPOSE	+ Spark curiosity + Build emotional connection	+ Clearly explain business opportunity + Earn the investor meeting
CONTENT FOCUS	+ Your "why" + Personal story + Passion for the problem	+ Slide-by-slide pitch + Core 10 sections
TONE	+ Authentic, informal, compelling	+ Clear, confident, informative
USED WHEN	+ Cold outreach + Social posts + Networking follow-up	+ With deck after intro call + Accelerator applications + When investor asks for pitch overview
FORMAT	Face-to-camera only	Split-screen: your face + slides
PRO TIPS	+ Let personality shine + Focus on connection, not perfection	+ Make eye contact + Keep slides clean + Practice your flow
GOAL	Make them want to learn more	Make them want to take a meeting

Table 26.1

QUICK REMINDER: TRAILER VS. SUMMARY

Think of your intro video as your *movie trailer*—it hooks people emotionally.

Your pitch video is your *executive summary*—it delivers the core opportunity.

HOW TO FILM IT (AND LOOK LIKE YOU KNOW WHAT YOU'RE DOING)

You don't need a studio, fancy equipment, or a film crew. Below are some founder-friendly tips on the process and tools.

GEAR (SIMPLE, EFFECTIVE, AFFORDABLE)

+ **Camera:** Your iPhone/Android smartphone or a high-quality webcam is perfectly fine.
+ **Microphone:** If you can, use a $20–$40 USB mic or lavalier mic (small, discreet microphone that clips onto your clothing). But your phone's mic in a quiet room also works.
+ **Lighting:** Natural light is best. Face a window. Avoid overhead lighting that casts shadows.
+ **Stability:** Use a phone tripod or prop your phone on books. No handheld wobble.

SETTINGS AND BACKGROUND

+ Clean, uncluttered background (bookshelf, plants, solid wall, etc.).
+ Avoid office or home chaos behind you; it distracts from your message.
+ No props needed unless *highly* relevant (e.g., your physical product).

RECORDING SETUP

+ For the intro video, keep it framed on you from roughly your midsection up.
+ For the pitch video, use a split-screen layout where one-half shows you speaking framed like the intro video, and one-half shows your slides. This keeps the viewer engaged and feels closer to a real conversation. There are many online video tools, both free and paid, that allow you to easily record in this format.

IMPORTANT DETAILS

+ Make your face prominent; avoid being a tiny square or circle in the corner.
+ Speak directly to the camera lens, not below it.
+ Keep your energy up! Video flattens enthusiasm, so raise your tone by 5–10%.
+ Use a clicker or notes for pacing, but don't read a script word-for-word.

This should feel like a real presentation. That means:

+ You're visible the entire time.
+ Your slides are clearly shown.
+ Your energy and passion come through.

A pitch video is a way to ensure no matter who is watching, they experience your story the way you intend. It turns passive deck browsing into active engagement and puts you at the center of your pitch, where you belong.

YOUR HUMAN ADVANTAGE

Videos humanize what a deck flattens. They let people **see** you, **hear** you, and **feel** something, which matters even more if you're not already in someone's network or don't fit their mental template of a "typical founder."

A little science to back this up:

* Crowdfunding campaigns with a video were 85% more likely to achieve their funding goal.[69]

* There is a 7-55-38 rule of communication: words only convey 7% of a message, while body language (55%) and tone of voice (38%) do the heavy lifting in persuasive communication.[70]

* In a study of over 1,000 startup pitches, those with a passionate, warm, and enthusiastic delivery saw a 35% increase in their probability of receiving funding. [71]

So if you want to stand out in a pile of pitch decks? Video. If you want to be remembered by someone who forgot what they ate for breakfast? Video. If you want to be evaluated on your opportunity rather than someone's snap judgment of your résumé, accent, or hometown? You guessed it. Video.

---

69 Clark, B. (2017, September 27). *Why your video is important for your equity crowdfunding campaign. MicroVentures.* https://microventures.com/why-your-video-is-important-for-your-equity-crowdfunding-campaign

70 Mehrabian, Albert. (1971). *Silent Messages: Implicit Communication of Emotions and Attitudes,* volume 8 (Wadsworth Belmont, CA).

71 Hu, A., & Ma, S. (2020). *Persuading investors: A video-based study.* https://songma.github.io/files/hm_video.pdf

BUT WHAT IF I HATE BEING ON CAMERA?

You're in excellent company. Most people dislike being on camera at first. You're not weird, you're just human.

Keep in mind that the goal of a pitch video isn't to be photogenic or perfectly polished. Your goal is to be real, prepared, and create just enough emotional connection that someone wants to meet you live. That connection builds trust, and trust opens the door to actual conversations.

You don't need a production studio or a charismatic TED Talk presence. You need intention, practice, and your own personality. That's it. Let's break down how to get there.

WHAT GOES INTO A PITCH VIDEO

This section aligns directly with the Inform pitch mode: clear, focused, and conversational. Treat the camera as the first investor in the room.

SAY WHAT YOU MEAN (AND MEAN IT)

Before you record anything, write down your talking points. For each slide in your deck:

+ **Identify the main takeaway:** This should mirror your header statement.
+ **Lead with that takeaway out loud:** Say it first, clearly and confidently.
+ **Add 1–3 supporting statements:** Don't enter a monologue or stray off-topic.

Truly, write the way you talk. If you wouldn't say "synergistic go-to-market motion" to a friend, don't say it in your video.

READ IT OUT LOUD. TO A THING THAT HAS EYES.

I repeat this all the time because it works: SAY YOUR PITCH OUT LOUD. Not in your head. Not while scrolling social media.

Saying your pitch OUT LOUD is the single fastest way to remember it and feel comfortable with it. It forces you to confront the parts that feel awkward or unnatural. It surfaces tangents. It reveals where you sound like a human, and where you accidentally sound like a bot or someone else.

If a live human makes you too nervous at first, use a workaround:

- A row of framed pictures in front of your computer.
- A stuffed animal with good eye contact.
- Coffee mugs with faces drawn on them.
- Generate an image using a tool like Nano Banana, Canva, DALL-E, Midjourney, or whatever is popular at the time you're reading this and display it full screen on your computer. Try using this prompt: "A photograph of an active four-way Zoom call. The four-video feed shows people who are demographically diverse. All participants are looking at their cameras with warm expressions and have office backgrounds. The Zoom interface with names and the bottom toolbar is visible."

The great thing about these workarounds is the people are consistently supportive, nonjudgmental, and never interrupt. Jokes aside, looking at someone's face while you're presenting evokes the same feelings as when you're pitching in a live situation. It instantly helps you hear what doesn't sound like you, catch rambling in real time, and get comfortable enough that you don't freeze when the record light turns red. There just isn't a substitute for this step. I'll gladly read your thank you note when you realize how critical it is in developing your pitch talk track and overcoming anxiety.

If you're feeling particularly courageous, record yourself and watch it. You might hate it at first; most people do. But nothing accelerates your delivery like seeing your own habits, filler words, rushed sections, or stiff posture reflected back at you.

SPEAK LIKE YOU CARE (BECAUSE YOU DO)

+ **Your tone matters:** If you sound like you're reading a phone book, people will have a hard time believing you're passionate about your business.

+ **Modulate your voice:** Shifts in pitch, pacing, and volume keep people engaged and signal that you care about what you're saying. A flat or monotone delivery, especially on video, will lose your audience, and once someone zones out, it's extremely hard to pull them back in.

+ **Project with intention:** You don't need to be loud or theatrical, but you do need to sound like someone who believes in what they're building. Quieter, introverted, or more reserved speakers can still communicate strength; it just takes practice and a deliberate focus on how you project. Being introverted isn't a disadvantage; it simply means you build the muscle differently. If you don't sound like you believe in what you're saying, why would anyone else?

MOVE YOUR FACE AND HANDS

Everything reads flatter on camera. When we pitch live, our presence, movement, and energy fill the room. On video, all of that gets compressed. If you default into "formal mode" and strip out your natural expressiveness, you risk coming across as detached or low energy even when you don't feel that way internally.

A little animation goes a long way.

- Use your face. Change your expression to match what you're saying. Genuine excitement draws people in.
- Use your hands. Natural gestures make you seem more dynamic and more confident. They also help emphasize key moments.

These adjustments shouldn't make you "performative." They help the viewer feel what you feel, which is essential in a medium that can strip away nuance.

LOOK STRAIGHT AT THE WEBCAM

You can tell the difference when someone is looking slightly below the lens of their web camera and when they look directly at it. This can make a meaningful difference to the viewer. When someone feels like you're looking at them, they instinctively listen more closely. They trust you more and stay with you longer.

Let your enthusiasm shine through! You wouldn't have started your company if you weren't passionate about its potential. Move your hands around and exaggerate your facial expressions to help your video really come alive and establish that emotional connection with the investor.

LET YOURSELF BE SEEN

Your pitch video works only if you show up in it. Not the stiff, hyper-polished version of you, but the real, intentional, mission-driven you.

You started this company for a reason. Let the camera feel that.

Move your hands. Use your face. Look into the lens. Let your excitement slip through the edges of your voice. These aren't tricks, they're tools that help your investor connect with you as a human, not just as a deck curator.

I want to be clear that "be animated" does not mean "perform a version of yourself that feels fake." We all experience and express emotions differently, and forced expressiveness might feel like a caricature, especially if you are neurodivergent. That's not the goal here. We're looking to increase your chances of forming a connection with someone in a virtual format.

If your natural presence is calmer, quieter, or more contained, keep it. Just make sure the video doesn't flatten your energy so much that your conviction disappears. That compensation can look different depending on your wiring:

+ Subtle hand movements instead of big gestures
+ A fidget tool off camera to stay regulated (I keep a heavily utilized stress ball on my desk)
+ More intentional vocal variation instead of more facial animation
+ Eye contact with the webcam in short, comfortable intervals

Dial yourself up, not into someone else.

YOU'RE NOT PITCHING FOR EVERYONE, JUST THE RIGHT PEOPLE

Ease some of the stress by reminding yourself that you don't need *every* investor to say yes, nor should you want that. You need the *right* ones to see you clearly and want to get to know you better. Go ahead and unclench your jaw and lower those shoulders.

Your video shouldn't be a perfectly polished, one-size-fits-all performance designed to appeal to the masses. It should reflect your actual personality and leadership style because that's what allows potential partners to decide whether working with you will feel aligned. Remember, investors aren't just evaluating whether your business is compelling; they're also trying to understand what it would be like to collaborate with you for years.

Don't sand off the edges that make you *you*. If you're high-energy, let that come through. If you're calm, analytical, or understated, lead with that. If you're mission-driven and express emotion when you talk about the problem, don't hide it.

Your video becomes more than presentation; it becomes a filter. It attracts the people who are genuinely excited by your energy, values, and vision, and filters out the ones who were likely never going to be good partners for you. That's the point. A pitch video isn't about winning everyone. It's about helping the right people see you clearly where they otherwise might not have been able to.

HOW IT'S DIFFERENT FOR *THE REST OF US*

For *The Rest of Us*, showing up on camera can feel like a lot. Maybe you're self-conscious about how you sound, or worried that you don't look like the founders who go viral in pitch competition clips. Maybe you're worried an investor won't take you seriously if you record your video in your kitchen with a toddler toy in the background.

I've been there. Most of the founders I work with have been there. And here's what I'll tell you:

None of that disqualifies you.

*The problem with **imposter syndrome** is that it assumes the issue lies within the individual, ignoring the system in which that person operates.*

70% of people experience imposter syndrome (International Journal of Behavioral Science), yet it rarely reflects our true abilities or potential.

Stop questioning your worth. Start questioning the system that makes you feel unqualified to pursue your ambition. It's not always about working on yourself. It's often about identifying or building a more functional system.

So, instead of saying you have imposter syndrome, say you're in an imposter system. Then take steps to get out of it or change it.

In fact, it's often your hidden advantage.

A pitch video does something the traditional fundraising process almost never does for *The Rest of Us*: It lets people meet you before they judge you. When people skim decks in two minutes and bias creeps in long before someone hears your voice, video can shift the power dynamic. It gives you the first word, first impression, and first emotional connection on your terms.

The data in the first part of this book highlights that *The Rest of Us* get fewer warm intros, at bats, and meetings where someone is willing to sit down and actually hear us out. When you're not already plugged into investor circles, you're often judged by a cold email, a quick skim of your deck, or your LinkedIn, none of which communicate your drive, clarity or lived experience as it pertains specifically to your startup and investment opportunity.

Video is a form of access that gives you visibility and context, and perhaps more importantly, a chance to be remembered. Don't let fear or *impostor syndrome* (see sidebar) keep you from hitting the "record" button. Your story matters. Your voice matters. Someone out there, the right someone, is just waiting to see and hear you.

Key TAKEAWAYS

Investors skim decks in under 3 minutes.

A static deck alone doesn't give you enough space to convey your conviction, clarity, or human story. A video restores that missing context.

People absorb more from video than text.

Seeing and hearing you together increases attention, comprehension, and emotional resonance, which are all things that drive investor curiosity.

Use two video types for two different jobs.

- **Introduction video** (1–2 minutes): Your "why" trailer, ideal for cold outreach, intros, or social posts.
- **Pitch video** (~5 minutes): A full deck walkthrough that lets you own the narrative and ensures every viewer gets the same clear, consistent story.

Your delivery should reflect who you are.

Authenticity doesn't mean performing; it means presenting in a way that highlights your natural strengths. Neurodivergent or more reserved founders can adapt techniques (lighting, pacing, fidgets, gestures) to make video feel comfortable and genuine.

A video is a relationship tool, not a replacement for meetings.
It sets context so live conversations can focus on dialogue, not slide narration, which usually leads to richer questions and stronger connections.

For *The Rest of Us*
A pitch video is a structural advantage in a system where we often get fewer warm intros, fewer meetings, and fewer chances to be seen as full humans rather than résumés. It gives every investor the same first impression, on your terms, countering bias, expanding access, and letting your voice and presence do work a deck can't.

LOOKING GOOD ON CAMERA (EVEN IF YOU FEEL AWKWARD)

You can have the world's strongest pitch, but if your internet cuts out, your face is in shadow, or your audio makes you sound like you're speaking from inside a cereal box, the investor will focus on that instead of what you're saying. Whether you're recording a pitch video or meeting live over Zoom, your setup shapes the first impression as much as your words do.

This chapter is the tactical twin to Chapter 26. You don't need a studio, a ring light wall, or the gear of a TikTok creator. You just need to control the basics, so your setup disappears into the background, and the spotlight stays where it belongs: on *you*.

Figure 27.1

Here's a picture of my setup as an example. This chapter will walk through why these elements matter and how to use them to your advantage.

+ **Background:** Clean, simple, and uncluttered. A few elements add depth, but nothing pulls attention away from the speaker. No virtual filters.

+ **Clothes:** Solid color, no distracting patterns, chosen to contrast with the background so my face stays the focal point.

+ **Position:** Centered in the frame with the camera at eye level to create natural, direct eye contact.

+ **Lighting:** Bright enough to avoid graininess. The window behind me has a shade pulled down so I'm not backlit. A light source in front of me (behind the camera) illuminates my face evenly.

+ **Sound:** Not visible in the screenshot, but I use a small external microphone just below camera height.

This chapter breaks down how to create a clean setup at home with minimal gear so nothing about your environment distracts from your message or your presence.

YOUR CAMERA SETUP

BACKGROUND: KEEP IT SIMPLE

We've all been in online meetings where someone's shoulders are dissolving into a virtual Golden Gate Bridge or their bookshelf looks like it's trying to win a personality contest. It's entertaining on a team happy hour (is it, though?) but distracting in a pitch. Investors should be focused on your face and your words, not trying to read the titles on the bookshelf behind you.

Choose a clean, neutral background that doesn't compete with you. If you want a hint of your real environment behind you, that's fine, but let it be quiet and intentional. If your usual space is chaotic (kids' art, laundry, a plant mid-collapse), record somewhere calmer or adjust your framing.

APPEARANCE: YOU, NOT YOUR CLOTHES

On camera, what you wear matters far less than whether you're visible and easy to read. Bold patterns and neon colors might work in person, but on video they can shimmer, strobe, or muddy your silhouette. Solid colors that contrast with your background tend to read best.

If you wear glasses, test for glare that might obscure your eyes entirely, which makes it harder for the viewer to feel connected to you. Adjust lighting or tilt your frames until your pupils are visible. Unless jewelry is central to your product, skip anything reflective or jangly.

CAMERA: EYE CONTACT WITHOUT GOING CROSS-EYED

Camera position sounds trivial until you see the difference it makes. If your webcam is tilted upward or pointing into your nostrils, you're unintentionally signaling inexperience, distraction, or lack of preparation. Investors won't consciously articulate this, but they will feel it. A thoughtful frame, on the other hand, instantly elevates your presence and credibility before you even speak.

Figure 27.2

Aim for this setup:

+ **Camera at eye level or slightly above.** Stack your laptop on books if necessary.
+ **Sit about an arm's length away.** You want your head, shoulders, and a little breathing room visible.
+ **Center yourself with your eyes in the top third of the frame.** This mirrors photography's rule of thirds and creates a balanced, natural look.

+ **Look at the camera, not at yourself.** Harder than it sounds. A small sticker or dot next to your webcam can anchor your gaze and help simulate eye contact.

These choices aren't about vanity. A well-framed shot makes you appear grounded, confident, and prepared, all of which reinforce the leadership signals investors are subconsciously scanning for.

LIGHTING: BRIGHT FACE, DARKER BACKGROUND

Good lighting doesn't need to be expensive, but it does need to be deliberate. When lighting is bad, it becomes the only thing viewers notice: shadows across your face, bright light blowing out half the frame, a glowing window turning you into a silhouette. When lighting is good, no one notices it at all because they're focused on you.

Keep these principles in mind:

+ **Light should be in front of you, not behind:** Facing a window is ideal. If that's not possible, place a lamp or ring light behind your laptop.
+ **Avoid bright windows behind you:** Backlighting turns you into a shadow and forces the viewer to squint.
+ **Fix graininess with more light:** Grain is almost always a lighting issue, not a camera issue. Add another lamp or bump up your ring light brightness.
+ **Aim for a brighter foreground and a slightly darker background:** This creates depth, highlights your face, and keeps attention where it belongs.

Think of lighting as removing friction. The clearer your face, the easier it is for someone to read your emotion and stay engaged, which is critical in both recorded videos and live investor meetings.

SOUND: YOUR SECRET CREDIBILITY ENHANCER

Bad audio can be worse than bad video. If people can't hear you clearly or if the sound quality makes you feel distant, muffled, or echoey, it becomes harder for them to follow your reasoning, track nuance, or stay engaged. Whether we like it or not, poor audio subtly signals a lack of preparation. Clear sound, on the other hand, makes you instantly more compelling and credible.

Here's how to get it right:

+ **Eliminate background noise:** Silence your phone, turn off desktop notifications, close windows, and kill fans or AC units pointed at your mic. Even small sounds get amplified on recordings and can pull focus at the worst possible moment.

+ **Use any external mic over your laptop mic:** Seriously, *any* external option is better. Wired earbuds you forgot you owned? Great. A $20 plug-in USB mic? Perfect. Your AirPods? Totally fine. Investors are used to seeing headphones in meetings. No one is judging your gear, they're judging whether they can hear you clearly.

+ **Reduce echo with soft surfaces:** Rooms with bare floors bounce sound around, making you echo like you're presenting from a tiled bathroom. If you can, record in a room with carpet or curtains. If not, throw a blanket on the floor or under your laptop. It makes a real difference.

+ **Test before you record:** Do a 10-second test clip. Play it back. Make sure you're not too far from the mic, too close, or your computer decided it was going to mess with your settings and not capture the audio (it happens to everyone).

TECH HYGIENE: DON'T LET GLITCHES STEAL THE SHOW

You don't need to be an IT wizard, but a few small checks can be the difference between a smooth, credible pitch and one derailed by distractions that have nothing to do with your abilities.

Before recording or doing a live pitch:

+ **Plug in your laptop:** Nothing breaks flow like a low-battery warning flashing mid-sentence.
+ **Check your internet:** Sit close to the router or use an Ethernet cable if possible. Stability > speed.
+ **Quit unnecessary apps and silence notifications:** Slack pings, email chimes, and calendar alerts pull attention away from you.
+ **Open your deck in advance:** Keep it at the ready so you can screen-share instantly without fumbling through tabs.
+ **Do a 10-second test recording:** Check your lighting, framing, and sound before you hit "go." It's the fastest insurance policy you'll ever take out.

Ninety seconds of prep can save you thirty minutes of distraction, frustration, and preventable credibility leaks.

LIVE VIRTUAL MEETINGS VS. RECORDED PITCH VIDEOS

Here's where Chapter 27 builds on Chapter 26. Your recorded pitch video is your calling card; it's the thing investors can watch when you're not in the room. Your live meeting is where you build the relationship.

By the time you're in a live meeting, you don't need to walk through the entire deck again. If they haven't seen the video, give a crisp 2–3 minute recap to set context, then spend the rest of the time answering questions, reading the room, and going deeper, which are things that move an investor toward yes.

QUICK PREFLIGHT CHECKLIST

Use this before every recording or meeting:

- ☐ Quit apps + silence notifications.
- ☐ Plug in your computer (laptops always die at the worst moment).
- ☐ Light in front of your face, not behind.
- ☐ Camera at eye level, about an arm's length away.
- ☐ Mic test: Speak one sentence and listen back.
- ☐ Close the door/ask for quiet time.
- ☐ Open your deck in its own window (not full screen) so you can share it quickly.
- ☐ Water within reach; phone on silent but accessible.

HOW IT'S DIFFERENT FOR *THE REST OF US*

For *The Rest of Us*, showing up on video comes with layers many founders never have to think about. Your "office" might be your kitchen table, your accent might make you nervous, maybe you've gotten feedback that your tone, hair, or style is "unprofessional" or "too much." All of that sits on your shoulders before you even hit record or start the online meeting.

You don't have to contort yourself into someone else's idea of what a founder should look or sound like. You definitely don't need to reshape yourself for people who were never going to understand your context, your community, or your opportunity in the first place.

That doesn't mean all investors will fall into that category. Many will see you clearly if you give them the chance, and video can help with that. It creates a more level first impression by giving everyone the same context. Conserve your emotional energy for the people who could become true partners.

So, don't chase perfection or universal approval. Connect with the investors who recognize your leadership when they see it and who align with the company you're building. Video, even if awkward, vulnerable, or imperfect, can be one of the most powerful ways to make that connection.

Professional presence is about clarity, not perfection.
Good lighting, clean audio, and intentional framing remove distractions so the investor stays focused on you.

Video quality shapes credibility more than people realize.
Smooth sound and a well-framed shot signal preparation and reliability, which are subtle cues investors often (consciously or not) associate with strong execution.

Preparation reduces nerves and increases control.
Managing your setup, including camera height, lighting direction, and microphone choice, frees your brain to focus on your pitch, not whether something looks off.

You don't need expensive gear.
Free tools, natural light, and basic earbuds are often enough.

For *The Rest of Us*
You don't need a studio or a Pinterest-perfect backdrop to be taken seriously. By optimizing the basics and showing up with authenticity, you create a level first impression where investors can see your conviction and leadership without your environment getting in the way. Your presence becomes an asset, not something you have to compensate for.

AFTER THE PITCH: KEEPING MOMENTUM GOING

You made it through the meeting. You told your story, answered the tough questions, and you didn't flinch even when someone tossed out one of those vague-but-existential ones like, *"So … what's your moat?"*

Take a breath. That was a big deal.

Of course, fundraising doesn't end when the Zoom window closes. The *after* is often where deals are won, lost, or left to drift so slowly that you start contemplating a new life selling B2B black licorice subscriptions (don't tempt me with a good callback).

This is where investor differences become real. Remember back in Part I, when we broke down angels, angel groups, VCs, corporates, and other sources of capital? Up to this point, those categories shaped how you pitch. Here, they shape what happens next. Different investor types move at different speeds, ask for different materials, and require different nudges to keep momentum alive. Knowing who you're talking to, and what their process typically looks like, helps you stay calm and strategic instead of reactive and anxious.

Let's talk about how to keep things moving after the pitch.

THE FOLLOW-UP: BE CLEAR AND PROMPT

Send a same-day thank-you. Keep it short, direct, and forward-moving. Something like:

> *Thank you for your time today. As discussed, I'm sending [the deck/data room link/intro to customer] and will follow up next week on next steps. Please let me know if you'd like anything else in the meantime.*

A great follow-up does three things at once:

+ **Signals professionalism:** You look organized and buttoned-up, qualities investors value more than they admit.
+ **Reduces their cognitive load:** Investors take dozens of meetings. You're helping them remember where your conversation landed.
+ **Keeps control of the clock:** You set the next touchpoint and keep the process moving.

No paragraphs of re-pitching. You're demonstrating that working with you is easy and efficient.

READING THE SIGNALS

Founders often torture themselves trying to decode investor behavior. *Did they smile? Did they say "interesting"? Did they ghost me because they secretly hate me?*

The reality is simpler and less personal. Investors are busy, distracted humans. Even genuinely interested ones can go quiet for weeks. Silence doesn't automatically mean no but it does mean you shouldn't wait passively for them to reappear.

Signals aren't judgments of your worth. They're data points about the investor's capacity, process, and level of conviction. These are the signals that matter:

- **Fast follow-up questions → real interest:** Curiosity is the strongest buying signal in early-stage investing.
- **Introductions to partners, other investors, or operators → diligence has begun:** They're expanding the circle, which is meaningful.
- **"Let's circle back in six months" → usually a polite no:** Treat it as closed for now unless they give a concrete reason tied to *their* timing, not yours.
- **Ghosting after multiple nudges → also a no:** Don't waste months chasing it.

Suelin Chen described her own instincts for reading investor interest:

To not waste your own time, you need to trust your gut. I got better at that through pitching hundreds of investors. I could tell, sometimes within minutes, when they weren't going to invest. I would sometimes cut the call short, thank them for their time, and say I didn't think it was the right fit.

When they start asking only prevention questions or have an attitude, I'm just thinking, why are we even talking? Life is too short!

> I've had all sorts of rejections and weird things happen. A quick no is always appreciated. Some people told me to my face that my company was dumb and no one was interested in end-of-life. I welcome honest and direct feedback, but I did not tolerate unnecessary nastiness.
>
> There was one particular angel group that was so gratuitously rude that I actually followed up with a note explaining that the way I was treated was not okay. Surprisingly, they actually apologized and explained they had just gotten off an upsetting board call with one of their portfolio companies right before our call, and mistakenly brought all that energy in, but you have to wonder whether they would have emotionally dumped on a male founder like that. You have to maintain respect for yourself and call out disrespect. Another time an investor, who happened to be a woman, fell asleep during the Zoom pitch. Fundraising can feel dehumanizing at times.

She's describing signal sorting as a survival skill *The Rest of Us* often develop faster than others because we receive a wider range of tone, bias patterns, and interaction quality.

TIMING BY INVESTOR TYPE

Not all investors move the same way. Their timing reflects their structure, not your quality. Knowing this helps you plan the round instead of getting blindsided.

Angel investors: Unlike VCs, this isn't their full-time job. They may be juggling day jobs, families, or other commitments, and their capacity to focus on diligence ebbs and flows. If they go quiet for a bit, it doesn't always signal disinterest, sometimes life just gets in the way. Stay polite, stay organized, and keep nudging gently, but don't stall your entire process waiting for them. This happens to me all the time as an angel investor. Sometimes I genuinely like a founder's idea but just don't have the capacity for diligence right then. It's not about them, it's about timing.

Corporate VCs: CVCs are often even slower. Their process usually involves multiple layers of approvals, strategic alignment reviews, and sometimes even board sign-off. It doesn't mean they don't like you, it just means they move at corporate speed, which is to say, glacial. If you're talking with a CVC, build that into your timeline from the start.

Investor type determines incentives, bandwidth, internal process, and approval layers. Here's how that generally plays out after the pitch:

INVESTOR TYPE	WHAT TO EXPECT	WHY IT MATTERS
Solo Angels	Can be very fast or very slow; pace depends on their personal bandwidth.	It's not their day job. Life events, travel, or work can pause momentum. Silence doesn't always mean no. Nudges help.
Angel Groups/ Syndicates	Slower—often 1–3 months. Group discussions and votes take time.	One pitch can unlock multiple checks, but you're at the mercy of group calendars and consensus.
Early-Stage VCs	Usually faster to show interest, but full diligence can still take weeks to months.	This *is* their job. They screen quickly but juggle dozens of deals. Unprompted silence often means they're unsure, not opposed. Staying top of mind matters.

INVESTOR TYPE	WHAT TO EXPECT	WHY IT MATTERS
Corporate VCs (CVCs)	Slowest of the bunch. Decisions often take months.	Multiple internal approvals, strategic alignment reviews, and sometimes board-level sign-off. If you include CVCs, build that timing into your raise.
Impact/ Mission-Driven Funds	Highly variable. Fast when you're a mission fit, otherwise similar to VC timelines.	They may weigh values alignment alongside returns, so your story matters as much as your metrics.

Table 28.1

If you're raising on a tight timeline, focus on angels and early-stage VCs who can move faster. Keep groups, CVCs, and slower funds in the mix, but don't hinge your whole round on them.

DUE DILIGENCE: DON'T PANIC

If an investor is serious, they'll move into diligence. This stage can feel like an exam you didn't study for, but that's rarely the reality. Diligence is simply a deeper look at the business you've already pitched, giving the investor a chance to check the details and answer any remaining questions. It's not a trap; it's a continuation of the same conversation.

A helpful way to think about it is to remember the last time you made a major purchase or commitment. You probably researched your options, narrowed them down, and then dug deeper into the final contenders to make sure there were no open questions before committing. Investors do the same thing. Before wiring money, they want to confirm what they heard, understand your assumptions, and make sure they feel confident about partnering with you. Same concept, just with higher stakes.

Typical diligence requests include:

+ Financial model or projections
+ Customer pipeline, contracts, or LOIs (letters of intent are non-binding agreements showing a customer plans to buy once the product is ready)
+ Cap table and incorporation documents
+ Team bios, advisor list, and references
+ Product demo, screenshots, or technical review

Show what you have, explain what you don't, and frame gaps as things you're actively working on. Investors don't expect perfection, just honesty and progress. If you frame diligence as collaboration rather than interrogation, you'll project confidence instead of defensiveness.

HOW TO STRUCTURE IT

Think of your diligence materials as a digital filing cabinet that investors can easily browse. The most common format is a data room, which is a shared folder with cleanly organized documents. You don't need to have a Fortune 500-level data room (please don't build one).

A straightforward structure might look like this:

+ **Pitch materials:** Deck, pitch video, one-pager
+ **Corporate documents:** Articles of incorporation, bylaws, cap table

+ **Financials:** Financial model, historical data, profit and loss (P&L) statements, balance sheets, and cash flow statements
+ **Market:** Research, TAM/SAM/SOM, industry insights
+ **Product:** Demo video, screenshots, road map
+ **Traction:** Metrics, customer contracts, pipeline
+ **Team:** Bios, org chart, advisors
+ **Legal:** IP filings, key agreements

You don't need every folder filled before you start pitching. Most early-stage rooms begin partially complete and evolve as the conversations deepen. Empty folders are fine as long as you flag what's coming.

WHAT TOOLS TO USE

You do *not* need an expensive virtual data room to look credible. Early-stage founders can absolutely use:

+ **Google Drive or Dropbox:** free or cheap, easy to share and update
+ **Notion:** Good for embedding decks + documents in one place
+ **DocSend:** useful for deck tracking to see who opened what

If you're raising a larger round with heavy diligence, you may graduate to a paid data room platform with granular permission levels, but don't overcomplicate it early.

Pro tip: Set your docs to view-only or PDF download only. Watermark your financials and protect your information without creating friction for the investor.

FOUNDER-TO-FOUNDER REALITY CHECK

Build your data room in parallel with your round. Keep your documents clean, current, and labeled clearly ("Q2_2025_PnL.pdf" is better than "new financials FINAL FINAL v2.pdf"). Investors care far more about whether they can find what they need than if you have a logo on your folder system. It shows you're running operations with discipline.

WHEN THE GOALPOSTS MOVE

Shifting goalposts are one of the most disorienting and demoralizing parts of fundraising. You think you're aligned, you think you understand what's being evaluated, and then, suddenly, the criteria change. It's not always malicious, but it's destabilizing. And yes, it disproportionately affects *The Rest of Us*.

After raising substantial angel funding for Scroobious, I decided to engage selectively with VCs who were values-aligned. One firm felt like a really good match. We spent two months in diligence. Every requested document was reviewed, every metric and projection was reinforced, and the team repeatedly told me we checked their boxes.

At the end, they passed. They now wanted to see us scale *without* the capital required to make that happen.

It wasn't just the no that stung, it was the retroactive rewrite of expectations. From the beginning, the focus had been on market size and long-term projections, all of which we met, by their own admission. At the finish line there was suddenly a brand-new requirement to hit near-term sales traction unrealistic for a pre-seed stage without the funding that the round itself was meant to provide.

I sent a thoughtful reply (see figure 28.1), more for my own integrity than expecting a response (I never heard from them again). I shared how the experience landed from the perspective of a woman entrepreneur, and how shifting criteria undermine trust in a process already opaque for so many of us.

These shifts aren't always deliberate. Many investors aren't aware that they're moving the bar, but that doesn't make it any less exhausting or less costly for founders, especially those who rely on clarity because we don't have insider networks translating the "unspoken rules" for us.

Allison Byers <abyers@scroobious.com>

Thank you for your email. Yes, it is disappointing because I genuinely believed we could have made great partners. It's disheartening to read that you would like to see us scale the business without the capital required to make that happen and that you realize the paradox of that decision.

My understanding after our last conversation was that we checked every box apart from determining if we have a venture scalable business. Our market size and projections check that box, but now there is a new box to check about meeting near-term sales goals at the pre-seed stage.

Women entrepreneurs are constantly presented with what we call shifting goalposts. I say this with a spirit of constructive openness, as that's how the current situation appears from my vantage point. Like you, I value transparency and recognize this outcome is driven by factors you have carefully assessed, but I'd like to share how it's perceived on my end.

It's notable that your portfolio predominantly consists of companies with male founder CEOs, and only a small fraction includes female founder CEOs – five out of twenty-eight if I'm not mistaken. Please understand that I'm not implying any wrongdoing here, but rather underscoring the broader context. This is significant because my motivation behind founding Scroobious stems from a desire to enrich the entrepreneurial landscape by fostering diversity. This entails not only encouraging underrepresented entrepreneurs but also educating and reshaping the funding landscape.

While I respect your decision and your commitment to what you believe is best for your fund, I believe it's valuable to share perspectives from both sides. Your insights are undoubtedly grounded in your fund's objectives, and I wish to offer mine as well. Thank you once again for considering our partnership and for engaging in this exchange of viewpoints.

Allison

Figure 28.1

Jen Saxton faced a nearly identical situation, only stretched across a longer timeline with even higher stakes. After early traction and strong investor interest, she received a term sheet from a major fund. Then the war in Ukraine broke out, disrupting a planned retail partnership launch. The fund pulled out. She explains:

> I was told, 'Come back when you launch a retailer.' It took a while, but I finally did. Then they said, 'Come back when you get 1% share.' I somehow hit that goal too, without having raised, running on fumes.
>
> I came back again. Then it was, 'Come back when you have *X* revenue.' And I'm thinking, I'm going to be out of cash by then. At some point, it's just not worth my time to chase these VCs and their constantly shifting goalposts.

Instead of continuing the cycle, Jen doubled down on her business. She paused her salary, laid off her team, and hung in just long enough to close a massive new deal with a different national retailer.

> Of course, now they're all knocking on my door.

These stories are not uncommon, but they're rarely told in full or in public. We're conditioned to believe that if an investor doesn't say yes, we must not have been ready. That's not always true. Sometimes the bar moves. That doesn't mean you failed. It means the system isn't as objective or consistent as it claims to be.

I posted my experience on LinkedIn, and it clearly struck a nerve. It has over 92,000 impressions, 300 comments, and 22 reposts at the time of writing.[72] If you're a founder who has experienced this, I strongly recommend reading through the comments for an instant sense of understanding and camaraderie. In fact, Jen's response to this post is how we met!

---

72 Allison Byers, LinkedIn post, https://www.linkedin.com/posts/allison-byers_two-months-of-diligence-then-a-pass-activity-7361018652256526336-_S8l?utm_source=share&utm_medium=member_desktop&rcm=ACoAAAAs6SkBtAqodqDMX5u7uNUiNz-Vyn6OPnY.

This is why understanding all your funding options matters, which you're already doing by reading this book, so good on you! When a door closes or a goalpost shifts out of reach, you don't have to stop. You can take back control.

For me, that meant slowing down, proving out our model by working directly with founders, building our education platform without outside capital, and raising gradually through a rolling angel round on terms that made sense for us. For Jen, it meant bootstrapping, staying alive through grit and creativity, and letting growth speak for itself.

Whatever your path looks like, remember that you do not need to earn investor approval to validate your worth. If the rules keep changing, you are not obligated to keep playing the same game. Choose the path that works for you.

MANAGING MOMENTUM

One of the hardest parts of fundraising is the in-between time when you're waiting for investors to decide, while still running a company that can't afford to pause. This limbo feels especially brutal for *The Rest of Us* because the stakes often feel higher and the timelines more ambiguous.

A few principles help keep you in the driver's seat:

- **Keep adding to your pipeline:** Never stop pitching because one investor "might" commit. Momentum attracts momentum, and a broad pipeline prevents you from becoming dependent on any single decision-maker.

- **Share small wins:** New customer? Partnership signed? Product shipped? Send a brief update. It signals progress, reduces perceived risk, and reminds investors that you're moving forward with or without their capital.

+ **Don't camp out in ambiguity:** If it's been weeks with no clarity, you're allowed to ask directly: *Given your process, would you say we're in diligence or should I assume this isn't the right fit right now?* Protect your own time.

+ **No response *is* a response:** This isn't personal; it's common given people's realities of overcommitments and competing priorities. If follow-up after follow-up goes unanswered, log the no, archive the thread, and move on. Your mental bandwidth is precious.

RELATIONSHIPS OVER TRANSACTIONS

Even if someone doesn't write you a check, the relationship still matters. A no today doesn't mean a no forever. Investors switch funds, change theses, and develop new focus areas. How you handle yourself after the pitch leaves an impression. You aren't just raising money in this process; you're building a network of people who know what you're building and trust how you operate. That network becomes a long-term asset and fuel for future intros, hires, partnerships, advice, and, eventually, capital.

Ricquelle Jeffrey emphasized the value of authentic connection:

It is really important when I am working with first-time founders to understand that I have helped others raise money. I have received investment from friends, former colleagues, people I have met at networking events, even virtual meetings where I was just giving someone advice. An investor can be anywhere.

These people might not be a potential investor today, but they'll come to you when they are, because you're a trusted connection. When I talk about networking, I really mean building authentic relationships. As a founder, you need to spend one-third of your time doing that, not just for investment, but for hiring, resources, and more. Relationships save you money on your bottom line.

Whether or not someone becomes an investor today, real connection builds long-term value. The connections you make now often shape the opportunities you have later.

Ricquelle shared more about how she forms these deeper connections:

I work in both London and Boston, so I do a lot of virtual coffee chats for 15–30 minutes. I always let people talk about themselves. A surprising number of founders are shy, and it's a great strategy to jump in and ask someone to tell you about their journey. People get excited to talk about themselves when they sense you are genuinely curious about their 'why.'

I was just talking to someone from Silicon Valley Bank for what was supposed to be a 20-minute chat. I asked him about his 'why' and we spoke for over an hour. He was giving me all these free tidbits. We weren't just networking; we were having an authentic conversation. I used that time to learn, and now he wants to schedule another chat in a month.

This story mirrors something we've explored throughout the book. Investors are evaluating what it would be like to work with you, but you're evaluating them too.

WHEN RELATIONSHIPS WORK AGAINST YOU

Occasionally, a relationship that looks like "support," "expertise," or "experienced guidance" can turn into something manipulative or destabilizing. These situations don't start as dramatic breaches of trust. They start small with an overstep here, a subtle dismissal there, and escalate because founders feel pressure to stay agreeable, grateful, or coachable. These examples aren't common, but they're not rare either, and they disproportionately affect *The Rest of Us*. The more attuned you are to early red flags, the more confidently you can protect yourself and your company.

The story you're about to read is heavy. I'm not sharing it to scare you, but to shine a light on the darker corners of fundraising that too many founders navigate in silence. This is about helping you build your own internal radar, your Spidey sense, so that when something feels off, you trust yourself to pause, question, and protect what you're building.

In 2016, Jennifer Kushell had strong momentum: a bestselling book, product demand from over 100 schools, and a $1.5 million investment commitment from a trusted angel investor. She was not the best operations person, so she brought in an experienced executive, someone who had led a major advertising firm as a stand-in operator to support growth.

That executive introduced her to a venture capitalist he knew, someone Jennifer coincidentally went to high school with. The VC offered to match the existing $1.5 million, bringing the potential total raise to $3 million. Though she wasn't ready for venture capital, they pressured her to pursue it.

> They said, 'You'll never have to raise again. It'll be wonderful.' But I knew I wasn't ready for venture, that type of capital needs structure.

Things quickly spiraled. The VC and the executive turned out to be close friends. A third person, a high-profile industry "expert" with a reputation for billion-dollar exits, was brought in under the guise of helping. Behind the scenes, the three began manipulating projections and removing Jennifer from financial decision-making.

> They started building numbers on top of mine, saying, 'You can hit a million,' when I had a realistic $700,000 pipeline.

Then came deception. The industry expert offered to help set up tech infrastructure and merchant accounts, but instead began siphoning company funds through an account tied to another business where he was chairman. She was shut out of financial reporting.

> We had schools running programs, students paying. The revenue was coming in, but I couldn't get a single report. My investors started screaming at me.

As pressure mounted, the team backchanneled with investors and corroded her credibility. They demanded she hand over control or risk the investment falling through. At one point, the board chair, who was also embezzling, threatened to withhold his signature unless she signed a $7,000/month contract for him.

> I told him I hadn't even confirmed compensation levels for the core team. He said, 'Do it or I won't sign.' I said, 'You're blackmailing me.'

The manipulation climaxed when she was beside her mother's deathbed and received calls threatening legal action unless she signed over full operating control.

> They said they'd sue me or put us out of business. While I'm with
> my dying mother.

Eventually, the board gave her a vote of "no confidence." Everyone involved exited the company, leaving her and her partner to pick up the pieces. Years later, she learned that the board chair had a history of predatory behavior, dismantling at least seven other female-led startups, which was confirmed by investigative reporting. He remains active in the ecosystem today, advising new founders.

> We were the only ones who survived.

This traumatic experience left deep scars. Her co-founder relationship was damaged, her cap table remains distorted, and the manipulative executive still holds significant equity, despite never generating revenue.

> I live with that. He brought in no dollars. But he still owns a piece
> of my company.

Even today, transparency can cost her. When she discloses what happened to prospective investors, many shy away, saying they want to wait and "see how things shake out." "I'm penalized for being honest. Even with projections, I stick to reality. But they want inflated dreams." The misogyny is still present as well. "In meetings, I've heard comments like, 'Throw your dick on the table.' I told them, 'Don't ever say that in my presence.'"

I've heard far too many stories like this that are painful, enraging, and completely avoidable. Jennifer's stayed with me not just because of its severity, but because of how familiar it felt. The manipulation, the gaslighting, the erosion of trust; it's not a rare outlier. It's what happens when power is unchecked, and the fundraising ecosystem lacks accountability.

Relationships are at the heart of fundraising, but they only work when they're built on trust, respect, and shared values. When they're not, they can do more harm than good. No amount of capital is worth the cost of emotional trauma, loss of control over your own company, damage to your reputation, your team, your cap table, and in some cases, your personal life.

WHAT *LEAD INVESTOR* REALLY MEANS

At some point in your fundraising journey, someone will inevitably say, *You need to find a lead investor.* It sounds simple, right? Find one person to believe, and the rest magically falls into place. If you've already been down this road, please feel free to take a moment for your eye roll, hollow laughter, or primal scream.

A lead investor isn't necessarily the one writing the biggest check. They're the person or fund who takes point on the deal. The one who drives the diligence process, reviews your materials in depth, validates assumptions, negotiates terms, and signals to everyone else, *I've done the work; this is real.*

Everyone else gets to "follow" with less effort and less perceived risk. That's why you'll often hear investors say they're interested, but only if someone else leads. It's not that they don't like your company, but that they don't want to take on the work or responsibility of being first.

A lead investor can be:

+ An experienced angel who knows your market
+ A micro-VC or small fund willing to take on the diligence
+ An accelerator, syndicate, or early institutional fund that wants
  to help formalize your round

This can create a frustrating loop for founders, especially those without a deep network. Everyone is waiting for someone else to validate you first. It also puts the lead investor at the center of your fundraise and gives them influence over the other investors. Joel Mutua experienced this dynamic in full effect:

> We had $4 million in commitments for a $2.5 million round. But none of it came in. Everyone was waiting for our lead investor to close, and they didn't. Their due diligence dragged on for three months. When they pulled out, everything else collapsed.

This is the reality behind the scenes of so many failed rounds. If you don't appreciate the difference between a committed investor and a lead, you miss the nuance that the lead signals trust based on their ownership of the diligence.

Joel also experienced how a smaller investor can step up and provide outsized value as a lead.

> We had a VC ready to put in $600,000, but they wouldn't lead. Our $250,000 lead investor had deep experience in Africa and their network was worth more than money. That $250,000 could unlock 10x more.

If you can't find a traditional lead, it absolutely does not mean that you can't raise a round. A lead is not a requirement. Many founders bring rounds together without a lead by running a clear, transparent process. Share your diligence materials proactively, communicate progress, and create your own momentum. In doing so, you effectively become the "lead" in your own round, and that kind of initiative and organization signal leadership and accountability investors respect.

HOW IT'S DIFFERENT FOR *THE REST OF US*

For *The Rest of Us*, the after-the-pitch period can feel especially heavy. We often don't have a deep bench of investor friends we can "circle back to," and we don't get infinite at bats. When an investor goes silent, it can feel personal. When someone nitpicks or pushes unreasonable diligence asks, it can feel like another test we didn't sign up for. And when the timeline drags on, it's not just frustrating, it's destabilizing.

But remember this: You're not here to convince every investor. You're here to find the ones who lean in, who ask thoughtful questions, who get excited when you talk about your business. If someone ghosts you, or nitpicks you to death, or asks you to perform backflips they'd never demand of someone else, that's simply not your person.

Your job isn't to please the gatekeepers. Your job is to keep moving, keep building, and keep showing up until you meet the right partners who see you clearly and want to build *with* you. They are out there. When you do find them, the yes will feel different. It won't be conditional or performative. It'll feel like alignment.

I asked Rica Elysée to name the one thing that truly changed for her from all the accelerators and investor experiences. This is what she said:

> I used to think the grind was all about saying yes. Yes to meetings, yes to mentors, yes to 'opportunities.' Now, I've learned the real flex is saying no. After the wild terms, the ghosting, and the 'we love what you're doing, but … ' moments, I started asking myself a new

question. Not, 'Do they want me?' but, 'Do I want them?' That shift changed everything. That's founder energy.

Suelin Chen echoes this with a story about treatment from others involved in the fundraising process, like service providers:

One of our corporate lawyers (who we paid, by the way!) disparaged me and even aggressively shouted at me in front of other people. I think people sometimes feel like because I'm an Asian woman, they can push me around and there are no consequences to their bad behavior. I don't think they would ever talk to a white man the way they did to me. When both my CMO and CFO witnessed this wild behavior, they encouraged me to report this lawyer, and my VC actually helped escalate it to resolution.

These aren't side stories. They're part of the real fundraising landscape for *The Rest of Us*. The work isn't just about meetings, decks, or data rooms. It's about navigating power dynamics, maintaining your center when the system tries to shake you, and refusing to shrink when someone tests your boundaries.

Fundraising for *The Rest of Us* is about resilience, discernment, and ownership. It's about choosing partners, not chasing approval. It's about remembering that you're not here just to raise money; you're here to build something that wasn't designed with you in mind, and to carve a path others will walk more easily because you were here.

Now that we've talked about how to navigate the messy, human, often unspoken parts of this process, let's step back one more time and look at the bigger picture—the future you're stepping into, the movement you're part of, and how everything you've learned threads into the conclusion of this book.

The pitch is the beginning, not the finale.

The real decision-making happens after the meeting in the follow-ups, the diligence requests, and the conversations investors have when you're not in the room.

Momentum is its own data point.

Quick follow-up questions, intros to partners, and steady engagement are strong buying signals. Dragging feet, shifting criteria, or repeated delays are also signals pointing the other way.

Your follow-up shapes the process.

Clear, timely, concise next steps communicate that you are running a professional process. Investors respond differently when you lead with structure rather than waiting for them to decide the pace.

Diligence isn't a test of worth; it's a workflow.

You're not being graded; investors are simply trying to understand how your business works. Organization and transparency matter more than perfection.

Relationships compound.

Even a no can become valuable later. Treat every interaction as part of a long-term ecosystem, not a one-off transaction.

Bias often shows up strongest after the pitch in who gets fast replies, who gets endless requests for "more proof," who gets ghosted, and who gets shifting goalposts. Don't internalize the noise. Silence or delays are often about bandwidth, bias, or institutional habits, not your worth or your company's potential. Maintain boundaries, manage your pipeline with intention, and remember that you're not waiting to be chosen. You're choosing the right partners.

CONCLUSION

If you've made it this far, you've done something that most founders never do. You've slowed down long enough to understand how fundraising works in real life, and how it works for *you*. That alone sets you apart.

By now, you've seen the pattern. The venture capital system wasn't built for *The Rest of Us*. If you've ever walked into an investor meeting and wondered whether you needed to change yourself to be taken seriously, let this be your reminder: you don't. You never did. You are not the thing that needs fixing. The system is.

THE REDEMPTIVE ARC

The arc of an entrepreneur's journey is, at its core, redemptive.

We experience pain, we observe injustice, or we see a problem that nobody else is fixing and instead of turning away, we decide to do something about it. We transform frustration into invention, exclusion into access, injustice into progress. That's the work of entrepreneurship.

Investors, at their best, also play a redemptive role. They are the fuel that powers these transformations. But right now, that fuel is highly concentrated in one type of founder. Diversify the fuel, and you diversify the engines.

Diversify the engines, and you diversify whose problems get solved. This isn't just about who gets funded. It's about who we trust to build the future.

Rajia Abdelaziz brings this to life:

> After my mom and dad's intervention, I was in my room crying, doubting myself, wondering, 'What if declining Google is the worst decision? What if they're right? What if I'm throwing my future away? What if we can't raise that $150,000?'
>
> Now, not only did we raise $150,000, but we've raised millions. I'm on the cover of *Forbes* "30 under 30 Social Impact" list; I'm on billboards in New York's Times Square; *Inc.* named us as one of the fastest-growing companies in America; and the *Boston Globe* named me to their Tech Power Players list.
>
> Some days, I truly feel like I'm living my wildest dreams. I wish I could go back and give 21-year-old Rajia who's crying in her room a hug and reassure her that turning down Google would be the greatest decision she ever made.

This is the emotional truth for so many of *The Rest of Us*. The fear, doubt, and pressure to play it safe. In the face of it all, we still leap.

Representation in entrepreneurship and investing matters because it expands the permission space. It reminds every founder still sitting in their bedroom wondering if they made the worst mistake of their life that someone like them has done it and thrived.

YOUR AGENCY

Here's the part I want you to hold tight: You have agency. There are no rules, only patterns. "The way fundraising is done" is not physics, but habits. Habits can be changed.

New structures and methods are being created in real time. Things like rolling funds, revenue-based financing, community syndicates, crowdfunding, and more are already reshaping the landscape. These aren't fringe experiments; they're the early signs of a system evolving because founders like you and me are demanding it.

A smart woman once told me there are no rules for how fast or slow you build your business. You get to decide. That's true in fundraising, too.

SYSTEMS AND RESILIENCE

The real risk isn't that startups close. Startups winding down is normal and expected. The real risk is that our systems keep assuming only the "survivors" were ever worth betting on, which means they keep betting on the same narrow slice of founders again and again.

If we design for resilience, reflection, and recirculation rather than just return on investment, we get something far more powerful. We get an ecosystem that grows stronger through "failure" because lessons, networks, and opportunities are redistributed instead of extracted. That's how we build a system that doesn't just survive pressure but grows stronger because of it. A community is strengthened every time one of us tries, not just when one of us succeeds.

Resilience isn't just about bouncing back after rejection or persisting through the next fundraise. It's about how we handle the moments when persistence means letting go. For many founders, the hardest test of resilience comes not in scaling up, but in shutting down and facing the emotional and relational weight of closing a company with honesty and grace.

WHEN THE END IS ALSO A BEGINNING

The way you end can define your reputation more than any pitch ever could. Startups close for all kinds of reasons, including timing, market shifts, burn, health, family, or, of course, lack of access to resources and capital. Sometimes it's simply a hard acknowledgment of reality. Yet we don't talk enough about what happens next or how to navigate those final conversations with investors, employees, and yourself.

Joel Mutua told me this story about the hardest email he ever wrote:

> When we decided to shut down, I couldn't write the email to our investors. I stared at it for three months. These were people who had become mentors, friends. When I finally hit send, I was shocked. The support I received—it was more than I expected. Even though some didn't invest in my new company, many of my original investors are still helping me. One is helping with go-to-market. Another runs three-hour strategy sprints with me. That's trust. That's long-term capital.

That moment of hitting send is one of the most courageous choices a founder can make. It means you're choosing honesty over avoidance and accountability over shame. Reputation is another type of capital. When founders act with transparency and integrity, even in difficult moments, it builds something more valuable than a check. You grow a network that wants to see you win, whatever you build next.

The mythology of entrepreneurship tells us to glorify grit and survival at all costs, but real resilience is about integrity. We all need to own the full arc of our stories, including when chapters end. Joel's experience shows that transparency and humility don't close doors, but do the opposite, and keep them open. His investors respected him more for communicating clearly and responsibly than if he had gone silent or disappeared.

You don't need to have a viral success story to be remembered well. The founders who show up with honesty and care, even in a shutdown, are often the ones who get funded again later. Investors aren't just betting on a company; they're betting on your character. The system rarely gives founders the space to grieve, reflect, or honor the effort it took to try. That space is a critical part of resilience, too. You can "fail" with integrity and still be proud of what you built. Sometimes, closing one door is how you learn to open the next one with intention.

If I had succeeded in raising our Series B funding at my last company, I'd probably still be running it. I wouldn't have founded Scroobious. I wouldn't have co-authored a groundbreaking law requiring venture capital firms to disclose demographic data. I wouldn't have met the thousands of founders and investors who make up my network today. I wouldn't have written this book. I wouldn't have acted with the passion, conviction, and intention I do today to change how we access innovation capital.

CHECKS FOLLOW RELATIONSHIPS

Let's clear up one last myth: that you have to always be pitching. The truth is that checks follow relationships, not the other way around.

Many angels don't even think of themselves as "investors" at first. They mentor a founder, advise a little, get to know the business and watch a founder operate, and *then* they decide to write a check. That's why funding sometimes comes when you're not formally raising and why it can feel elusive when you are. When you build real relationships and let people see your leadership in action, you create the conditions for investment rather than forcing it.

Even if money doesn't come, those same relationships can open doors, sharpen your thinking, and broaden your network in ways that matter just as much.

Suelin Chen reflected on something she noticed only after the fact, but it says a lot about how bias, trust, and identity show up in early-stage investing:

> I had a lot of people on my cap table. I find it so interesting that almost all of the men who invested have daughters. My theory is that having daughters humanizes women to them, or they see how capable women are and it helps chip away at some of the patriarchal conditioning. I didn't seek out girl dads on purpose, but I randomly noticed it one day.

You don't need to go recruit a bunch of dads with daughters, but this is how you find your people. The ones who already see part of themselves, or someone they love, in you and what you're building. Shared identity, lived experience, mission, values—whatever it is, familiarity reduces perceived risk. You're not "risky" to someone who already understands you.

You don't need to convince everyone. You just need the right people in your corner, the ones who say yes because you feel inevitable to them.

CARE LESS, BUILD MORE

So here's where I want you to land: Focus on your business, on the work that brings you energy and confidence. You're not building to impress investors. You're building to solve the problem you couldn't ignore.

If you can grow without investors, even better. If you choose to raise, walk into meetings with your whole energy and conviction, but don't hand investors the power to validate your worth. Care less about persuading every person across the table. Care more about building the thing that excites you. If they get excited alongside you, great. If they don't, move on.

Nobody is coming to save you, which is fine, because you're not in distress and you don't need saving. You are taking action and driving change. Entrepreneurship is ever-evolving. Capitalism is ever-evolving. New methods of building and funding are being devised every day, and you are part of that evolution.

The locus of control is always shifting, but it is not absent. Systemic issues are real, and many lie outside your control, but many things remain within it. Identify them. Act on them. Don't assume you're powerless, because you're not.

As Deanna Meador put it:

> You have to talk about what you're doing. Sometimes that's not comfortable. I'm very introverted; this is not my ideal thing, and it takes a lot of energy for me to do it. But the more you talk about what you're doing, and you connect with other people, you just never know where those connections to either customers or investors are going to come from. You have to share your story and be intentional about how you do that.

Your story is part of your strategy. Share it, own it, and build with purpose.

THE REST OF US

Fundraising for *The Rest of Us* isn't about enduring within a broken system. We are reshaping the system so more of us, with all our stories, our lived experiences, and our communities, get to participate in building what comes next.

So yes, this work is hard. You will be rejected. You will get ghosted. You will question yourself. But you will also experience the redemptive arc. The moment someone gets it, the moment a check clears, the moment you realize you've built something nobody can take away from you.

That's why you keep going. That's why you raise. That's why you build.

Go raise. Go build. Go take up space. We need you here.

ACKNOWLEDGMENTS

This acknowledgment section was actually the hardest thing to write out of everything in the book. I ended up writing it far past when it was due, which I'm sure required a lot of self-restraint on my publisher's part, since he was much too polite about it.

Sitting for uncomfortably long periods of time, looking at a blank, white document screen, I found my thoughts looping through introspection, self-evaluation, and almost crushing gratitude for those I want to thank. This section, to me, is more than just acknowledging the challenge of writing this book and the people who helped make it possible. This book is the result of over a decade of toiling in the startup ecosystem, learning everything the hard way, and carrying the weight of others' pain and anxiety by fostering safe spaces and a sense of belonging.

How do you acknowledge that much time and effort? How do you acknowledge everyone who played a critical role in vastly different ways?

The short answer is: You can't. I have a compulsion to overcommit myself, hold myself to impossibly high standards, and pour myself into everyone around me with very little regard for the volume of what's left in my own cup. Lest you think I'm attempting to portray myself as a martyr, the point is I can only continue to act this way because I have a network of people who recognize when I need refilling and who take it upon themselves to support me.

I won't lie; writing this book was far more challenging and time-consuming than I had anticipated. When people congratulate authors for the achievement of publishing a book, I totally get it now. Writing a book like this meant consistently checking that I was putting forth the most valuable and accessible content possible to help you, the reader, who is in a place of learning and need. It meant doing that in stolen pockets of time amid running my company, policy and advocacy work, serving on boards, and being with and taking care of my family.

So, I can't possibly thank everyone, but I'm going to acknowledge some pillars in my life who were critical to my ability to develop into the person I am today and in my ability to put out this book.

FAMILY

To my husband, **Steve**. You are my true partner in every part of my life. After 23 years together, you still make me laugh every single day. You amaze me with your thoughtfulness, morality, kindness, generosity, humor, and unwavering belief in me. You make everyone around you a better and happier person. It took me way longer than it should have to write your acknowledgment, because for one of the very rare times in my life, I was at a loss for words. I don't think I could sustain my passion and dedication to my work without the unconditional love and mutual respect we have for each other. Thank you for being you, without compromise, all of the time. You are incredible.

To my kids, **Zach and Hannah**. You tell me how proud you are that your mom is speaking up and taking a stand for others, and that pride goes both ways. You've grown up watching me build hard and meaningful things that make the world better, and I've watched you both mature into values-driven teenagers who, thank goodness, adopted our love of 90s alternative rock. Just like how I couldn't do what I do without your dad, I am also motivated to continue because you remind me why my work matters. Being your mom is my greatest joy.

To my dad, **Phil**. You've always been my compass. You help me zoom out, put things in perspective, and stay focused on what really matters. You taught me how important it is to treat people with respect and approach everyone with good intentions. I've watched you give people your full attention and curiosity—from your students, to the local diner owner, to your business partners—and take the time to engage in meaningful conversations. You've supported me in all my endeavors, and I am profoundly grateful to have you as my dad.

To my grandma, **Mickee**, who turns 98 years old the week this book is published. You've always embodied strength, humor, and unwavering independence. You were born just eight years after women were granted the right to vote and have forged your own way through personal and professional identities throughout your life. Your belief in yourself when it would have been easier to accept what others expected of women and your dedication to always finding laughter in any situation have shaped me more than you realize. I am endlessly proud to be your granddaughter.

To **Toni**, my platonic life partner. Yup, you're in the family section, deal with it. We ran a company together, were dubbed the couple name Allonia, and forged a lifelong bond. Our time working together was full of insane, difficult challenges (only a small portion of them described in this book), and any one of them would have sunk the company if we hadn't been so incredibly in sync and maintained 100% trust in each other. You give me confidence, camaraderie, understanding, empathy, and shared rage over oh so many things. I can be my full self around you—and I know you can be yours around me—and that means everything. I wish everyone could have a Toni.

MENTORS

To **Cynthia**, my mentor for nearly 20 years. When I won your scholarship during my first year of business school at BU Questrom, I bet you didn't think I'd hold you to the lifelong mentorship part of it! You have been one of the most impactful people in shaping my professional life, guiding me through every career chapter with the tough love and unvarnished advice I sorely needed (and still do). Nobody walks her talk quite like you. You advance your own work while paving the way for others, always tackling obstacles by making yourself indispensable and bringing other women into every room you enter. You have inspired thousands, and I hope you know that.

To **Kelly**, who has proclaimed us as "ride or die." You managed to change the course of my life and self-identity in just a few years. Whatever I did while teaching the Harvard Business Analytics Program pitch workshop that drew you to my energy, thank f'n goodness I did it. You have an uncanny ability to see right through to a person's core and detect their authenticity—all while maintaining the driest wit I have ever encountered. I never would have considered entering the world of policy advocacy without you pulling me into it. You helped me understand the exponential impact regulations can have when paired with commercial and economic efforts and fundamentally shifted my view of how to create change. I cannot properly express how much you mean to me and how much I respect the way you show up in this world. In your words, here's to not being insignificant, which is something nobody in their right mind would ever use to describe you.

FOUNDERS AND SCROOBIOUS COMMUNITY

To the founders, investors, partners, providers, and everyone who has supported me over these past 6 years: I've never felt so fulfilled by my work as I do today, and it's because of the people I get to connect with. Founders are a special group. We're called crazy for good reason. Creating change of any kind is hard. Starting a company to do that is harder. Being an underestimated profile while doing those things is the hardest. We're in this together. Many of you take time out of your day to let me know that my work helps you or has an impact, and that, without exaggeration, is what motivates me to keep going and to do things like write this book so I can reach and help even more people.

A special thank you to the 20+ founders and investors featured in this book. You trusted me to tell your stories in a way that honors what you experienced, amplifies your insights, and inspires readers.

READERS

What value is a book if nobody reads it? I wrote this for you, and I thank you for reading it. An enormous thank-you to the 100+ people who participated in my beta reading program and gave me such thoughtful feedback along the way. You came along on this journey with me, reading chapter by chapter, and helped shape the book's utility.

WANT TO GO DEEPER?

Readers can access a private resource library at

ALLISONBYERS.COM/RESOURCES

including stories and materials referenced in this book, downloadable templates, and additional video content. Use the password *FFRU* to unlock everything!

ABOUT THE AUTHOR

Allison Byers is the founder of Scroobious and co-author of California's Fair Investment Practices by Venture Capital Companies Act (FIPVCC). She co-founded a medtech company spun out of MIT, raised nearly $10 million, and brought an FDA-registered product to market, only to watch the all-male team that acquired it raise $55 million. She serves on multiple boards, speaks on startup ecosystem redesign, and invests as an angel. Her work has been featured across leading outlets, including Bloomberg, The Boston Globe, and TechCrunch.